RETHINKING ABORTION

RETHINKING ABORTION

EQUAL CHOICE,
THE CONSTITUTION,
AND REPRODUCTIVE POLITICS

Mark A. Graber

PRINCETON UNIVERSITY PRESS   PRINCETON, NEW JERSEY

Copyright © 1996 by Princeton University Press
Published by Princeton University Press, 41 William Street,
Princeton, New Jersey 08540
In the United Kingdom: Princeton University Press,
Chichester, West Sussex
All Rights Reserved.

Library of Congress Cataloging-in-Publication Data
Graber, Mark A.
Rethinking abortion : equal choice, the Constitution,
and reproductive politics / Mark A. Graber.
Includes bibliographical references and index.
ISBN 0-691-01142-7 (alk. paper)
1. Abortion—Political aspects—United States.
2. Abortion—Government policy—United States.
3. Abortion—United States—Moral and ethical aspects.
I. Title.
HQ767.5.U5G734   1996
363.4′6′0973—dc20   95-25448   CIP

This book has been composed in Galliard

Princeton University Press books are printed
on acid-free paper and meet the guidelines
for permanence and durability of the Committee
on Production Guidelines for Book Longevity
of the Council on Library Resources

Printed in the United States of America by Princeton Academic Press

1   3   5   7   9   10   8   6   4   2

To My Parents: for everything,

and

To Jerry and Liza: for J.B.

Contents

Acknowledgments

RETHINKING ABORTION defends and elaborates the traditional American antipathy toward special privileges in any area of law. Fortunately for me, the principle of equality under law has never extended to personal relationships. While writing this book, I was frequently reminded of how specially privileged I have been to have faithful friends, learned associates, and a loving family. Without their inspiration and help, this book would have been a substantially inferior work.

I am particularly grateful for the advice and comments I received from my colleagues and graduate students at the University of Texas and the University of Maryland. David Braybrooke, Scott Powe, Sandy Levinson, Henry Dietz, Bob Hardgrave, Brian Roberts, Wallace Mendelson, Jim Gimpel, Doug Laycock, Sarah Weddington, Mike Sharlot, Paul Herrnson, Fran Buntman, and Lewis Ringel read and improved parts or all of this work. Jim Fishkin and Jon Wilkenfeld each created a supportive academic environment and provided summer money. Friends too numerous to be named chipped in with helpful asides and consistent encouragement.

Rogers Smith, Andy Koppelman, Philippa Strum, Steve Helle, and Jennifer Davidson offered additional and important suggestions when I went outside my universities for assistance. Leslie Goldstein merits special mention for giving me the opportunity to test an early version of the manuscript at the American Political Science Association and in her anthology, *Feminist Jurisprudence: The Difference Debate* (Rowman and Littlefield, 1992). The *Virginia Journal of Social Policy and the Law* graciously published a version of chapter II in their Spring 1994 edition.

Rethinking Abortion exists because Malcolm DeBevoise had the confidence to see the manuscript through some very dark days. Linda McClain and two anonymous readers for Princeton University Press all extended themselves generously in their analyses and recommendations for improvement. I am also grateful to Alice Falk, for the superb job she did copyediting the manuscript, and to Molan Chun Goldstein, for smoothly expediting its production. Heidi Sheehan deserves extra plaudits for promptly addressing my innumerable nervous concerns with her usual professional grace.

My family is the most special privilege I enjoy. Without Julia Frank's emotional and editorial support, this book would have been little more than scrap paper for the children. Dr. Frank served as my medical advisor and read more versions of the manuscript than I would like to admit. Her sharp eye is the reason why Humean philosophers will not ponder the nature of a "sceptic" abortion. Any fault you may find with *Rethinking Abortion*, however, probably resulted from the attention I paid to Naomi, Abigail, and Rebecca. Of course, any fault you may find with Naomi, Abigail, and Rebecca probably resulted from the attention I paid to *Rethinking Abortion*.

RETHINKING ABORTION

Sublime Theories, Ugly Facts

WHENEVER the Supreme Court reconsiders *Roe v. Wade*[1] or pro-life forces win major elections, well-meaning friends and pro-choice organizations[2] become concerned about the future welfare of my family. If that decision is overruled, they warn, my wife and three daughters will be unable to secure safe abortions should they be confronted with an unwanted pregnancy. "Voices from the illegal abortion era" ominously portend that these are the "traumatic circumstances . . . in which [we] will soon be conducting [our lives] if the forces of reaction . . . are victorious in their attempt to deny women the right to choose."[3] Julia and I could be compelled to exhaust our financial and emotional resources raising a severely deformed child. Naomi, Abigail, and Rebecca might have to abandon their promising educational and professional careers in order to mother an untimely baby. Even if they are fortunate enough to find an abortionist, Julia and the children will risk serious injury, even death, should they decide to hazard a terrifying and humiliating black-market procedure.

These dire prophecies are difficult to take seriously. My wife and I earn substantial salaries and our families have money. Julia is a medical doctor, well established in both liberal and feminist medical circles. Should *Roe* be abandoned, we will have the connections and wherewithal necessary to terminate any unwanted pregnancy safely, either locally or in some jurisdiction where abortion remains legal. A series of improbable political or economic events might severely curtail these reproductive choices. I confess, however, to having greater fears about a nuclear holocaust or an environmental disaster, both of which are more catastrophic and more likely to occur than social policies that significantly impair the ability of upper-middle-class professionals and their children to obtain safe abortions.

Social science literature enhances my confidence that Julia, the children, and I will not suffer severe harm should *Roe v. Wade* be overruled. Studies published in medical, public health, and policy journals uniformly conclude that statutory bans on abortion are selectively administered. No matter what the formal status of abortion rights, persons of high socioeconomic status have almost always been able to terminate unwanted pregnancies without substantial medical, legal, or financial complications.[4] Prominent analyses of contemporary trends in American politics suggest that access to abortion services remains fairly secure for affluent citizens; no serious nationwide prohibition is likely to be implemented in the near future. Republican presidents and presidential candidates talk a good deal about restricting abortion, and many leading politicians oppose the use of public resources to pay for or otherwise encourage that procedure. The core business and suburban constituency of the GOP, however, studiously avoids measures that promote governmental interference with privately financed methods of family planning.[5] Attitudes toward abortion vary among regions: committed pro-life activists dominate some local legislatures, but pro-choice policies enjoy substantial legislative support in other areas of the United States. Connecticut and Maryland are among the states that have passed new statutory and state constitutional provisions that provide additional guarantees for abortion rights.[6] Should *Roe* be overruled, persons financially able to travel to those communities will still enjoy legal abortion on demand.[7]

Remarkably, much legal and popular literature presents a very different picture of my family's stakes in the ongoing debate over *Roe v. Wade*. Pro-choice scholars and their political allies frequently write as if they believe that hardly anyone had access to safe or legally sanctioned abortions before *Roe* was decided, and that hardly anyone will have such access should *Roe* be overruled. Although law professors presumably enjoy high socioeconomic status, legal commentaries consistently suggest that prominent attorneys expect to be affected directly should the federal judiciary cease protecting abortion rights. A 1989 article in the *Harvard Law Review* states that the Supreme Court's willingness to reconsider *Roe* "has threatened women across class and racial lines." "The answer to the question why is it so important that abortion access be constitutionally protected is obvious," an academic lawyer who teaches at an elite law school proclaims: "because I or someone I care about may desperately need one, and the vagaries of electoral politics do not guarantee access." Many pro-choice advocates seriously contend that Margaret Atwood's *Handmaid's Tale*, an account of a fictional society in which religious fundamentalists seize power and reduce women to child bearers and child raisers, offers "an understanding that should and could have supported the morality of *Roe* and that can still illuminate its application."[8]

The contemporary debate over abortion rights and restrictions is permeated with other claims that are similarly belied by common experience and social science. Pro-life commentators who maintain that the Supreme Court should not prevent the people's representatives from making abortion policy routinely ignore evidence suggesting that many of the people's representatives would prefer that the Supreme Court make abortion policy.[9] Pro-choice commentators who assert that *restrictions on* abortion violate women's right to equality routinely ignore evidence suggesting that approximately half the women in the United States believe that abortion *on demand* violates their right to be treated as equals.[10] Quite frequently, pro-choice and pro-life activists act on the same erroneous assumptions. Bitter struggles take place annually over Medicaid funding for abortion because both proponents and opponents of reproductive choice think that "by foreclosing . . . governmental reimbursement," federal and state legislatures "make it impossible for an indigent woman to obtain an abortion."[11] Much research, however, demonstrates that governmental subsidies have little impact on the abortion rates of poor women.[12] Commentators who celebrate or condemn the changes *Planned Parenthood v. Casey*[13] and *Webster v. Reproductive Health Services*[14] made to abortion law on the books seem oblivious to studies suggesting that those decisions have had little influence on abortion law in action.[15]

Recent years have witnessed an enormous outpouring of writing on both the politics and the constitutionality of abortion regulations. The history of abortion policies, contemporary abortion politics, and public attitudes toward legal abortion are well documented; the philosophical and legal arguments for and against abortion rights are well explored. So far, however, neither the empirical nor the theoretical literature significantly addresses the concerns of the other. As a result, social science studies of abortion are frequently politically and legally sterile. Likewise, philosophical and constitutional commentaries too often seem little more than extended discourses on hypothetical abortion policies enacted and implemented in a fictional society that bears only a passing resemblance to the present-day United States.

Rethinking Abortion seeks to bridge this gulf between descriptive and prescriptive analyses of abortion rights. This study explores what moral and legal theorists would see if they seriously investigated how actual abortion policies are implemented and considers how such investigations might affect their philosophical, constitutional, and democratic arguments. Late-twentieth-century American abortion law in action raises distinct constitutional issues from abortion law on the books, issues too frequently ignored by professors and activists concerned with the status of reproductive rights in all possible worlds. By analyzing how bans on abortion have been and are likely to be administered, I hope to identify those policies that might be adopted in the present political climate and evaluate their relative merits. Rather than reproduce yet another metaphysical critique of privacy, the following pages examine the philosophical, constitutional, and democratic adequacy of the two systems of abortion regulation that existed in the recent past and might exist in the near future: pre-*Roe* statutory prohibitions on abortion and *Roe*'s ban on significant state interference with the market for safe abortion services.

Equal choice, a new philosophical and constitutional defense of legal abortion, is a child of this union between descriptive and normative analyses. Abortion should remain legal in the near future, this argument maintains, because statutory bans on abortion during the twentieth century were selectively or arbitrarily enforced in ways that intentionally discriminated against poor persons and persons of color. Sympathetic police officers, prosecutors, judges, and juries in the years before *Roe* routinely ignored and sometimes assisted those physicians who discreetly terminated pregnancies for their private patients. The same law enforcement officials, however, often prevented competent abortionists from offering their services to the general public. Although affluent white women were granted practical immunities from pre-*Roe* abortion law on the books, the law in action frequently forced poor women and women of color to choose between a dangerous abortion and an unwanted child.

Such discriminatory practices violate the fundamental human and constitutional right of all Americans to equal justice under law. No social class or racial caste should enjoy special dispensations from generally applicable criminal laws. This basic right to legal equality has powerful roots in the American political tradition, was the major concern of the framers of the equal protection clause of the Fourteenth Amendment, and is a central requirement of democratic governance. Americans have historically demanded to be governed by general laws, laws that on their face and as applied bind the rich and the poor, white citizens and citizens of color. Policies that consciously distribute the right to purchase abortion services by race and class do not satisfy this fundamental political norm. Recent Supreme Court decisions do sustain laws that have a disparate impact on poor persons and persons of color. When, however, enforcement practices that serve no legitimate interest severely burden poor persons and persons of color, both constitutional precedent and common sense compel finding state actors guilty of intentional discrimination.

Equal choice promises equal opportunities, not equal results. Persons remain formally equal before the law when states prevent all persons from purchasing certain goods or refuse to assist all citizens who cannot pay the market price for necessary services. Hence, impartially administered bans on abortion, regulations of abortion, and restrictions on governmental funding for abortion do not violate equal choice principles. Such policies meet present equal protection standards, even when they have a disparate impact on the capacity of poor women and women of color to procure safe and legal abortions. Equal choice principles prohibit legislative efforts to recriminalize abortion because statutory bans on abortion have not and will not be administered constitutionally, but they provide no independent grounds at present for constitutionally condemning the measures sustained by the Supreme Court in *Webster* and *Casey*. Contemporary abortion regulations do not intentionally discriminate against persons of color and the poor. The Hyde Amendment and similar state measures ban governmental funding for both rich and poor women who seek medically unnecessary abortions. Law enforcement officials in states that regulate abortion are not administering such policies in ways that give affluent white women and only affluent white women a de facto exemption from statutorily mandated waiting periods or informed consent requirements.

Nevertheless, equal choice policies remain the best practical means for making abortions available to poor women and women of color. Research done in states that regulate abortion belie claims that the right to a privately financed abortion is "a cruel deception" for the poor or that "formalistic legal rules seldom lead to justice."[16] Judicial decisions permitting states to regulate but not ban abortion have had little impact on the availability of safe legal abortions. *Webster* and *Casey* may have changed abortion law on the books, but abortion law in action has remained substantially the same since the early 1970s. Most states have not exercised their judicial permission to reregulate abortion. Many regulations that passed are not being enforced, while others are being enforced in ways that do not burden women seeking abortions. It is true that federal and state regulations forbidding the use of governmental funds to pay for abortions seriously inconvenience many women. Such policies, however, have had little effect on the legal abortion rates of the poor and racial minorities. Thus, the evidence indicates that as long as abortion is not prohibited by law, women of all economic classes are usually able to hurdle the legal obstacles that hostile states place in front of their efforts to terminate an unwanted pregnancy.[17]

The most important practical issue in contemporary reproductive politics remains whether abortion should be legal. Abstracted from all political and social contexts, the choice between procreative liberty and fetal life is difficult, if not impossible. Once accurate analysis of twentieth-century reproductive law in action is incorporated into the abortion debate, however, the case for preserving *Roe* becomes compelling. Statutory bans on abortion have consistently violated a principle whose constitutional pedigree is undeniable, the principle that the founding fathers placed at the heart of the Constitution. "The genius of the system," James Madison asserted in *Federalist* 57, is that our governing officials "can make no law which will not have its full operation on themselves and their friends, as well as on the great mass of society."[18] Until our elected officials become seriously committed to denying abortions to their family members and friends, judges, lawyers, scholars, and citizens should not permit our leaders to deny that choice to anyone.

THE ARGUMENT FOR EQUAL CHOICE

Equal choice changes the focus of contemporary debates over reproductive policy. Rather than concentrate on the philosophical and constitutional status of procreative liberty or fetal life, equal choice discusses the political and constitutional justice of a phenomenon best described as a "gray market." Gray markets develop when law enforcement officials, from police and prosecutors to judges and juries, make conscious decisions not to enforce a criminal statute because they believe the offending conduct is not wrong or, at least, not sufficiently wrong to merit penal sanctions. Proponents of equal choice insist that state officials in the years before *Roe* helped establish and maintain a particularly intolerable kind of gray market in safe abortions. As chapter II documents at length, police officers did not arrest, district attorneys did not prosecute, juries did not convict, and judges did not sentence physicians known to be terminating pregnancies for well-off citizens. The persons responsible for administering abortion policy did, however, take steps that prevented competent abortionists from offering the same services to the general public. The resulting exclusive gray market, chapters III and IV demonstrate, violates the philosophical and constitutional principle that persons must be governed only by general laws, rules of universal application made by their elected representatives.

This turn to the philosophical and constitutional deficiencies of the exclusive gray market in safe abortions highlights the philosophical and constitutional standards that should govern state officials who enforce any criminal statute. In sharp contrast to liberal and feminist defenses of legal abortion, equal choice is agnostic on whether Americans have a fundamental right to control their reproductive capacities. Some proponents of equal choice may also endorse more conventional pro-choice arguments; others may not.[19] Women have the constitutional right to equal choice, advocates of that defense of keeping abortion legal maintain, only because all persons have the right to be governed by general rules. Even if states may ban abortion, law enforcement officials cannot prevent some women from procuring an abortion in those communities that by law or custom permit women of other races and economic classes to make that reproductive choice. Proponents of equal choice condemn any intentional official action that helps establish or maintain an exclusive gray market, whether the nominally proscribed good or service be abortion, pizza, cancer treatments, or access to cable television. The exclusive gray market in abortion services is more intolerable than a similarly exclusive gray market in pizza only because having control over their fertility is more important to most people than having access to a particular food, and because the consequences of the former gray market were often fatal.

Full or rigid enforcement of every provision in the penal code is, of course, impossible. Small gray markets inevitably and legitimately dot the landscape of the criminal law. All communities vest their police officers, prosecutors, judges, and juries with some discretion as to how strictly and when to administer legal rules and regulations.[20] Yet official discretion can be abused. In derogation of the principle that all citizens are equal before the law, law enforcement officials made conscious decisions not to arrest, prosecute, convict, or sentence persons for known violations of laws prohibiting abortion when those perpetrators belonged or provided services to certain favored social castes. In derogation of the principle that no person may be punished except in accordance with the duly made law of the land, law enforcement officials arrogated to themselves the power to determine which citizens were permitted to buy and sell safe abortion services.

The philosophical and constitutional case against twentieth-century abortion prohibitions in action is much stronger than similar attacks on other inequitably administered criminal prohibitions. Discriminatory enforcement of bans on abortion creates far greater racial and class inequalities than discriminatory enforcement of laws banning, say, litter or parking in the red zone. Unlike relatively trivial offenses that are sporadically enforced, statutory bans on abortion threaten to impose lengthy prison terms for performing an act that is often necessary to preserve another person's capacity to compete as an equal in the public world of work and power. Being forced to park farther from the shopping mall may be a temporary nuisance, but being forced to bear and care for an unwanted child can severely and permanently damage one's prospects for education and career.

Malenforced prohibitions on abortion also pervert the processes of democratic deliberation and decision making. Unlike other fairly serious offenses that are selectively enforced, statutory bans on abortion are violated by millions of persons, often with the tacit consent of state officials. More equitable enforcement of the death penalty would probably not inspire calls for repeal of capital punishment, because few politically influential citizens commit first-degree murder.[21] The discriminatory implementation of laws prohibiting abortion, however, may seriously infect public debate. Pro-choice citizens who enjoy this indulgence from the criminal law may not invest their scarce political resources fighting for legal abortion and may even support pro-life candidates who advocate other social policies that they find more desirable.[22] Some affluent citizens who are nominally pro-life may never seriously consider whether they are really prepared to bear and care for any child they conceive. Significantly, persons who oppose legal abortion are as likely as pro-choice advocates to choose abortion when faced with an unwanted pregnancy.[23] Thus, pro-life policies may be relatively immune to legislative revision only because many persons know that even when the law on the books bans abortion, they can safely terminate an unwanted pregnancy without legal complications.

The argument for equal choice must admit of one significant qualification. Equality rights are powerful, but they do not trump the sanctity of human life. Few persons would abandon a commando raid on a Nazi death camp if the prejudiced military forces available were only willing to save white or more affluent inmates from the gas chambers. Pro-life advocates who sincerely believe that *Roe* gave legal sanction to another Holocaust will understandably think that the limited number of human lives restrictive abortion policies save outweighs the seeming intractable political injustices endemic to restrictive abortion laws in action. As Representative Henry Hyde has declared, "a life is a life."[24]

The following pages do not speak directly to those who draw no distinction between Dachau and the abortion clinic down the street. Repeating the usual litany of reasons why abortion differs from murder is not likely to be very persuasive; most sophisticated pro-life advocates have already heard and rejected such recitals. Moreover, no accepted mathematical or philosophical formula exists for determining how many fetal lives pro-life policies must save to justify their discriminatory impact on poor women and women of color.[25] Hence, proponents of equal choice must politely agree to disagree with committed opponents of legal abortion and turn their rhetorical attention to the rest of the populace. Equal choice advocates do not think that strong pro-life advocates are irrational or that the abortion debate is incapable of rational resolution. Their point is simply that Americans have temporarily run out of new things to say to each other on whether abortion is a fundamental human or constitutional right.[26]

Equal choice arguments are primarily pitched to those persons who cannot decide whether abortion is a fundamental human right or who think that abortion, while morally wrong, cannot be equated with murder or some other horrible evil. Rather than attempting to shake the confidence of persons who are convinced that abortion is a gross iniquity, equal choice provides reasons why persons who are not confident that abortion is a venal sin should support the result in *Roe*. This rhetorical strategy is politically significant because surveys suggest that most Americans, even most Americans who question *Roe*, reject basic elements of both strong pro-life and pro-choice positions. One study found that the "people who are between the extremes or inconsistent [on abortion] constitute over one-half to two-thirds of the public."[27] These conflicted citizens occupy the crucial middle ground in the abortion debate.[28]

Previously ambivalent Americans may be persuaded by equal choice arguments. This defense of legal abortion does not claim that persons have a fundamental human or constitutional right to terminate an unwanted pregnancy. Equal choice is an equality right, and having a right to equal X does not entitle a person to any X. For example, students at the University of Maryland do not have the right to have the state pay their college tuition; but should Maryland pay the tuition for all white students at the state university, then all students of color would have the same right to be educated at the public's expense. This principle of formal legal equality also governs abortion policy. Even if persons have no right to a legal abortion, when state officials allow substantial segments of the population to enjoy a de facto right to abortion on demand, then these state officials must extend that privilege to all citizens.

Equal choice provides broader constitutional grounds for attacking pro-life policies than do conventional pro-choice defenses of Roe. The equal choice attack on exclusive gray markets is relatively indifferent to contemporary debates over the best method of interpreting the Constitution. Depending on their tastes and those of their audience, proponents of equal choice may rely on historical, textual, doctrinal, prudential, structural, or ethical arguments when defending the result in Roe.[29] Anti-originalists who think that constitutional law should not depend on remote history will emphasize the central role the principle of general laws plays in both the American political tradition and Western moral philosophy. Citizens who reject Ronald Dworkin's call for "a fusion of constitutional law and moral theory"[30] may be persuaded by evidence that the principle of general laws has powerful roots in the plain and original meanings of the Fourteenth Amendment. Of course, no argument is equally compelling in every constitutional language. Strong pro-life supporters will raise ethical objections to equal choice, and proponents of McCleskey v. Kemp[31] have a doctrinal bone to pick. Still, even if equal choice cannot convince all persons that the result in Roe was correct, its attack on pro-life laws in action will appeal to more members of influential schools of contemporary constitutional thought than conventional pro-choice arguments that, having little specific foundation in the plain, original, or historical meanings of the Fourteenth Amendment, must rely on very controversial theories of constitutional interpretation.

Equal choice also strengthens the case for judicial protection of reproductive autonomy. Opponents of Roe frequently insist that courts have no business second-guessing the values chosen by elected officials unless the legislature's decision-making process was somehow defective. Jurists who maintain that federal justices must let the people's representatives decide whether to ban abortion, however, might be more sympathetic to the claim that evenhanded enforcement of laws against abortion is essential to a fair democratic process. Laws that are selectively or arbitrarily enforced illegitimately weaken the groups that might otherwise be strong enough to repeal the offending legal provision. Moreover, such selective enforcement places responsibility for policy making in the hands of unelected and often unaccountable police officers, prosecutors, judges, and juries. By declaring erratic efforts to enforce generally neglected criminal laws unconstitutional, Supreme Court justices prevent unauthorized policy making by unelected law enforcement officials and maintain the rule of law. Anti-*Roe* theorists cannot validly accuse the Supreme Court of failing to defer to reproductive policy choices made by legislatures. Restrictions on abortion were enforced in ways that did not reflect any such decisions. Indeed, most legislatures refused to make any clear policy choices on abortion. To the extent that many legislatures did make a policy choice, they typically chose to defer to whatever policy the judiciary made.

Equal choice arguments are not good for abortion only. Bans on homosexual conduct, stop-and-frisk practices, and other controversial policies may also in practice violate the principle of general laws.[32] Democratic and constitutional theory as a whole will be enriched by greater attention to the standards that ought to govern the law in action. Societies, after all, are only democratic to the extent that laws passed by the people's representatives are enforced. Moreover, meaningful democratic deliberation cannot take place when influential political actors know they will enjoy practical exemptions from constitutionally controversial policies. *Rethinking Abortion* reminds Americans that capricious, discriminatory, and unconstitutional law enforcement inevitably occurs when constitutional democracies keep statutes on their books that most citizens are allowed to violate with impunity most of time. This lesson retains its vitality whether the precise issue being considered is the existence of abortion rights, particular policies regulating abortion, more general questions of sexual privacy, or even more general issues of constitutional law.

THINGS TO COME

Chapter I of *Rethinking Abortion* examines the abstract, often mythical character of conventional efforts to support or attack *Roe v. Wade*. Both proponents and opponents of reproductive choice usually discuss the constitutional status of arguments developed by philosophers interested in deducing certain universal truths about the morality of abortion. Rarely do major participants in the abortion debate consider how actual abortion policies are implemented, justified, and politically maintained. "Concrete facts" in many constitutional commentaries are too often derived from normative beliefs about abortion rights rather than from any serious empirical investigation into contemporary life.

Chapter II explores the functioning of the exclusive gray market in safe abortions that developed before *Roe* and the mildly regulated market in safe abortion services that flourished after that decision. Using evidence from academic medicine, public health, political science, sociology, and anthropology, the chapter constructs a more accurate picture of how statutory bans on abortion actually work in practice, the impact of legalization on access to abortion, the limited influence of contemporary regulations on abortion, and the probable social consequences of judicial decisions further modifying *Roe*. This investigation into twentieth-century abortion law in action reveals a political milieu quite different from that presupposed by previous commentaries on reproductive policy. The precise wording of abortion law on the books, in this universe, has little relationship to the total number of abortions performed at a given time and place. Rather, state decisions to legalize or criminalize abortion primarily affect the quality and cost of abortions available to poor women and women of color. Contrary to popular wisdom, regulations that do not ban abortion outright do not affect access to abortion services significantly. When abortion is legal, abortion rates are far more influenced by the location of abortion clinics than by the absence of public financing.

Chapters III and IV discuss the philosophical and constitutional status of exclusive gray markets with particular emphasis on traditional American concerns about how criminal laws should be enforced. Chapter III maintains that pro-life laws in action violate our constitutional commitment to equal justice under law. Basic principles of justice require that the persons responsible for administering the penal code treat all citizens as legal equals. The Constitution may not guarantee all women the right to choose whether to carry a pregnancy to term. Nevertheless, the equal protection clause forbids law enforcement officials from intentionally distributing the legal right to choose on the basis of the wealth and race of the pregnant woman. Market societies such as ours do allocate many goods on the basis of one's ability to pay for them. Americans, however, have historically resisted suggestions that persons should be allowed to purchase exemptions from the criminal law. Chapter IV develops a related rule-by-law attack on pro-life laws in action. The due process clause requires that laws be regularly enforced and that the persons responsible for administering the penal code be guided by the policy choices embodied in duly authorized statutes. When police and prosecutors selectively or capriciously enforce criminal laws on the books, law enforcement agencies unconstitutionally make public policy.

Chapter V returns to the politics of abortion, an arena in which strategies for keeping abortion legal have been perverted by the same flawed assumptions that weaken arguments for keeping abortion legal. Seduced first by the myth of an independent judiciary and later by Bill Clinton's victory in the 1992 election, advocates of reproductive choice have adopted political tactics that leave abortion rights at the mercy of the nation's economic condition. Pro-choice presidential candidates win when pro-life presidents are blamed for a recession; they lose when pro-life presidents create economic booms. Legal abortion will be more secure in the United States only when proponents of reproductive choice sever the present electoral connections between abortion rights and economic policy. To do so, proponents of reproductive choice must abandon their effort to forge a coalition of women, poor persons, and racial minorities, groups whose members have no special affinity for abortion on demand. Instead, abortion rights activists must, paradoxically, make political efforts to depoliticize abortion. When both major parties are dominated by politicians who would rather not decide when women should have the right to terminate an unwanted pregnancy, the status quo remains good law—and legal abortion is the present status quo. In such a political environment, the Supreme Court may be the only national institution willing to make abortion policy. That tribunal is ordinarily staffed by elite professionals, and American elites strongly support abortion on demand. Unless the federal courts are packed with justices known to favor abandoning *Roe*, the federal judiciary can be trusted to keep abortion legal.

Equal choice arguments alter the intellectual focus of the abortion debate, but such claims will never fully uncouple reproductive policies from those issues of sex, religion, and politics that engender our deepest passions. Given the fervent commitment many persons already have to pro-choice or pro-life policies, no new analysis of procreative issues will suddenly enable all citizens to think dispassionately when comparing abortion policies. One suspects that if some political activists demonstrated that basic propositions of arithmetic supported their side of the abortion debate, the other side would immediately question whether one plus one really equals two.

Still, participants in the abortion debate might gain some perspective by thinking about the philosophical and constitutional justice of an exclusive gray market in some good or service less contentious than abortion. Imagine, for example, that one hundred years ago every state had passed a law forbidding doctors from offering certain medical services to senior citizens. Some historians claim that this policy was intended to husband scarce medical resources for younger persons who might profit more in the long run from medical treatment. Others claim the laws reflected illegitimate ageism. Whatever their original purpose, however, these statutory bans were never strictly enforced and an exclusive gray market in geriatric medicine soon evolved. Most well-off senior citizens at present find competent doctors who, often under color of legally sanctioned practice, provide them with high-quality medical services. The elderly poor, however, normally must forgo medical treatment for certain serious ailments or pay inflated prices to obtain inferior services on the black market. Many experienced physicians are perfectly willing to offer their services to less affluent citizens. They do not do so because a law enforcement community that typically tolerates doctors who discreetly provide geriatric services to their private clientele is not willing to permit the same doctors to offer the same services for any senior citizen with the same medical needs. Organizing the political support necessary for repealing penal bans on medical services to the elderly has proven next to impossible. When asked, many affluent citizens favor a free market in geriatric medicine. Unfortunately, a clear majority of wealthy voters casts their ballots for candidates who promise to reduce their taxes rather than for politicians who promise to legalize medical services that the most fortunate Americans already enjoy in practice.

American citizens would clearly regard this exclusive gray market as making a mockery of their commitment to equality before the law. The official willingness to let doctors serve affluent patients but not the poor seems an intolerable violation of the equal protection clause. The law against geriatric medicine in action also violates basic democratic norms. Unelected law enforcement officials, not our elected representatives, are determining who will have access to important medical services. Surely the Supreme Court should recognize that legislative majorities cannot be trusted to diagnose and remedy these constitutional wrongs when the families of most legislators and their leading supporters already enjoy access to adequate medical care for their elderly. If these observations about American philosophical, constitutional, and democratic values are correct, what relevant difference between the hypothetical gray market in geriatric medicine and the actual gray market in safe abortion services would justify condemning the former but not the latter?

CHAPTER I

The Clash of Absolutes Revisited

THE CLASH OF ABSOLUTES

Those activists and academics who forge and wield the rhetorical weapons used in abortion wars[1] typically debate "whether the law should *ever* permit abortion" (emphasis added).[2] From this atemporal perspective, abortion appears to present a "clash of absolutes,"[3] a conflict between two fundamental values, fetal life and procreative autonomy. This tragic choice apparently transcends time, circumstance, and culture. "The questions that framed the abortion debate four thousand years ago," most commentators believe, "are the same questions framing it today."[4] Pro-choice and pro-life writings often suggest that the abortion rights of Cleopatra, Joan of Arc, Madonna, and every other woman who ever lived depend on the correct answers to these inquiries: "1) When is a fetus a person? 2) What circumstances justify an abortion? 3) Who decides?"[5]

This popular way of framing the debate over *Roe* slights important normative issues unique to twentieth-century American abortion policies. Determined to discover what timeless truths govern the regulation of pregnancy, few pro-life or pro-choice academics seriously compare how different abortion policies have actually functioned in the recent past and are likely to function in the near future. Constitutional thinkers often write as if Americans must choose abortion policies under a veil of ignorance,[6] denied the knowledge of how the rules they choose will be administered and interact with other public policies. Many influential philosophical and constitutional arguments about abortion rely heavily on absolute "gross concepts,"[7] symbolic words and phrases divorced from the social contexts that give language meaning. Political actors ostensibly concerned with fetal life seem strangely uninterested in how many unborn children restrictions on abortion actually save. Activists who proclaim their devotion to the liberty of all women seldom investigate whether most women want reproductive choice or inquire whose liberty to do what has actually been enhanced by abortion on demand. Such "facts," academics, activists, and Ronald Reagan apparently agree, "are stupid things."

Two rhetorical practices seem responsible for the overly abstract quality of most commentary on *Roe*. The canonical philosophical and constitutional analyses of legal abortion usually concentrate on those issues raised by the reproductive policies set out in authoritative legal texts, neglecting those issues raised by the actual administration of legal rules. Sophisticated attacks on abortion law on the books litter the pages of most law reviews. The constitutional attack on abortion law in action, by comparison, has remained underdeveloped for more than twenty years. When proponents and opponents of reproductive choice do attempt to construe abortion rights contextually, their presentations of the facts are frequently skewed by their larger theoretical agendas. Prominent pro-life and pro-choice commentators rationalize their normative predispositions by presenting as social reality popular myths that lack serious evidentiary foundation. In the looking glass world of abortion advocacy, specific facts are more often derived from general theories than general theories from specific facts.

Feminist practice warrants special treatment as both an exception to and a confirmation of the academic tendency to focus on abortion law on the books and derive social facts from moral theories. Such influential jurists as Catharine MacKinnon, Deborah Rhode, Robin West, Ruth Colker, and Frances Olsen agree that conventional analyses of abortion are remarkably abstract and apolitical. They maintain that feminist works offer more empirically grounded and historically contingent arguments.[8] Feminist legal theorists do document meticulously how restrictions on abortion harm many women. Nevertheless, leading feminist commentaries are often as oblivious as the standard liberal commentaries they scorn to the real world of abortion policies and politics. MacKinnon's claim that bans on abortion exacerbate the consequences of the forced sex that too many women must endure in our society is decisively refuted by the very study she cites as supporting her conclusion. The more conventional feminist claim that restrictive abortion policies result from patriarchal politics is belied by studies demonstrating that women are at least as likely as men to favor pro-life policies.

Standard constitutional and philosophical discussions of abortion do clarify how certain fundamental values and aspirations should influence public decisions about reproductive choice. Fetal life and procreative autonomy do not, however, exhaust the competing principles, rights, and interests affected by contemporary abortion policies. The pro-life activist who opposes sex education in the schools does not experience abortion on demand solely as threatening the lives of unborn children. The pro-choice activist who can travel to any jurisdiction where abortion is legal does not experience restrictions on abortion solely as threatening her right to control her fertility. Too often, these common experiences are not taken into account by the canonical pro-life and pro-choice arguments, which rarely discuss what Americans in the twentieth century actually say and do when making and administering abortion policies.

ABORTION LAW IN BOOKS

Americans generally think of law in two ways, as "law in books" and as "law in action."[9] The law in books consists of such authoritative legal texts as legislative enactments, executive orders and judicial decisions. These legal sources are often referred to as "blackletter law." Official utterances, however, are not the only legal phenomenon that persons must consider when making private decisions or public policy. As a perceptive legal historian points out, "law needs to be examined in terms of how it is put into practice and enforced on a daily basis at the local level and how it affects the citizenry."[10] Thus, legal philosophers point to an alternative sense of "law," the law in action. The law in action describes how police officers, prosecutors, judges, and juries administer legal norms. "What these officers do about disputes," a leading American legal realist declares, "is, to my mind, the law itself."[11] The difference between law on the books and law in action should be obvious to any motorist who drives seventy miles an hour on interstate highways or, for that matter, to any licensed physician who performed a hospital abortion in the years before *Roe*.

The law of abortion in contemporary academic writing and popular argument is almost always law on the books. Legal and political commentators determine whether the law prohibits abortion by examining the language found in the appropriate legislative enactments, executive orders, and judicial decisions. Professors and pundits regard abortion as illegal before 1973 because most states had statutes declaring that abortion was a criminal offense.[12] Abortion, in this view, was "legalized" in 1973 when the Supreme Court declared that restrictions on abortion interfere with the exercise of constitutional rights.[13] Everyone agrees that abortion will again be illegal should a judicial opinion overrule *Roe* and states subsequently pass legislation prohibiting most efforts to terminate unwanted pregnancies.[14]

Mary Ann Glendon's controversial *Abortion and Divorce in Western Law* (1987) clearly illustrates how this fixation on abortion law on the books handicaps sound policy analysis. Glendon, a professor at Harvard Law School, limits her discussion of abortion law to cross-national comparisons of legislative enactments and judicial doctrine. After surveying various legal documents, Glendon concludes that European laws are superior to American laws because only the former contain explicit provisions expressing the sanctity of life. Glendon admits that the precise wording of blackletter law does not have an appreciable influence on the accessibility or frequency of abortions in different countries. Several European countries do require that "two doctors . . . certify the existence of the grounds for abortion," but Glendon recognizes that "in practice, so long as the woman can freely choose her doctor or doctors, medical discretion does not effectively restrict her choice." Nevertheless, without citing any empirical evidence to support her hypothesis, Glendon suggests that such laws "communicate a message which *may* enter, along with other social forces, into the way in which [Western Europeans] think . . . about how one should conduct one's life" (emphasis added).[15]

Glendon's treatment of European abortion policies illustrates the penchant constitutional commentators have for speaking as if abortion law on the books accurately describes abortion law in action. All parties to the abortion controversy assume that actual differences in access to abortion in the United States may be deduced from the wording of different statutory provisions. States with more liberal statutory polices respecting abortion, many writers suggest, must be the states in which persons can most easily procure abortions. John Hart Ely of Stanford Law School finds the "disparity among state laws regulating abortion . . . most troubling" because he mistakenly thinks that the variation in state laws was the primary reason why affluent persons before *Roe* were frequently able to terminate a pregnancy without legal complication.[16] In fact, wealthy citizens usually had access to safe abortions even in jurisdictions with draconian restrictions on abortion on the books.[17] No scholar includes California as among the states that legalized abortion immediately before *Roe*, because the state penal code after 1967 declared that abortion was legal only when bringing a child to term would "gravely impair" maternal health. The officials responsible for administering that provision, however, permitted abortion on demand. As a result, legal abortion rates in California by 1973 were higher than in some states that had repealed all restrictions on abortion in their statutory books.[18]

This blind faith in the efficacy of legal language partially explains the exaggerated rhetoric that many academics and activists use when describing the probable impact of a judicial decision overruling *Roe*. Pro-choice advocates who should know better often proclaim that no one will enjoy secure access to safe or legal abortions if authoritative written laws again ban that procedure. "When the state prohibits abortion," an influential feminist professor prophesies, "*all* women of childbearing age know that pregnancy may violently alter their lives at any time" (emphasis added).[19] Abortion rights activists who issue these predictions make no effort to refute evidence suggesting that affluent women typically enjoy practical immunities from statutory bans on abortion.[20] Robert Burt of Yale Law School makes the opposite mistake when he assumes that all persons can easily obtain an abortion whenever the procedure is legal. Seduced by abortion law on the books, Burt suggests that as long as "free access" exists in some states "*every* women who want[s] an abortion [can] travel to find one" (emphasis added).[21] In fact, more than one hundred thou sand women annually cannot obtain a legal abortion at present because they live too far from the nearest abortion provider.[22]

The academic tendency to deduce facts about legal and social practices from legal texts has particularly serious consequences when pro-choice commentators criticize how wealth influences access to safe abortion services. Proponents of legal abortion insist that as long as the Supreme Court sustains legislation banning government funds for abortion,[23] only "pregnant adult women with the means to pay for it retai[n] their freedom." "The abortion right has already been lost" for "poor women," Catharine MacKinnon asserts, "by deprivation of governmental funding for abortion."[24] Current restrictions on government funding, however, have in fact had relatively little impact on access to safe abortions. Contrary to Justice Marshall's dissent in *Harris*, "denial of Medicaid-funding abortion is [not] equivalent to denial of legal abortion altogether" for approximately 94 percent of all women eligible for Medicaid.[25] Sympathetic abortionists and private charities frequently assist those women who cannot otherwise afford to terminate an unwanted pregnancy. Legalization drastically reduced the cost of safe abortions, making that reproductive choice affordable for most women. For these reasons and others, poor women and women of color have been the primary beneficiaries of state policies and judicial decisions that decriminalized but did not fund abortion.[26]

Pro-choice advocates may generally be unaware that funding bans have a limited impact on legal abortion rates, but most proponents of reproductive choice recognize that the system of abortion regulation in pre-*Roe* America was "a regime of manifest economic discrimination."[27] What pro-*Roe* commentators know about how abortion regulations actually affect (or do not affect) social practices in the United States, however, rarely influences their philosophical or constitutional defenses of legal abortion. Confined to commenting on abortion law on the books, pro-choice commentaries typically imply that communities treat affluent and poor women differently only when their written laws say so.

THE LOOKING GLASS WORLD OF ABORTION ADVOCACY

The major combatants in "the clash of absolutes" rely on normative beliefs as their second source for obtaining facts about twentieth-century reproductive policies and politics. Apparently confident that life must imitate their moral and constitutional theories, leading proponents and opponents of legal abortion often forgo the onerous task of investigating how restrictions on abortion in the United States have actually been implemented, justified, and politically maintained. As a result, influential abortion commentaries are saturated with pseudo-empirical proposi-tions—statements purporting to describe social reality, but that, in fact, are derived from the author's antecedent philosophical convictions.

Consider the claim, made by both pro-life and pro-choice activists, that the federal judiciary in 1973 removed abortion issues from electoral poli-tics. Scholars who believe that *Roe* was wrongly decided accuse the Supreme Court of inhibiting public debate on abortion.[28] Scholars who support reproductive choice maintain that the justices properly curtailed that debate in order to limit the baneful effects that single-issue abortion politics have on democratic processes.[29] In fact, these assertions are histor-ical and political nonsense. *Roe v. Wade* was largely responsible for insert-ing abortion into electoral politics and sparking the rise of the right-to-life movement.[30] No intelligent person who during the 1970s and 1980s oc-casionally looked at a newspaper or glanced at television news could be-lieve otherwise. Claims that the Supreme Court either did or should act to prevent abortion from influencing political campaigns are thus not serious empirical assertions about the nature of American politics. Instead, these theses are actually normative statements about which branch of govern-ment should resolve abortion disputes.[31]

All parties to the abortion controversy rely heavily on other pseudo-empirical claims derived from their moral and constitutional theories. Critics of *Roe* assert that pro-life measures protect the unborn and reflect a social consensus that abortion should be banned. Liberal pro-choice activists maintain that pro-life measures force persons to become parents against their will and result from undemocratic single-issue politics. Femi-nists maintain that pro-life policies falsely assume that women control sex and that such measures stem from the male domination of American polit-ical life. These claims seem intuitively obvious to true believers and their allies, yet none survives any serious investigation of twentieth-century abortion law and politics.

Pro-Life/Anti-Roe Arguments

Pro-life activists maintain that all genetic humans have the right to be born. Abortion is immoral, in their view, because life is "an almost abso-lute value in history." "Direct and voluntary abortion is intrinsically wrong," an editorial in the *Catholic Lawyer* states, "since it is the direct killing of an innocent human being."[32] Many philosophers who oppose legal abortion advocate an even broader pro-life ethos. No public policy, in their view, should sacrifice human lives to achieve other social goals. Sidney Callahan, an influential moral theorist, describes her "prolife con-victions" as "stem[ming] from a feminist, Quaker-influenced, pacifist tradition." Another pro-life ethicist professes to "write in opposition to abortion, infanticide, the death penalty, and war."[33]

Although some pro-life advocates maintain that states must ban abortion because the Fourteenth Amendment protects unborn humans,[34] most leading critics of *Roe* reject claims that fetuses have a constitutional right to life. Instead, such influential legal scholars as former Judge Robert Bork and Professor John Hart Ely contend that states *may* ban abortion because the state interest in potential personhood is a sufficient legislative justification for outlawing that procedure in the absence of any constitutional clause that affirmatively protects the right to terminate a pregnancy. "The protection of fetal life," Professor Michael Perry of Northwestern Law School points out, "is surely more than a trivial good."[35] This communal desire to preserve the unborn distinguishes restrictions on abortion from the restrictions on birth control that some critics of *Roe* admit may be unconstitutional. Previous judicial decisions striking down state bans on contraception, a law professor notes, were "not of special importance" in *Roe* because "it was precisely the claims of the fetus and its status to assert them that raise the greatest difficulty in abortion cases."[36]

Critics of *Roe* do not think that constitutional authorities must investigate how abortion policies actually function before ruling that the state interest in protecting fetal life is a legitimate constitutional justification for limiting reproductive choice. They believe the point of pro-life measures should be obvious to any person who can understand the state penal code. Every abortion necessarily destroys a genetic human. Therefore, one can logically deduce that statutory bans on abortion must protect the unborn, or so most anti-*Roe* arguments suggest.

This facile assumption is based on a faulty syllogism. From the normative premise that the social interest in protecting fetal life justifies statutory bans on abortion, one cannot reach the empirical conclusion that all statutory bans on abortion are primarily designed to preserve the unborn. Concern for fetal life may serve as a convenient pretext for more dubious official purposes, purposes that can be detected only by exploring state reproductive policies as a whole. Indeed, much evidence indicates that "states have never mandated policies, statutes, or enforcement procedures that would display anything approaching a compelling interest in protecting all potential human life."[37]

Conventional attacks on legal abortion do not explain why communities so committed to the unborn never strictly enforced their statutory bans on abortion.[38] Academic lawyers who maintain that restrictions on abortion are constitutional means of protecting fetal life ignore numerous studies that document how state officials before *Roe* routinely allowed many women to terminate a pregnancy, as long as the procedure was performed discreetly.[39] Pro-life attempts to refute claims that past restrictions on abortion did not save many fetal lives are transparently inadequate. Opponents of legal abortion religiously cite statistical analyses that even a lay reader should recognize as resting on absurd assumptions. The most influential pro-life study reaches the conclusion that no more than 210,000 illegal abortions were performed annually from 1940 to 1972 by relying on Center for Disease Control (CDC) data on abortion fatalities that CDC officials admit represent "a minimum estimate." The authors then calculate the relative risk of the *average* criminal abortion by using a survey of "the nonwhite population of New York City." That study was done at a time when 94 percent of the women who died from criminal abortions in that community were women of color. Nowhere do the authors explain why one would assume that black women in Harlem had access to anything remotely resembling the same quality abortion services as had white women who lived in such affluent suburbs as Scarsdale and Great Neck.[40] More generally, no article published after 1960 in a respectable medical, public health, or scientific journal supports the claim of pro-life advocates that less than 200,000 abortions were being performed annually in the United States during the period when abortion was illegal.[41] The most reliable studies, which admittedly are not very reliable, suggest that approximately one million illegal abortions were performed annually in the years before *Roe*.[42]

Pro-life philosophers and their legal defenders also do not ponder why elected officials ostensibly concerned with protecting fetuses often adopt other policies that make abortions more frequent. Although moral and constitutional theorists may think the social interest in potential life distinguishes bans on abortion from bans on contraception, conservative American reproductive policies usually combine both measures. The anti-abortion Reagan and Bush administrations ranked contraception last in their priorities for family planning services. Yet, as a means of preventing both unwanted pregnancies and abortions, contraception is six to seven times more effective than the natural family planning methods that were given first priority by recent Republican administrations.[43] Many pro-life activists also oppose federal and state programs that increase access to contraceptives. The American Life League, for example, denounces all forms of birth control, even those that cannot be characterized as abortifacients.[44] Not surprisingly, studies find that abortion rates are "far lower" in virtually every other developed country "than in the United States." Only in America, family planning researchers bemoan, have "abortion laws [not] been designed as part of comprehensive practices intended to reduce the demand for abortion by facilitating access to contraceptive methods, sex education and related health services."[45]

Indeed, Americans seem uninterested in any measure other than restrictions on abortion that might prevent the death of unborn humans.

Father Theodore Hesburgh, the former president of the University of Notre Dame, points out that "many candidates who agree with [the Catholic Church's] position on abortion in this country advocate foreign policy positions that increase the likelihood that women in the Third World will seek abortion."[46] State and national legislators who oppose legal abortion rarely play a significant role in domestic political struggles to retain and expand governmental programs that further fetal health by providing nutrition and nutritional information to pregnant women. Most critics of *Roe* never note that socially conservative officials who proclaim that fetal life trumps procreative choice apparently regard lower taxes or a balanced budget as an even higher social value. "Pro-life representatives," one survey found, "are reluctant to vote for higher federal spending for programs designed to prevent unwanted pregnancies or to assist pregnant women."[47]

This ignorance can be bliss. Thus, evidence that American reproductive policies taken as a whole are destructive of potential life rarely disturbs conventional critics of *Roe*. Indeed, Bork suggests that constitutional theorists need never explore why persons actually oppose abortion. "Knowledge that [abortion][48] is taking place," he declares, "can cause moral pain." In Bork's opinion, courts in a democracy have no authority to prevent persons from enjoying the "gratification" that comes when bans on abortion ease this "moral pain," unless abortion rights are "covered specifically or by obvious implication by a provision of the Constitution."[49] Bork nowhere indicates that the particular source of this moral pain might matter. He apparently does not care whether anti-abortion activists are horrified by the death of unborn children, disgusted that other persons are committing acts that their religion regards as mortal sins, or fear that legal abortion will reduce the numbers, significance, and influence of their racial group.[50] By definition, it seems, if persons oppose abortion, then constitutionally sufficient reasons must exist for restricting that procedure.

Critics of *Roe* feel no greater need to examine actual political contexts to support their arguments that existing laws on the books reflect a present pro-life social consensus or an inherited political tradition. That abortion bans remain in state penal codes, they maintain, is conclusive evidence that the American people favor limiting their reproductive choices. Ely treats the mere presence of pro-life policies in authoritative legal texts as establishing a nearly irrebuttable presumption that restrictions on abortion satisfy the constitutional requirement that majorities generally rule. "There exists a societal consensus that [abortion] is . . . immoral," Ely asserts, because "this is what is counted crucial to get the laws passed and keep them on the books."[51] The presence of abortion restrictions on the books, however, is the only evidence Ely offers to prove that "there exists a societal consensus that abortion is immoral." Bork relies on the same tautologous criteria for democratic adequacy when he maintains that the very existence of legislation regulating abortion constitutes sufficient proof that "*Roe* [is] the greatest example and symbol of the judicial usurpation of democratic prerogatives this century."[52] Scholars who oppose *Roe* also deduce the traditional status of reproductive liberties from the legal language found in authoritative writings. "Justices," Jeffrey Rosen of the *New Republic* insists, should "anchor their search for the 'conscience of our people' by looking for a consensus among the state constitutions and state laws that are currently on the books."[53] That these laws were not strictly enforced does not strike him as a relevant part of our constitutional heritage.

Bork, Ely, and others quickly dismiss claims that statutory bans on abortion passed in the late nineteenth century might not reflect the views of late-twentieth-century majorities on sound public policy. That contemporary restrictions on abortion no longer serve their original purpose of protecting maternal health, they claim, has no bearing on sound constitutional analysis. "New justifications," after all, "can be advanced for old statutes." "There is no reason," a prominent law professor states, "to require a legislature to protect or rehabilitate an old statute with a new preamble."[54] Nor, apparently, is there any reason to study late-twentieth-century American politics to determine whether, in fact, elected officials did consciously decide to retain restrictions on abortion because they believed such policies serve worthy purposes other than the protection of maternal health.[55]

Critics of *Roe* also substitute hypotheticals for evidence when claiming that abortion restrictions can withstand constitutional scrutiny even when pro-life policies do not reflect the views of popular majorities. Coalition politics, Ely notes, are hardly unconstitutional in the United States. "There is nothing unusual, and I was not aware there was anything wrong," he argues, "with an intense minority's compromising on issues about which it feels less strongly in order to gain support on those it cares most passionately about."[56] Speculative assertions that legitimate logrolling politics might explain the existence of restrictive abortion policies, however, cannot obviate the need to investigate whether such bargains have been struck, and what the nature of such bargains might be. Once again, theoretical demonstrations that abortion politics could satisfy democratic standards replace empirical demonstrations that contemporary abortion politics do satisfy democratic standards.

The canonical constitutional defenders of pro-life policies rely heavily on unrealized potentialities. Restrictions on abortion, Bork and others hypothesize, *may* protect the unborn, *may* communicate messages about the sanctity of life, *may* reflect present majoritarian values, and *may* result from legitimate pluralist bargaining. As long as some plausible justification exists for restrictive abortion laws on the books, the most prominent critics of *Roe* believe that justices should sustain pro-life measures. Whether abortion law and politics in action actually pass constitutional or democratic muster is an issue critics of *Roe* do not address.

Pro-Choice Arguments

Pro-choice advocates claim that restrictions on abortion necessarily violate fundamental human and constitutional liberties. Many proponents of reproductive choice endorse the *Roe* Court's declaration that the "right of privacy . . . encompasses a woman's decision whether or not to terminate her pregnancy." Ronald Dworkin, the most influential liberal constitutional thinker of the late twentieth century, maintains that "all citizens have a general right, based in the Fourteenth Amendment's guarantee of due process of law, to decide for themselves ethical and personal issues arising from marriage and procreation."[57] Abortion does not violate any fundamental human or constitutional right to life, these pro-choice advocates insist, because fetuses have no right to be born[58] and because "the word 'person,' as used in the Fourteenth Amendment, does not include the unborn."[59]

Other liberal proponents of reproductive choice derive abortion rights from the more general right not to have one's body occupied and used by an unwanted, albeit innocent, invader.[60] One version of this argument condemns restrictions on abortion for violating the right to bodily integrity protected by the due process clause of the Fourteenth Amendment. Professors Robin West and Deborah Rhode charge that anti-abortion measures permit invasions of "the physical boundaries of the body and the psychic boundaries of a life."[61] A second version of the argument from bodily autonomy claims that pro-life policies unjustly and unconstitutionally conscript women for the good of others. Professor Cass Sunstein maintains that "the government cannot impose on women alone the obligation to protect fetuses through a legal act of bodily cooptation." Requiring women to shoulder this responsibility is particularly offensive to the values protected by the Thirteenth Amendment and the equal protection clause because men have no comparable legal obligation to be Good Samaritans. "The law of abortion," Laurence Tribe of Harvard Law School declares, is the "one place in the law where a really significant and intimate sacrifice has been required of anyone in order to save another."[62]

Liberal defenses of legal abortion maintain that any decent community must recognize that "the right to privacy is inherent in the right to liberty." "Keeping Reproductive Choice in Private Hands," a bold heading in one law review article proclaims, "is Essential to a Free Society."[63]

Mainstream pro-choice arguments suggest that a simple syllogism demonstrates that all flat bans on abortion are necessarily unconstitutional. Every abortion decision entails two choices: whether one's body will be occupied by a (somewhat) distinct entity and whether to bring a fetus to term. Hence, by outlawing all procedures that terminate pregnancies, all pro-life policies force women to succor an unwanted being and become mothers against their will. Given this inexorable logic, evidence that bans on abortion do or do not protect unborn life cannot bear on the validity of *Roe*. Thus, the constitutional defects in recent attempts to regulate abortion are inherent in any substantial effort to limit reproductive choice.

The rhetoric of "choice," however, obscures questions concerning when persons must exercise their right to privacy or bodily autonomy.[64] The overwhelming majority of women who have abortions became pregnant after engaging in voluntary sexual activity; victims of rape and incest account for only a minute percentage of all women procuring abortions.[65] Hence, pro-choice claims that early cutoff dates for abortion deny women the time necessary to make responsible abortion decisions[66] do not take seriously anti-*Roe* assertions that most persons are already free to consider at length "ethical and personal issues arising from marriage and procreation." Barring rape, sexual abstinence is an infallible form of birth control. As Bork points out, an individual "has, as a matter of fact, the freedom to decide whether to bear or beget a child . . . because he or she has the right to choose whether or not to copulate."[67] Persons who cannot decide whether they want children may postpone this decision indefinitely by avoiding heterosexual intercourse.[68]

Insisting that only "religious ascetics do without sex"[69] is both inaccurate and misleading. Psychologically healthy people are celibate for long periods of time. The most recent *Diagnostic and Statistical Manual of Mental Disorders* (DSM IV; 1994), the authoritative nosology used by American psychiatrists, does not list voluntary sexual abstinence as either a symptom of a mental disorder or a disorder itself.[70] Even if sex is a basic human need, the connection between any right to sexual activity and abortion is more complex than pro-choice advocates so readily suggest. Many forms of heterosexual lovemaking do not risk pregnancy. Advice columnist Ann Landers was stunned by the number of women who, in response to her survey, wrote that they preferred cuddling as their exclusive form of lovemaking.[71] Permanent sterilization is another option for persons who want to enjoy sex "without consequences." More to the point, many Americans, indeed many Americans who support pro-choice policies, engage in heterosexual intercourse with the understanding that they will not have an abortion should conception occur.

The failure to explore at length when and whether persons have a constitutional right to engage in heterosexual intercourse is particularly unfortunate because the political struggle over abortion is ultimately grounded in different attitudes toward human sexuality. Pro-life supporters are no more likely than pro-choice supporters to take positions solicitous of the health or existence of the unborn when they evaluate policies other than abortion: dramatic differences appear only when both are questioned about sex. One study found that National Abortion Rights Action League "members are 15 times as likely as [National Right to Life Committee] members to support sex education in the schools and four times as likely to favor making birth control available to teenagers." Pro-choice activists are also seven times more likely to see nothing wrong with premarital sex, fifty-three times more likely to see nothing wrong with extramarital sex, twenty-two times more likely to see nothing wrong with homosexuality, and ninety-nine times more likely to see nothing wrong with voluntary sterilization.[72]

Roe cannot be adequately justified by lengthy analyses of the right to procreate voluntarily or the right to bodily autonomy that, at best, make only cursory mention of any right to engage in sexual intercourse. If the Fourteenth Amendment does not protect the right to engage in amative sexuality—that is, lovemaking motivated by pleasure or intimacy rather than procreation—then people must exercise their right to control their fertility by remaining celibate or by being sterilized. Yet mainstream pro-choice advocates rarely discuss the constitutional status of human sexuality. Indeed, the omission of sex in most commentaries on abortion epitomizes what Thomas Reed Powell once described as the capacity of the "legal mind" to "think about a thing, inextricably attached to something else, without thinking of the thing it is attached to."[73]

Liberal pro-choice advocates present a similarly incomplete picture of abortion politics when they charge that pro-life policies result from narrow-minded partisan behavior that adversely affects the ability of the American political system to reflect majoritarian sentiments on other, more important issues. In several articles published by the *New York Review of Books*, Ronald Dworkin catalogues how "the corruption of single-issue [abortion] politics" has damaged "American democracy." "The sudden dominance of the abortion issue in state politics and elections in all regions of the country," he declares, "has driven crucial economic and social issues from the political agenda." In his view, pro-life activists wield this disproportionate power over what policies are subject to democratic control because they are "dedicated and single-issue minorities who in many parts of the country can destroy politicians they single out for attack, not because their views are so popular but because most voters are concerned with a variety of issues and are unwilling to allow their politics to be governed by any one."[74] Given that no political system can resolve every political controversy that divides a society, Dworkin notes that granting elected officials the authority to restrict abortion will weaken the capacity of American institutions to represent the majority will on more vital domestic and foreign policy questions. If *Roe* is overruled, he warns, "political decisions will be less sensitive to the complexities of the popular will, because ordinary voters are in a worse, not better, position to express their convictions and professions across the range of political issues when politicians are forced to treat one issue as the only one which counts."[75]

Even if these dubious assertions about the political potency of pro-life forces are correct,[76] the spectacle Dworkin and others present of a pitched battle between primitive pro-life voters and the more sophisticated electorate is a political fantasy. Pro-life citizens are concerned with a wide variety of issues, from school prayer to pornography.[77] Although early scholarship depicting most American voters as grossly uninformed about politics has been challenged by more recent research,[78] no evidence supports the assumption that the average citizen is politically more astute than the average anti-abortion activist. Major elections frequently turn on economic issues,[79] but few persons think that the pocketbook voter or the Chamber of Commerce engages in single-issue politics. Thus, proponents of legal abortion have no factual basis for believing that the pro-life movement is a distinct and powerful single-issue interest group. Assertions that the Christian Coalition must be judicially neutralized are rooted in normative beliefs that politics should be about political economy rather than Christian moral virtues (particularly when abortion has been "removed" from that politics by a judicial ruling that women have a constitutional right to terminate their pregnancies).

A quick glance at contemporary culture wars over sex education, religion in schools, and homosexuality would have suggested to conventional pro-choice advocates that pro-life activists are not simpleminded single-issue voters. Of course, were pro-life philosophers willing to look in the same direction, they might begin questioning whether most opponents of legal abortion are primarily concerned with protecting the unborn. This unwillingness of mainstream theorists to talk about how twentieth-century citizens experience pro-choice and pro-life policies provides the grist for much feminist theory. Unfortunately, in the guise of examining how statutory restrictions on abortion actually oppress women, many feminist theorists reproduce much of the abstracted analysis found in more conventional pro- and anti-*Roe* commentary.

Feminist Pro-Choice Arguments

Pro-choice feminists[80] promise more realistic justifications of legal abortion. "One distinct feature of feminist legal analysis," practitioners maintain, "is . . . a grounding in practical problems and a reliance on 'practical reasoning.'"[81] Unlike male academics who "elaborate yet more arcane abstractions of ideas building on ideas,"[82] feminist jurists maintain that they consider "people's actual experience of themselves in the world." "Feminist jurisprudence," Catharine MacKinnon of the University of Michigan Law School insists, "is accountable to women's concrete conditions and to changing them." MacKinnon, an extraordinarily influential legal theorist and political activist, claims that her legal writings and those of other feminists are about "what *is*, the meaning of what is, and the way what is, is enforced."[83]

Pro-choice feminists defend legal abortion in ways they claim "accurately correspond to the experience of women."[84] According to MacKinnon, pro-life policies ignore the close relationship between rape and sex under present conditions of gender inequality. All pro-choice feminists maintain that limiting access to abortion oppresses women by preventing or severely inhibiting their efforts to achieve political, economic, and social equality. Statutory bans on abortion, they contend repeatedly, would be repealed immediately if women had the same political power as men.

ABORTION AND FORCED SEX

Catharine MacKinnon aspires to correct *Roe v. Wade*'s disregard of actual social circumstances. "Liberals," she charges, "have supported the availability of the abortion choice as if the woman just happened on the fetus."[85] This, her readers are informed, is mere male abstraction. MacKinnon argues that "abortion policy" must be "explicitly approached in the context of how women get pregnant," which, she believes, is a "consequence of intercourse under conditions of gender inequality." Feminists who wish to improve the constitutional foundations of abortion rights must "talk about sex, specifically about intercourse in relation to rape in relation to conception."[86]

Attention to the concrete reproductive choices actually open to women, MacKinnon asserts, reveals that abortion is "an issue of forced sex." Her "feminist investigations" suggest that "sexual intercourse . . . cannot simply be presumed coequally determined."[87] Women today remain physically and culturally vulnerable to male lovers, acquaintances, and rapists. MacKinnon claims that some women endure sex to obtain life's necessities. "Poverty and enforced economic dependence," she contends, "undermine women's physical integrity and sexual self-determination."[88] More often, subtle social pressures exploit female sexuality in ways that limit the capacity of women to refuse intercourse. "Women," MacKinnon states, "are socially disadvantaged in controlling sexual access to their bodies through socialization to customs that define a woman's body as for sexual use by men. Sexual access is regularly forced or pressured or routinized beyond denial."[89]

MacKinnon supports her claims about how women become pregnant by pointing to studies documenting that many women with the financial resources and knowledge necessary to practice effective birth control nevertheless do not use contraception consistently.[90] These systemic failures to prevent pregnancy, she maintains, must occur when women engage in sexual intercourse reluctantly. "I wonder," MacKinnon declares,

> if a woman can be presumed to control access to her sexuality if she feels unable to interrupt intercourse to insert a diaphragm; or worse, cannot even want to, aware that she risks a pregnancy she knows she does not want. Do you think she would stop the man for any other reason, such as, for instance, the real taboo—lack of desire?[91]

Contraceptive risk-taking, MacKinnon emphasizes, cannot be explained by social proscriptions resulting in "women's repressive socialization to passivity or coolness."[92] In her view, decisions not to contracept raise questions about whether "sex, hence its consequences, [is] meaningfully voluntary for women."[93] Feminists, MacKinnon stresses, must "rethin[k] the problems of sexuality, from the repression of drives by civilization to the oppression of women by men."[94]

Remarkably, MacKinnon offers no study of "concrete reality" that supports her claims about the relationship between abortion and forced sex in modern society. She correctly asserts that persons can be compelled to have sex in the absence of violent threats and presents convincing evidence that forced sex in such circumstances is an important social problem.[95] Nevertheless, MacKinnon does not refer to any research, feminist or otherwise, demonstrating that a significant number of unwanted pregnancies result from sexual intercourse that women were compelled to have (however "compelled" is defined). The only feminist investigation she cites is Kristin Luker's *Taking Chances: Abortion and the Decision Not to Contracept* (1975).[96] Luker does conclude that contraceptive risk-taking cannot be explained without reference to social policies and attitudes that are "oppressive to women."[97] *Taking Chances*, however, does not support and frequently belies the "concrete realities" that ostensibly ground MacKinnon's critique of *Roe*.

Taking Chances offers many excerpts from Luker's interviews with contraceptive risk-takers, but in only two cases do her subjects indicate that they did not consent to sexual relations.[98] Instead, Luker found that the "biological and medical side-effects" of birth control explain why many women take contraceptive risks. Other researchers have reached similar conclusions.[99] Moreover, two-thirds of Luker's subjects had been told that they would have difficulty becoming pregnant. This information encouraged contraceptive risk-taking both by tempting women to see if they were fertile and by leading them to believe they were unlikely to become pregnant after engaging in unprotected sex.[100] Although MacKinnon cannot imagine why anyone would refuse to "interrupt intercourse to insert a diaphragm," some women Luker interviewed admitted that they willingly risked pregnancy when the delay necessary to use contraception interfered with the pleasures of lovemaking.[101]

Luker recognizes that social attitudes toward feminine sexuality contribute significantly to contraceptive risk-taking. Many women, she found, hesitate to contracept regularly because birth control "socially proclaims the user to be a sexually active women, a 'cold-blooded' planner, a hard-eyed realist with no romance in her soul, and a woman who is perhaps too sexually active to be a lady."[102] MacKinnon, however, maintains that a different sexual double standard has deleterious effects on contraceptive risk-taking. "Women," she claims, "feel compelled to preserve the appearance . . . of male direction of sexual expression, as if it were male initiative that women want, as if it were that which women find arousing. Men enforce this."[103] *Taking Chances* provides no support for this claim. No male or female subject quoted in the study suggested that a desire "to preserve the appearance of male initiative" influenced their contraceptive risk-taking. Although many women Luker interviewed indicated that male attitudes contributed to their decision not to contracept, they blamed male ignorance of basic facts about human reproduction or passive toleration of their contraceptive risk-taking for their failure to use birth control.[104]

Taking Chances also presents evidence inconsistent with MacKinnon's claim that women and men whose consciousness has been raised will recognize that abortion is a result of forced sex.[105] Contrary to MacKinnon's bald assertions, Luker found that contraceptive risk-taking is more likely to occur when women have some desire to have children and, hence, want sex.[106] Women who failed to use birth control, she repeatedly points out, "were attempting to achieve more diffuse goals than simply preventing pregnancy."[107] Many women quoted in *Taking Chances* took contraceptive risks, *in part*, because they believed that becoming pregnant would establish their fertility and femininity, force lovers and significant others to redefine their relationship, and enable them to receive psychological counseling.[108] To be sure, these contraceptive risk-takers, after consciousness-raising, may question their reasons for wanting to become pregnant.[109] Women who had some desire to become pregnant, however, are not likely to rethink whether they actually consented to engaging in unprotected sex.

Finally, MacKinnon and Luker dispute whether the failure to use birth control is deviant behavior. MacKinnon implies that contraceptive risk-taking is pathological. "Sex doesn't look a whole lot like freedom," she bluntly declares, "when it appears normatively less costly for women to risk an undesired, often painful, traumatic, dangerous, sometimes illegal, and potentially life-threatening procedure, than it is to protect oneself in advance.[110] Luker disagrees. She characterizes as "unscientifically misogynist" those persons who treat "women who fail to protect themselves contraceptively as qualitatively different from people who fail to protect life or health in other ways." Women who take contraceptive risks, *Taking Chances* points out, behave no differently than men (and women) who take chances on the ski slopes. Luker observes that "Americans smoke, drive when they've been drinking, and steadfastly refuse to fasten their seat belts." "Why should we expect contraceptive behavior to be of a higher standard," she asks, "when everyone agrees that correct behavior in these other areas can literally save lives?"[111]

American contraceptive and sexual practices do provide much fodder for potential attacks on pro-life measures. Conservative reproductive policies leave too many women, teenagers in particular, without adequate access to birth control services and information.[112] Various sexist practices help explain why many sexually active women fail to contracept regularly.[113] Many women, teenagers in particular, have difficulty resisting male advances in circumstances that do not technically constitute rape.[114] No evidence, however, supports MacKinnon's claim that women take contraceptive risks because they are reluctant to engage in sex. Her claim that pro-life policies fail to acknowledge the constant pressure on women to have sex is based on a theory that sees little difference between normal sex and rape, not on the actual experiences of women who procure abortions.

ABORTION AND THE OPPRESSION OF WOMEN

The most popular feminist defense of *Roe* claims that restrictions on abortion oppress women. State efforts to restrict reproductive choice, prominent feminists insist, "reflect and broadly reinforce the subordination of women" by "leaving women involuntarily pregnant and unable to act as freely as men do."[115] All pro-choice feminists agree that pro-life policies "integrally contribut[e] to the maintenance of an underclass or a deprived position because of gender status." Restrictions on abortion, Professor Sylvia Law asserts, "pervasively affec[t] the ability of women to plan their lives, to sustain relationships with other people, and to contribute through wage work and public life."[116] The burdens that unwanted pregnancies place on women do not simply result from human biology or "the nature of things." Rather, as Law and other feminists recognize, "where the state denies access to abortion, both nature and the state impose upon women the burdens of unwanted pregnancy that men do not bear."[117]

The conventional feminist defense of reproductive choice maintains that women's interests in abortion rights will be consistently discounted in public life as long as men disproportionately dominate the electoral and legislative processes. "Men don't get pregnant," pro-choice women proclaim, "they just pass the laws." This political imbalance is fundamentally undemocratic because one essential safeguard of democracy is that representatives must be subject to the laws they enact. But as feminist lawyers point out, "every restrictive abortion law has been passed by a legislature in which men constitute a numerical majority." Worse, they claim, "every restrictive abortion law by definition contains an unwritten clause exempting all men from its strictures."[118]

Communities that empower women, feminists maintain, will quickly abandon their pro-life measures. In their view, because "the interests, perceptions, and experiences that have shaped the law have not included those of women," abortion policies will be quite different when "women participat[e] equally in designing laws."[119] MacKinnon declares that "sex equality" as a norm "comes into being through the resistance of women as a people to their subjection." In a more egalitarian society, she and other feminists believe, elected officials (approximately half of whom would be women) would give greater weight to the women's interest in terminating her pregnancy and less weight to preserving fetal life. "If women were taken seriously," Olsen asserts, "fetal life would not be valued by society at large unless and until the women carrying the fetus valued it."[120]

Legislative abortion policies, however, cannot be said to reflect in any simple sense the gross underrepresentation of women in American politics and public life.[121] Men are at least as likely as women to favor abortion on demand; most surveys find that men, if anything, have a slightly greater tendency than women to support pro-choice positions.[122] Moreover, the pro-life movement is not a conservative male crusade against liberated women. Women are disproportionately represented in the leadership and grassroots membership of anti-abortion organizations. One study found that "over 80 percent of the activists in both the pro-choice and the pro-life movement in California were women." Women even constitute two-thirds of the leadership of the National Right to Life Committee.[123]

One possible reason why women do not overwhelmingly support abortion on demand is that they tend to be more religious and less educated then men, characteristics strongly associated with pro-life views. Even when the influence of religion and education are accounted for, however, women are not substantially more likely than men to favor abortion rights. Gender, survey after survey reveals, has little or no effect on attitudes toward legal abortion.[124] Moreover, pro-life women do not appear to be somehow dominated by pro-life men. No evidence exists that "resistant women were actually brainwashed into adopting repressive male atti-tudes" toward abortion rights.[125] Indeed, the mass media, the institution most likely to promote such false consciousness, is controlled by persons who are overwhelmingly pro-choice.[126]

Gender does influence voting in state and federal legislatures: female representatives are significantly more likely than male representatives to oppose restrictions on abortion.[127] Although this disparity between the sexes does not reflect broader gender differences in attitudes toward abor-tion, the strong support most women officials give to pro-choice policies is rooted in several features of twentieth-century American gender poli-tics. Women who serve in state and national legislatures have several char-acteristics that are significantly associated with pro-choice views. Elected officials are better educated and more affluent then average citizens, and highly educated, affluent women are somewhat more pro-choice than highly educated, affluent men.[128] Furthermore, women who prefer tradi-tional, domestic roles are unlikely to pursue the full-time professional or political careers necessary to become national or state officials.[129] Finally, pro-life citizens who believe that women belong in the home and not in the House probably do not vote for any female candidates, no matter what their stance on abortion, whenever a politically palatable male alter-native exists.[130] Not surprisingly, therefore, even though women in gen-eral are no more supportive of abortion than men, female legislators gen-erally represent more liberal, pro-choice districts.[131]

American abortion politics would probably be different if the political power of women increased, but not in the ways that many pro-choice feminist predict. Women tend to feel much more strongly than men about abortion, both for and against.[132] Hence, a political system in which women were more equally represented might spend much more time and energy debating different abortion policies. Reproductive rights might at-tract the same legislative attention currently given to balancing (and not balancing) the budget.[133] Changes in the relative political salience of abor-tion would also influence political competition in the United States. The two major parties might be as divided over abortion as over economic issues. This realignment would give voters a clearer choice between pro-life and pro-choice candidates in more elections.

Pro-choice activists are wrong, however, when they suggest that such a political environment would necessarily be more conducive to abortion on demand. All other things being equal, developments that facilitate greater representation of women in American political life will primarily replace lukewarm pro-choice legislators with committed proponents of abortion on demand and lukewarm pro-life legislators with committed proponents of restrictions on abortion. More pro-choice policies will re-sult from the increased political empowerment of women only if such increases disproportionately benefit relatively affluent women, who are more inclined than their less fortunate sisters to favor legal abortion.

Some feminists grudgingly admit that pro-life women exist, although no pro-choice analysis fully acknowledges the central role women play in the pro-life movement. One general work on feminist jurisprudence asks, "How can feminists wedded to experiential analysis respond to women who reject feminism's basic premises as contrary to *their* experience?" (emphasis in original).[134] So far, no feminist who maintains that "anti-abortion rhetoric and policies are anti-women," or who "purports to speak to the diversity of women's lives,"[135] has responded to this troubling question. Pro-life women, in feminist writings, are often permitted to speak only through the mouth of Andrea Dworkin, the equivalent of relying exclusively on Phyllis Schlafly or Marilyn Quayle to articulate the views of pro-choice women. Citing Dworkin's *Right-wing Women* (1983), Professors MacKinnon and Olsen suggest that antifeminists actually support feminist ideals but see restrictions on abortion as the only means of improving women's lot in present society. Pro-life "assertions" that the availability of abortion eliminates women's most socially "acceptable reason for refusing sex," Olsen declares, "certainly reflect a deep pessimism regarding change in male-female relations and in the role and status of women."[136] When surveyed, however, pro-life women never claim that restrictions on abortion enable them to reject unwanted sexual demands. Such women are far more likely to express fear that abortion on demand will degrade what they believe is the vital feminine value of nurturance.[137] These concerns cannot be fully addressed as long as most feminists are unwilling to heed and analyze the unmediated voices of those women who oppose making abortion legal. Too many pro-choice feminists who claim that "whatever womanhood mean[s], women . . . need neither men nor intercourse nor babies to prove it"[138] fail to acknowledge that most American women believe otherwise.

Restrictions on abortion may oppress all women, even if many women cannot recognize their subjugation. Persons may also have a timeless human and constitutional right not to be pregnant against their will. For that matter, pro-life philosophers may have irrefutable arguments that all abortions are homicides. Nothing in this chapter discredits these universal claims. The point is simply that they *are* universal claims, that the conventional pro-life, pro-choice, and feminist arguments are ultimately grounded on abstract concepts and not on concrete realities. Robert Bork, Ronald Dworkin, and Catharine MacKinnon may not agree on much, but each insists that we can resolve the abortion controversy simply by applying certain timeless philosophical and constitutional principles. When we contemplate life, democracy, liberty, privacy, patriarchy, or the nature of women long enough, these thinkers seem to believe, we will not need to examine the relative merits of particular abortion policies. The basic questions raised by *Roe* have right answers, and these answers can be discovered by any person capable of the sort of rigorous metaphysical thinking that avoids being distracted by material conditions. For better or worse, however, contemporary abortion policies are administered by actual persons in particular social environments. Unless citizens are prepared to argue that no abortion can ever be justified or that states may never restrict access to abortion, utopian reasoning—whether pro-life, pro-choice, or feminist—cannot by itself determine what measures persons on earth should presently support.

THE THEORETICAL IMPASSE

The most influential proponents and opponents of legal abortion are oblivious to the details of contemporary social life in one last, more political, sense. Neither the standard defenses nor the conventional critiques of *Roe* can persuade a clear majority of present-day Americans that a particular abortion policy best reflects our society's philosophical and constitutional values. The canonical works in the pro-choice, pro-life, and anti-*Roe* traditions frequently treat as axiomatic philosophical assertions and theories of constitutional interpretation that most citizens question. Too much commentary assumes rather than defends controversial theories about when life begins, the role of women, the meaning of the due process clause, and the function of the federal judiciary. Many polemics do little more than reassure their small targeted audience that only a moral cretin or constitutional moron could doubt the unassailable justice of the author's position on reproductive policy. Pro-choice theorists treat pro-life advocates as misogynists bent on punishing women who have sex. Pro-life theorists treat pro-choice advocates as murderers intent on perpetrating a new Holocaust. Anti-*Roe* theorists treat pro-*Roe* advocates as dictators committed to destroying democratic processes. Such rhetoric, designed primarily to preach to and inspire the converted, cannot and does not appeal to those citizens who have grave reservations about pro-choice, pro-life, and anti-*Roe* claims.

Nevertheless, the main rhetorical obstacles pro-choice, pro-life, and anti-*Roe* advocates face are substantive, not stylistic. No argument at the present time, even one crafted by the most eloquent presidential speechwriter or the most sophisticated political advertising agency, is likely to persuade a substantial majority of citizens that basic principles of philosophical or constitutional justice provide clear answers to questions about abortion rights and policies. The foundational values of pro-choice, pro-life, and anti-*Roe* positions all enjoy broad popular support and all are deeply rooted in the American political and constitutional tradition. Americans cannot reach a consensus on abortion policy because they cannot choose among those values when they conflict.[139] The clash of absolutes—fetal life versus procreative choice, written versus living constitutions, and democracy versus judicial review—is, in the view of many citizens, philosophically, constitutionally, and democratically unresolvable.

The rhetorical failures of pro-choice, pro-life, and anti-*Roe* advocacy during the second half of the twentieth century have left American abortion politics at an impasse. Before *Roe*, pro-choice forces did not have the political strength to repeal restrictions on abortion, but pro-life forces lacked the political strength to have such measures carried out. After *Roe*, neither side could muster the power necessary to produce a clear social consensus on a particular abortion policy. Most elected officials continue doing everything in their power to avoid making policy on or even discussing abortion. When offered clear choices on abortion in political campaigns, a significant number of citizens vote on other grounds. Democratic Party presidential candidates now run on pro-choice platforms, but many Democratic candidates for Congress and state offices publicly announce their opposition to abortion on demand.[140] Republican Party presidential candidates now run on pro-life platforms, but many Republican candidates for Congress and state offices publicly announce their support for abortion on demand.[141] The best argument the present judicial plurality can muster for retaining *Roe* is that judicial precedents should rarely, if ever, be overruled, a consideration that does not deter Justices Souter, Kennedy, and O'Connor in other areas of constitutional law.[142]

Of course, highly controversial political claims may in time become political axioms, as the examples of slavery and school segregation demonstrate. Perhaps as human intelligence and probity increase, all persons will recognize that basic principles of justice and constitutional interpretation justify a particular abortion policy. History may vindicate the most radical wing of the pro-choice or pro-life movements just as history has vindicated the most radical wing of the abolitionist movement. Moreover, pro-choice, pro-life, and anti-*Roe* theorists may indeed be articulating timeless philosophical and jurisprudential truths, even though the general public has not yet seen the light. An abortion advocate "more right than his neighbor," Henry David Thoreau reminds us, "constitutes a majority of one." Nevertheless, proponents and opponents of legal abortion who hope in the near future to form popular majorities significantly greater than one must talk more about gray markets and general laws and less about fetal life and procreative liberty.

CHAPTER II

Abortion Law in Action

ANY REALISTIC appraisal of American reproductive policies during the twentieth century must recognize that abortion law in action rarely resembles abortion law on the books. Formal and actual abortion policies differ because those pro-life persons and groups who have had the power to enact or maintain restrictions on procreative choice have never had the power to ensure that those rules are enforced. Even when the procedure is nominally illegal, so many prominent citizens desire or tolerate safe abortions that state officials usually only prosecute incompetent abortionists who harm their clientele or physicians who openly advertise their abortion services.[1] Historians debate whether abortion bans were originally designed to save fetal lives,[2] but law enforcement efforts in practice clearly did not protect the unborn.

Although statutory bans on abortion never mentioned race or class, law enforcement officials in many communities created and maintained an exclusive gray market in safe abortion services that catered to affluent families. This gray market flourished in the twilight zone between black and free markets. Black markets exist when law enforcement officials are *unable* to prevent unlawful transactions. A black market in unsafe abortions thrived throughout the twentieth century because police efforts to deter amateur abortionists usually failed. Gray markets, by comparison, exist when law enforcement officials are *unwilling* to prevent unlawful transactions. A gray market in safe abortions thrived throughout the twentieth century because the great majority of law enforcement officials did not wish to arrest, prosecute, convict, or sentence qualified abortionists. Police officers, prosecutors, judges, and juries were usually well aware that certain doctors and hospitals in their community performed "illegal abortions." Nevertheless, the official legal community rarely inhibited competent practitioners, particularly when the offending physicians did not offer their services to the general public. Indeed, active official cooperation was often necessary to ensure that the local gray market in safe abortions survived.

The unofficial official actions responsible for the exclusive gray market helped economic and political elites enjoy a de facto right to abortion on demand throughout most of the twentieth century. No matter what the local law on the books stated, affluent adult women in all regions of the

United States who had ongoing professional or personal relationships with private physicians rarely faced substantial obstacles after deciding to terminate an unwanted pregnancy.[3] To be sure, obtaining an abortion was not always convenient and the practice was considered disreputable. Nevertheless, by the late 1960s, upper- and upper-middle-class women usually had access to safe and affordable abortions, even when the cost included transportation to a state or country where abortion was legal.

Lacking access to this exclusive gray market, poor women and women of color bore the brunt of statutory bans on abortion.[4] Such women not only had less access to "therapeutic" hospital abortions than their more affluent counterparts, they also had considerably less access to safe "criminal" abortions.[5] Women willing to hazard black-market procedures had no reliable method for determining the credentials and skills of whatever abortionist they might locate. Even when doctors performed illegal abortions, the operating physician might be incompetent, abusive, or drunk. As a result, women who relied on black-market abortionists often paid significantly more money for significantly worse services than more affluent women who had their abortions performed on the gray market.

Legalization destroyed the gray market and, in doing so, sharply decreased race and class disparities in access to safe abortions. Nevertheless, many women remain unable to terminate an unwanted pregnancy. Abortion is not equally available to all women, because abortion providers remain scarce; economic considerations and pro-life mayhem deter physicians from offering abortions in most American communities. Contemporary access problems, however, cannot be blamed on anti-abortion state laws or on judicial decisions sustaining those laws. When abortion is legal, hostile state regulations that fall short of legal bans have little impact on access to abortion services. Laws imposing funding bans, waiting periods, informed consent, parental notification, and other barriers to reproductive services are not yet preventing women from obtaining abortions. Pro-choice advocates may proclaim that "*Roe v. Wade* is dead,"[6] but the Supreme Court's decisions in *Webster v. Reproductive Health Services*[7] and *Planned Parenthood v. Casey*[8] have not affected the reproductive choices presently open to most poor women and women of color.

Future bans on abortion would reintroduce massive discrimination against poor women and women of color. Should the judiciary stop protecting abortion rights, many states will adopt so-called reform laws similar to those that dramatically increased racial and economic disparities in the past. Even if law enforcement efforts in restrictive states actually prevent all competent abortionists from plying their trade, affluent women will travel without fear of official interference to jurisdictions where abortion is legal. Indeed, a post-*Roe* gray market will probably dwarf its pre-*Roe* predecessor. During the 1950s and 1960s, only the most fortunate women experienced little trouble terminating an unwanted pregnancy. Should abortion again become illegal in a few states, only the least fortunate women in those jurisdictions will have significant trouble locating a competent abortionist. Opponents of *Roe* may have a plan to ensure more egalitarian implementation of flat bans on abortion, but if so, their strategy is the best-kept legal and political secret in American politics.

In this chapter, I discuss how governmental officials administer various abortion policies and I examine the effect that official behavior has on the distribution of both safe and legal abortions.[9] My conclusions are estimates because information about abortion before *Roe* is sketchy and unreliable. Criminal abortionists did not keep detailed records of their successes and failures, so scholars have had to rely on more speculative means for determining the extent, bias, and consequences of the abortion underground.[10] Those who demand proof to a near certainty should remember Aristotle's maxim that "we must not expect more precision than the subject-matter admits of." As the distinguished historian Fernand Braudel once commented, "real figures would be better, but they do not exist."[11]

ABORTION PAST

The Scope of Abortion Past

American abortion policies before *Roe* cannot be described simply as blanket prohibitions. From 1900 until 1970, the penal code in every state forbade abortion except in certain narrowly defined instances. Few governing officials and communities, however, exhibited any enthusiasm for enforcing those bans. As a result, abortion law on the books never accurately characterized the obstacles that women actually faced when seeking to terminate their pregnancies. A wide variety of demographic factors had a far greater influence than judicial opinions and legislative enactments on the distribution of abortion services, particularly those provided by competent practitioners. A leading work on American abortion practices observes that throughout the twentieth century, "depending on where a woman lives, on the attitudes and practices of the woman's physician and hospital, or on who she is and whom she knows, she may find it easy or difficult to obtain an abortion regardless of how restrictive or permissive the laws are."[12]

The precise wording in state penal codes typically had little influence on the relative availability of legal abortions in different communities. States that prohibited only some abortions often had lower legal abortion rates than states that prohibited virtually all abortions. Conversely, other states that prohibited some abortions had higher legal abortion rates than states with no restrictions on abortion.[13] Access to legal abortions before *Roe* differed significantly in jurisdictions that adopted the same legal language. In the late 1960s, California, Maryland, Colorado, Virginia, South Carolina, and North Carolina passed nearly identical reform measures based on the recommendations of the American Law Institute (ALI). The respective legal abortion rates in these states in 1970, however, were 135, 102, 41, 13, 7, and 7 per thousand live births.[14] Legal abortion rates even showed extraordinary disparities in different regions of the same state. Quite frequently, the vast majority of legal abortions in a given state were done in one major city and by one or two major hospitals. Two-thirds of all legal abortions performed in California during the late 1960s and early 1970s, for example, took place near San Francisco.[15]

Abortion law on the books had even less impact on the total number of abortions performed in the United States. Illegal abortions remained readily available throughout the twentieth century. American women who were determined to terminate their pregnancies were usually able to procure an abortion, although not necessarily a safe one, in virtually every region of the country. "While the legal norm is condemnation," lawyers and doctors realized that "the social fact is omnipresence, on a scale of which we are just beginning to become aware."[16] As the English sociologist Colin Francome notes, "despite legal prohibitions, abortion has been a common operation for well over 100 years."[17] This demand for abortion, legal or otherwise, was not confined to any particular class of women. "Those who apply for abortions," an early-twentieth-century physician complained, "are from every walk of life, from the factory girl to the millionaire's daughter; from the laborer's wife to that of the banker, no class, no sect seems to be above [it]."[18]

Scholars estimate that one of every three to five pregnancies in the United States was aborted during the first seventy years of the twentieth century. During the 1950s and 1960s, close to one million illegal abortions were probably performed every year.[19] Some public health specialists suggest that as many as two to three million abortions were performed annually in the United States during the early twentieth century.[20] Although the overwhelming majority of abortions were obtained by married women,[21] the abortion rate among single women was shockingly high. Studies done by the Kinsey Institute found that unmarried women were fifteen times more likely to abort a pregnancy than to give birth. Approximately 93 percent of those abortions were illegal.[22]

Women who endured illegal abortions often took terrible risks. Criminologists in the mid-twentieth century estimated that five to ten thousand women died each year from complications resulting from criminal abortions.[23] One local coroner recalls seeing "three or four deaths a year from illegal abortion" and believes that just in his county there were "three times that number that no one knew about."[24] The overall death rate from illegal abortion did decrease dramatically during the 1950s, at least among white women, and may have previously been overestimated significantly.[25] Nevertheless, criminal abortion remained the leading cause of maternal death in the United States until *Roe*.[26] The "only significant causes of [maternal] death," the 1955 annual report of the Los Angeles County Hospital declared, are "complications of induced abortion," which had a death rate seven times greater than "all other obstetrical conditions combined."[27]

Illegal abortion maimed as well as slaughtered. Some public health authorities estimated that 350,000 women were injured every year by criminal abortionists.[28] Many hospitals established special wards to handle this public health crisis. Obstetricians remember those "wards being full of septic abortion patients [i.e., women suffering from an often fatal uterine infection caused by unsterile or otherwise incompetent abortion procedures]."[29] Los Angeles County Hospital admitted over two thousand women a year for septic abortion during the mid-1950s; Cook County Hospital in Chicago admitted almost five thousand women annually for septic abortion a decade later. The frequency of hospital admission after illegal abortion was particularly stunning given the paucity of legal abortions then performed at municipal hospitals. From 1950 to 1955, Bellevue Hospital in New York performed only seventy-seven therapeutic abortions, but admitted 3,488 women for septic abortion.[30]

Precise figures on both the scope and social cost of illegal abortion are, of course, impossible to ascertain. Pro-choice advocates suggest that as many as 1.5 million abortions were performed annually before *Roe*; pro-life advocates claim that 200,000 is a more reasonable figure.[31] Similar disputes exist over maternal mortality and morbidity figures, with proponents of legal abortion relying on estimates geometrically greater than the numbers commonly cited by opponents of abortion on demand.[32] In the absence of any authoritative statistics, policy makers relied on rough estimates based on fragmented data or personal experiences that varied considerably from investigator to investigator.

Nevertheless, by the mid-twentieth century, both proponents and opponents of abortion reform agreed on three central propositions. First, illegal abortionists were thriving. Criminologists found that abortion had become the third most lucrative criminal enterprise in the United States, surpassed only by gambling and narcotics.[33] One investigator determined that some expert abortionists were performing as many as forty-five abortions a day and between four and five thousand abortions a year.[34] Second, the omnipresence of illegal abortion had created a substantial maternal health crisis. Doctors and lawyers described criminal abortion as a "hidden social canker," "a festering social ill," and "one of the major medical and social problems of the nation."[35] "Driving abortion underground," commentators pointed out, "the statutes have brought it about that abortion [is] performed by the women themselves, by incompetent midwives, or by doctors who, even though they may be skilled, must operate with a secrecy which precludes the subsequent attention to the safest performance of the procedure."[36] Third, and most important, significant statutory restrictions on abortion were unenforceable. "All efforts to control the incidence of criminal abortion by legislation," public health specialists concluded, had "resulted in failure." A 1963 law review article noted that "our nation's abortion laws have admittedly kept *legal* abortions to a minimum, just as the eighteenth amendment virtually eliminated the *legal* consumption of liquor." Nevertheless, the author continued, "the abortion enactments have been no more successful in preventing abortions than the eighteenth amendment was in eradicating drinking."[37]

Legal Enforcement

Given the extent to which the general public ignored laws prohibiting abortion, most commentators doubt whether a social movement committed to unborn life could have substantially reduced the number of illegal abortions performed before *Roe.*[38] The matter, however, is ultimately unresolvable. No sustained political effort on behalf of fetuses occurred during the first seventy years of the twentieth century. The physician sponsors of late-nineteenth-century abortion bans soon developed other priorities, and efforts to ensure enforcement of the restrictions they helped enact were immediately abandoned.[39] Subsequent crackdowns on local abortionists typically fizzled within a year of being initiated.[40]

The few committed proponents of statutory bans on abortion before *Roe* lacked the political power or will necessary to have such measures enforced. Most communities adopted a policy of looking the other way when unwanted pregnancies were discreetly terminated.[41] Frustrated antiabortion physicians and civic leaders came "to the conclusion that the public does not want, the profession does not want, [and] women in particular do not want, any aggressive campaign against the crime of abortion." "You cannot enforce laws," a prominent midwestern doctor sadly commented, "with which the public has little sympathy."[42] Dr. F. J. Taussig, the foremost medical authority on abortion in the middle of the twentieth century, could find "no other instance in history in which there has been such frank and universal disregard for the criminal law."[43]

This unofficial permissiveness kept court dockets relatively free of abortion cases. Women who had illegal abortions during this period were never arrested by state officials, even when the local penal code clearly declared a woman was criminally liable for procuring an abortion.[44] Legislatures and judges uniformly "regard[ed the woman] as the victim of the crime, not as the criminal, as the object of protection, rather than of punishment."[45] Members of the law enforcement community rarely paid significantly more attention to those who performed abortions for pregnant women. "For professional abortionists," medical and legal authorities observed, "there exists a low rate of prosecution and an even lower rate of conviction."[46]

Virtually every member of the law enforcement community helped shield abortionists from serious legal sanctions. The primary "impediment to the enforcement of abortion statutes" was the blunt refusal of aborted women to consider themselves "victim[s] of crime."[47] Lacking cooperative witnesses and complainants, law enforcement agents could not easily shut down known practitioners of criminal abortion. Moreover, many police officers and prosecutors "share[d] the widespread belief that the abortionist is in fact performing a useful service" and preferred spending their scarce resources preventing what they and their communities regarded as real crimes.[48] The few prosecutions that were instituted faced jurors unwilling to convict abortionists and judges unwilling to impose severe sentences. Anti-abortion advocates complained that "even the most outrageous abortionist" could not be convicted in a jury trial. One juror refused to convict a well-known abortionist because there was "nobody in Schuykill County that the doctor hasn't helped."[49] Half the abortionists convicted in New York between 1925 and 1950 were sentenced only to probation. Dr. Milan Vuitch, a prominent physician-abortionist, was arrested sixteen times for openly running an abortion clinic in Washington, D.C., but never went to jail.[50]

Even abortionists convicted and sentenced to prison at trial often escaped legal sanction. Some appellate judges placed an extraordinarily high burden of proof on the state to establish that insufficient medical grounds existed for the abortion.[51] After pointing out that "the defendant in this case was a doctor with substantial experience and background," the California court in *People v. Ballard* overturned a conviction for illegally performing an abortion because the jury was not told that "there is a presumption of necessity in the case of an abortion by a licensed physician."[52] In times and places not noted for their solicitude for the due process rights of criminal suspects, a significant number of convictions for illegal abortion were reversed on appeal for constitutional "technicalities," most notably entrapment.[53] Some executives used clemency to keep abortionists on the street. A New York campaign against illegal abortion during the first decade of the twentieth century came to a dismal conclusion when the only three abortionists convicted were immediately pardoned by the governor.[54]

Persons seeking or performing abortions in this legal environment could normally predict that they would not suffer the statutorily authorized penalty for their conduct, particularly if they did not call public attention to their actions.[55] As a result, most localities had someone willing to terminate pregnancies for resident women, and almost anyone could be an abortionist. "Every sub-community" in New York County, a study of criminal abortion observed, "has its abortionists who, by and large, offer their services on terms their fellow residents can afford." These practitioners ranged from physician-abortionists, many of whom were alcoholic or otherwise incompetent, to midwives, who were a particularly good source for fairly safe abortions during the early twentieth century, to "salesmen, elevator operators, prostitutes, barbers and unskilled laborers."[56] Various anecdotal accounts speak of abortions being performed by ministers, mothers, bookies, dairy farmers, and motorcycle messengers. One women interviewed years later by the journalist Gail Miller was convinced that a police officer performed her illegal abortion.[57]

Law enforcement officials did occasionally make considerable efforts to prevent rank amateurs from performing abortions that maimed their clientele. The police conducted serious criminal investigations after women died from abortions, and offending practitioners could expect to defend their conduct in court.[58] From 1867 until at least 1940, Chicago officials prosecuted abortionists who killed their patients, often relying "on dying declarations collected from women near death due to their illegal abortion." When patients survived their abortion, however, the county coroner permitted the operating physician to destroy all records of the procedure.[59] The vast majority of convictions in New York for criminal abortion were obtained after complaints about botched procedures.[60] Many abortionists attracted police attention only when they engaged in other criminal enterprises such as dealing drugs, issuing false death certificates, and selling black-market babies.[61]

By comparison, law enforcement officers rarely prevented women from obtaining safe, illegal abortions from competent abortionists. Investigators from the Kinsey Institute found that "police and other officials often allow known abortionists to practice since it is felt that there is a need for their services." "If . . . abortion was a need" in your community, a former district attorney recalls, "you looked the other way," but "only . . . for the cleanest and safest operators." The president of the Pacific Coast Obstetrical and Gynecology Society, Dr. Roy E. Fallas, observed that law "enforcement agencies recognize the law's inadequacy by failing to prosecute flagrant violations."[62] Police officers sometimes ignored abortionists because they had been bribed to do so.[63] In most cases, however, the dearth of willing witnesses and lack of communal support prevented meaningful implementation of statutory bans on abortion. Although spo-

radic exceptions existed, the official policy in most localities was that unauthorized abortions would be tolerated as long as the practitioner was
fairly competent and reasonably discrete. The pragmatic rule of "hands
off," a study of changing abortion policies notes, "usually applied."[64] Several historical accounts of "Jane," an "underground" abortion clinic in
Chicago, observe that " 'the police had known what they were doing and
had not intervened . . . since they were providing a necessary service for
policemen's wives, mistresses and daughters and for all policewomen,'
and did so in a manner that left women healthy and well rather than
bloody and dying."[65] The clinic was once raided, but only because a new
police captain "did not understand that there was an understanding not
to disturb Jane." All charges against Jane's organizers were quickly
dropped.[66]

In some regions of the United States, state policies facilitated abortion.
Many governmental officials consciously shielded competent abortion
providers who offered safe procedures to prominent members of the community. Although the "hacks, quacks, greedy and others who resisted
supervision were turned in to the police, respectable practitioners who
operated 'clean' approved settings were protected." "It was not unheard
of," one law enforcement official remembers, "for the police officer to act
as a sort of intermediary . . . and to actually arrange the abortion. . . . The
police in the community would know who in the community was doing
abortions and who was not so good." Persons providing safe, though "illegal," abortion services sometimes conducted off-the-record negotia-
tions with local prosecutors to satisfy official standards for "approved
site[s] and situation[s]" where "prestigious physicians" could terminate
pregnancies.[67] This protection was frequently necessary to maintain access
to safe abortions. In several states, one study of pre-*Roe* policies concludes, "the criminal abortion system could not have been sustained without the entire apparatus of legitimate structure."[68]

Law enforcement officials were especially cooperative with the clergy-
run abortion "referral services" established during the 1950s and 1960s.
In Michigan, "a clergy broker identified two notorious abortion 'rings'
for law enforcement on the condition that police would allow the clergy
a free hand to deal with respectable physician-abortionists."[69] Police officers in New York City helped the organizers of a prominent clergy-run
abortion service set up a sting that led to the arrest of persons who were
blackmailing ministers making abortion referrals.[70]

Licensed physicians, who fought successfully in the late nineteenth century for the power to control abortion,[71] were particularly immune to
legal scrutiny. Because law enforcement was generally limited to rooting
out unsafe practitioners, regular doctors rarely experienced any official
challenge to their decision that an abortion was "medically necessary,"

however that term was defined by the appropriate statute or judicial decision. Kristin Luker's pathbreaking study of abortion policies concluded that "if a reasonably plausible medical indication for abortion could be presented to a sympathetic physician, neither the medical society nor any other authority was likely to intervene."[72] According to her reading of the historical evidence, no matter what the particular statutory definition of a lawful abortion, physicians agreed that "if the characteristics of the practitioner and the conditions of the practice were 'reputable,' then the abortion was 'justifiable.'"[73] California activists looking to set up a test case challenging abortion bans discovered that the only physician in state prison for performing an abortion also had six narcotics and two murder convictions.[74]

Many physicians took advantage of their legal dispensation. Studies suggest that licensed physicians were responsible for as many as one-third of all illegal abortions performed before *Roe*.[75] One survey done in Chicago at the turn of the twentieth century found that approximately 40 percent of that city's most respected physicians would abort a stranger's pregnancy. Affluent families expected their private doctor to perform abortions as a matter of course. Doctors who refused to terminate pregnancies were promptly dismissed, thus losing the considerable revenues they would have otherwise gained by taking care of the family's other medical problems.[76]

Prominent physicians developed various techniques for disguising as spontaneous miscarriages the abortions they performed for their private patients. "What I did," one practitioner revealed years later,

> was to examine [the pregnant women] and try to initiate bleeding. . . . And then after starting a little bleeding I'd tell her to go home and call me back within twenty-four hours to let me know if the bleeding continued. If it did, which I expected that it would, I would then admit her as a threatened abortion and complete the process in a legitimate way.[77]

Given the high rate of miscarriages in normal pregnancies, slight increases in their frequency were not likely to be noticed by medical authorities already committed to not noticing abortion. As a physician who frequently relied on that subterfuge notes, "spontaneous abortion was . . . always going to be about 15 percent of your practice, so if you raised it to 20 percent, who would know?"[78]

Some physician-abortionists practiced openly, attracting police attention only when a female officer or a male officer's wife, womanfriend, or daughter needed their services. Persons familiar with the abortion underground were aware that "almost every city harbors one or several full-time illegal physician abortionists."[79] Calling too much attention to one's practice was rarely wise,[80] but a few licensed physicians performed more than ten thousand abortions each without being subject to legal sanctions.[81] The Kinsey Institute discovered an abortionist "who had considerable evidence to support his claim that he had performed 30,000 abortions without a single death in the course of his medical practice."[82] The winner of the illegal abortion sweepstakes, however, was clearly Dr. Robert Douglas Spencer of Ashland, Pennsylvania. Spencer did over one hundred thousand abortions from 1923 to 1967 in his eleven-room clinic. As his widow recalls,

> no one was out to get him because he was such a good doctor. Besides, he was benefiting the local economy. People were coming here from all over the United States. They spent money in the hotels and restaurants. The local merchants, no matter what their attitudes about abortion, knew a good thing when they saw it, and they weren't about to kill the goose that laid the golden egg.[83]

The one candidate for district attorney who promised to shut Spencer down was crushed in the next election.[84]

Doctors were never prosecuted for the abortions that they performed in hospitals. "Hospitals of unimpeachable reputation," Dr. Alan Guttmacher knew from personal experience, "[were] allowed to interpret and administer the abortion law of their respective states without supervision or interference from either the police, the courts, or medical agencies." Milton Helburn, the chief medical examiner of New York City, declared that he did not "know of a single instance in which an abortion done in an approved hospital, presumably for therapeutic purposes, was ever questioned by the courts." "The only cases" he was "sure that are prosecuted are frank criminal abortions."[85] Law enforcement officials, B. J. George of Michigan Law School commented, "are not anxious to lock horns with the organized medical profession."[86]

This official disinterest hardly reflected confidence in actual medical practices. Doctors and public health specialists familiar with policies at American medical institutions agreed that "the practice of abortion in American hospitals is inequitable, inconsistent, and largely illegal."[87] Physicians publicly confessed that a substantial majority of hospital abortions did not satisfy any reasonable interpretation of state statutes. "Most therapeutic abortions in this country," Dr. Jerome Kummer bluntly stated, "are in violation of the law." One survey of hospital practices in New York City between 1953 and 1958 concluded that 90 percent of all "therapeutic" abortions were illegal.[88] During the German measles epidemic of the early 1960s, many hospitals routinely aborted private patients who contracted rubella while pregnant, even though no law permitted abortion for fetal indications.[89] On the basis of these studies and his long personal experience, Dr. Guttmacher, the leader of the reform movement in the 1950s and 1960s, frequently declared that "abortion laws in the United States make hypocrites of us all."[90]

The Bias of Abortion Past

"LEGAL" ABORTIONS

This combination of restrictive laws and laissez-faire enforcement was responsible for the arbitrary and discriminatory distribution of "legal" abortions during the first two-thirds of the twentieth century. The almost complete withdrawal of state scrutiny vested the medical profession with the practical authority to control access to "therapeutic" abortion. This virtually unregulated monopoly on determining when an abortion met legal standards produced substantial variations in both the frequency with which and circumstances under which abortions were performed at various American hospitals. Differences in physicians' personal attitudes toward abortion explain some of the variation in abortion rates at different medical facilities. The overwhelming majority of hospital abortions, however, were performed for affluent white women, particularly when the indications for abortion were legally borderline or clearly inconsistent with statutory guidelines.

Randomness

Early proponents of abortion reform complained that laws banning abortion were unconstitutionally vague.[91] Most physicians, however, admitted that the precise language used by abortion laws on the books was fairly clear.[92] Vagueness lay in abortion law in action, in the criteria doctors actually used when responding to requests for abortions. Whether physicians terminated pregnancies typically depended on their attitudes toward performing abortions,[93] obeying the law, and running the minute legal risks involved in ending a pregnancy that did not threaten the life of the mother. These beliefs varied considerably from place to place and from doctor to doctor. Some doctors frequently performed abortions in circumstances that, at best, stretched statutory exceptions. Others rarely granted abortions even when the procedure was clearly legal.[94] Hospital administrators aggravated the arbitrary distribution of safe abortions by promulgating different abortion policies. Several major hospitals routinely performed abortions in cases of rubella or rape; others would not.[95]

The near-absolute medical autonomy that physicians enjoyed before *Roe* led to extraordinary variations in access to abortion at American hospitals. Dr. Robert Hall's nationwide survey of abortion policies at different medical institutions during the 1950s and early 1960s found that abortion rates varied from one per 36 births to zero abortions after 24,417 births. California hospitals during the 1950s had abortion rates ranging from one for every 126 live births to no abortions after 7,615 live births.[96] Given this range of medical practice, whether a pregnant women procured a hospital abortion usually depended on which doctor she asked. "A large percentage of women who now have criminal abortions," Dr. Harold Rosen of Johns Hopkins Medical School noted, "in all probability could have their pregnancies legally interrupted somewhere in this country if they had sufficient time, physiologically, to shop from physician to physician, from hospital to hospital, and from state to state."[97]

Physicians' attitudes toward abortion and the law were particularly influential when patients presented psychiatric indications for abortion. Before *Roe*, no medical or legal authority established objective criteria for determining when bringing a pregnancy to term would gravely impair the mental health of the would-be mother. When asked to certify a patient for abortion, therapists tailored their diagnoses to suit their predetermined conclusions. In virtually all cases, "enough strands of evidence were available to enable the psychiatrist, whether anti-abortion or pro-abortion, to rationalize his position."[98] As a result, the actual emotional condition of the pregnant women often had less influence on hospital abortion decisions than the mental state of her psychiatrist. "Whether or not a patient was provided with an opportunity for a therapeutic abortion," one psychiatrist acknowledged, "depended . . . on the philosophical point of view of the psychiatrist whom she happened to consult."[99]

A 1959 study done by Herbert Packer, a professor at Stanford Law School, and Ralph Gampell, a physician-lecturer at the same institution, documented the inconsistent standards that different hospitals used when deciding whether to perform abortions. Packer and Gampell devised eleven hypothetical examples of women who had various indications for terminating their pregnancies. Some situations presented clear legal grounds for an abortion; in other vignettes, Packer and Gampell presented evidence that plainly did not warrant abortion under existing statutory guidelines. When personnel in various California medical institutions were asked whether they would terminate the pregnancy in each hypothetical case, their answers demonstrated the "considerable diversity of opinion among hospitals as to the appropriate medical standards for the performance of TA's [therapeutic abortions]."[100] Packer and Gambell found no situation in which doctors or hospital administrators agreed on the criteria for a hospital abortion. Although the California penal code in 1959 permitted abortions only when "necessary to preserve life," one hospital rejected the hypothetical petition of a woman with severe heart trouble that had nearly proved fatal in a previous pregnancy, while another hospital accepted the petition of a healthy woman who was "sure that the enforced cessation of her work would cause the collapse of the family unit which she has worked so very hard to hold intact."[101] Twelve percent of the hospitals surveyed refused to perform legal abortions, but 35 percent were willing to perform abortions in circumstances that were clearly inconsistent with any reasonable interpretation of the California penal code.[102]

Discrimination

Although chance played an important role in determining who received competent medical care, the distribution of legal abortions before *Roe* was not random. Physicians were far more willing to terminate pregnancies for affluent white women than for their poor or black counterparts. Lawyers, doctors, and journalists familiar with medical policies in the first seventy years of the twentieth century recognized "the vastly disproportionate unavailability of legal abortions to poor and nonwhite women as compared to their wealthier and white sisters."[103] "There is no facet of medical care," Dr. Guttmacher observed, "in which social position and dollars play so ugly a role, as the acquirement of legal abortion."[104]

Wealthy women and, for the most part, only wealthy women had special access to abortion almost on demand because they had the connections and experience necessary to locate doctors willing to perform the procedure and the financial resources to pay them. Affluent citizens sometimes experienced problems locating a safe abortionist, but persons familiar with pre-*Roe* abortion law in action note that "the upper-income woman who knew her family doctor quite well, who had some semblance of a physical reason to avoid childbirth, and whose motivation for abortion did not fundamentally offend the values of the physician may have had little difficulty in obtaining an abortion."[105] Moreover, the affluence necessary to enjoy a de facto right to abortion on demand significantly decreased during the second half of the twentieth century. In the early 1950s, only upper-class women could be confident that a safe abortion would be available should they wish to terminate an unwanted pregnancy. By the time *Roe* was decided, many middle-class women had the knowledge and resources necessary to find a competent abortionist.

State policies made important contributions to the discriminatory distribution of gray-market abortions. After a period of benign neglect during the depression, law enforcement officials in many communities began discouraging physicians from openly and indiscriminately terminating pregnancies. As police work became more professional and many communities cracked down on flagrant violations of statutory bans on abortion,[106] competent abortionists became more selective and discreet. "You could get away with [abortion] unquestionably," mid-twentieth-century physicians recognized, "as long as you didn't do it as a business."[107] Physicians who performed abortions in this mildly restrictive environment generally accepted the minute legal risk inherent in violating the law only when they knew fairly well the women who sought their help in terminating a pregnancy. Obstetricians, Guttmacher observed, would frequently "breach an archaic law" to ensure that their private patients received "optimum, total health care." The very slight threat of prosecution, however, was sufficient to deter most physicians from "accepting the same degree of responsibility for clinic patients." Other public health specialists noted that "typically, only the private patients were likely to find physicians sufficiently interested in their welfare to bear the small risk involved in making a liberal interpretation of the abortion laws."[108] Not surprisingly, therefore, the more legally doubtful the indication for abortion, the greater the disparities between abortion rates for members of different economic and racial groups.[109]

Hospital records dramatically confirm medical and legal complaints "of a double standard for private and indigent patients."[110] Approximately 80 percent of all "legal" abortions before *Roe* were obtained by patients in private, proprietary hospitals or by patients on the private wards of voluntary hospitals. These women were overwhelmingly white and affluent.[111] Dr. Robert Hall's analysis of abortion practices in medical facilities throughout the United States found that voluntary hospitals were performing nearly four times as many abortions on their private patients as on their ward patients.[112] Every voluntary hospital Hall surveyed that performed a significant number of abortions had higher abortion rates on the private service than on the ward service.[113] The disparity at several prominent hospitals was particularly egregious. From 1960 to 1962, Women's Hospital of New York City performed one abortion for every 900 live births on the ward service, but the same doctors performed one abortion for every 20 live births on the private service. At Strong Memorial Hospital in Rochester, New York, the respective rates were 1:4,324 for the charity cases and 1:218 for the paying customers.[114]

Poor persons at voluntary hospitals were particularly discriminated against when they presented indications that did not clearly warrant an abortion under existing statutory definitions. Ward patients in New York City voluntary hospitals were almost as likely as private patients to obtain abortions when their pregnancies threatened to aggravate a previous heart condition. Private patients, however, were seven times more likely than ward patients to have abortions for psychiatric indications and twenty-nine times more likely to have abortions after contracting rubella, a disease that has no permanent effect on maternal health but that frequently causes fetal defects.[115] Records at Sloane Hospital in New York reveal that "abortions were more common among the private patients . . . for virtually all of the more debatable indications."[116] More than half the abortions performed on the ward service of that institution were clearly legal, but less than a quarter of the abortions performed on the private service could meet the state's statutory requirements.[117]

The differences between abortion rates at proprietary hospitals that only admitted private patients and municipal hospitals that only admitted charity patients were even greater than the differences between abortion rates on the private and ward services within voluntary hospitals. Although the same doctors were frequently on staff at both private proprietary and public municipal hospitals, physicians were "far more timid" when considering requests for abortions at municipal hospitals.[118] During the middle of the twentieth century, patients at proprietary hospitals in New York City were twenty times more likely than patients at municipal hospitals to have abortions because of heart trouble and twenty-six times more likely to have abortions for psychiatric indications. These findings, researchers noted, were particularly "surprising" given their understanding that these "indications" were probably "more prevalent among [clinic] patients."[119] Overall, the private patients at proprietary hospitals in New York City were nineteen times more likely than the charity patients at municipal hospitals to have "therapeutic" abortions. From 1960 to 1962 the gap widened, as abortion rates at propriety hospitals rose to thirty-nine times those at municipal hospitals.[120]

Women of color faced additional difficulties obtaining abortions from an overwhelmingly white profession that shared the prejudices of the general population. Not only did members of disfavored minorities suffer because most were poor, but race served as an additional barrier to hospital abortions. Betty Sarvis and Hyman Rodman observe that "the experience needed to deal with a large array of largely white and often hostile medical personnel in order to get approval for an abortion were generally less available to black women."[121] A study of Georgia practices found that in 1970 single white women were twenty-five times more likely to be granted a "therapeutic" abortion than single black women.[122]

Similar discriminatory patterns existed north of the Mason-Dixon line. A review of abortion practices in Buffalo published by the *Journal of the American Medical Association* concluded that "therapeutic abortions seemed rarely indicated among non-white patients."[123] From 1954 to 1962, 94 percent of all hospital abortions in New York City were obtained by white women. Pregnant white women were five times more likely to have hospital abortions than pregnant black women and twenty-six times more likely to have hospital abortions than pregnant Puerto Rican women. This disparity did not reflect the relative demand for abortion services. During the same time period, 93 percent of the women who died as a result of illegal abortions were black or Puerto Rican.[124]

Startling as these numbers are, they probably understate the extent to which affluent white women were more likely than poor women and women of color to procure gray-market abortions. Doctors at some private hospitals often performed a dilation and curettage (D & C) on a pregnant woman, ostensibly because "the patient is suffering from a peculiar infection and . . . a diagnosis of the uterus is necessary in order to define the illness." Although such procedures were not recorded as therapeutic abortions, the D & C terminated the pregnancy. This practice was a particularly useful device for performing abortions without labeling them as such for the benefit of legal or medical authorities. One small proprietary hospital performed 107 "diagnostic uterine curettages" in one year, and in 104 cases the patient turned out to be pregnant.[125]

Those poor women and women of color able to procure hospital abortions often paid a price not demanded of more affluent whites. Doctors before *Roe* frequently required poorly connected women to abjure future childbearing in return for receiving a safe abortion. "Some women," academic doctors and public health authorities point out, "were presented with a 'package deal'—the physician would agree to do the abortion if the women agreed to be sterilized."[126] Prominent physicians believed this practice was widespread, and possibly legitimate. Dr. Harold Rosen observed that many obstetricians "refuse to accept any recommendation for therapeutic termination of pregnancy unless it be understood in advance that they will hysterectomize or concurrently otherwise sterilize their patient."[127] One survey found that more than half the teaching hospitals in the United States routinely sterilized many abortion patients.[128] Although sterilization in some cases was clearly warranted for health reasons, doctors were aware that "many women are sterilized with no medical or legal indication for the procedure."[129] Poor women and women of color were particularly victimized by this practice. Dr. Hall's study of abortion practices at Sloane Hospital revealed that "sterilizations were two-and-one-half times more common on the ward service" than on the private service, and that doctors disproportionately sterilized women of color. The major municipal hospital in Los Angeles, Los Angeles County Hospital, sterilized 75 percent of all patients who had abortions.[130]

The Impact of Review Boards, Liberalized Laws, and Medical Advances

Changes in hospital practice, state policies, and medical technology during the 1940s, 1950s, and 1960s exacerbated existing inequities in access to therapeutic abortions. Three developments in particular had a profoundly discriminatory impact on the ability women of different economic and racial groups had to procure legal abortions in American hospitals: the institution of abortion review boards, the liberalization of restrictions on abortion, and the decrease in medical indications for terminating a pregnancy. Each "advance" multiplied the resources necessary to obtain a hospital abortion and increased the proportion of abortions done for nonmedical indications. By 1965, most poor women were in effect priced out of the market for abortions done for psychiatric or fetal indications, and sharp reductions in medically necessary abortions had largely eliminated the only circumstance in which private and ward patients had relatively equal access to hospital abortions. Economic and racial disparities in education, employment, housing, and political power may have decreased significantly during the middle of the twentieth century, but poor women and women of color found themselves increasingly unable to obtain safe, sanctioned abortions.[131]

Many hospitals responded to increased official concern about open violations of the laws against abortion by establishing internal abortion review boards. Strict oversight of abortion practices, medical administrators hoped, would prevent legal troubles and cut down on the number of abortions performed at their hospitals. Following institutional guidelines, abortion review boards approved abortions only when patients produced detailed documentation of their indications for that procedure.[132] Such complex procedural obstacles frequently proved too difficult for poor women and women of color. "Ward patients," prominent doctors observed, "are much less likely to have the necessary consultations requested, including the psychiatric, and to have the necessary recommendations made and accepted by a hospital board, than are their more well-to-do sisters."[133] Access to hospital abortions under this new regime also became dependent on access to medical advocacy skills. Abortion review boards "tended to become market systems, in which women with wealth, information, and medical connections were far more likely to be granted abortions than their poorer, less well-informed, and less well-connected peers."[134] Harriet Pilpel, a pro-choice activist familiar with medical practice in the 1960s, declared that "women of means are the only women, by and large, who can obtain hospital abortions" in the face of these procedural barriers.[135]

The so-called reform laws that states passed in the 1960s codified important elements of existing hospital practice and thus had a similarly discriminatory impact. Following the recommendations of the American Law Institute, many legislatures legalized abortion whenever two doctors certified that bringing a pregnancy to term "would gravely impair the physical or mental health of the mother."[136] In practice, this standard required pregnant women to find two physicians quickly who would testify that their condition met the statutory criteria for abortion. Not surprisingly, such attempts to ease restrictions on abortion were branded "middle-class reform." Doctors, journalists, and public health specialists recognized that "it was overwhelmingly the more educated and affluent women who were able to obtain legal abortions under these circumstances."[137]

Access to psychiatric services proved particularly important in reform states because over 90 percent of all hospital abortions in those jurisdictions were granted on psychiatric grounds.[138] Again, high-status women more easily obtained the services of physicians willing to make the dubious assertion that bringing a pregnancy to term would severely damage their mental health. Many psychiatrists proved willing to declare as a matter of course (and for a small fee) that their previously stable private patients would kill themselves immediately if forced to carry an unwanted pregnancy to term. Dr. Bernard Nathanson, an early advocate of abortion rights who later became a pro-life activist, recalls that

> every patient suffered from a "reactive depression . . . and all were immi-nently "suicidal." One particular psychiatrist was reputed to conduct his in-terview in five minutes and to charge $100 dollars a letter. . . . A few [psychi-atrists] held their ground, resisted the easy money, and even spoke out against their colleagues in the game. We quickly learned who these "reac-tionaries" were and struck their names from our lists [of psychiatrists to whom abortion-seeking patients were referred].[139]

Poor women were not so fortunate when they sought to have a psychi-atric indication validated. Advocates of reform laws learned that in Colo-rado a "state-imposed requirement of two psychiatrists was causing an effective discrimination against ward patients." "Private consultations," Dr. Guttmacher discovered, "were so expensive as to be available only to the wealthier patients, and psychiatric appointments in public facilities were booked solid for three months—far beyond the time limit for obtain-ing an abortion."[140] Similar problems plagued the operation of reform laws in other states. "Where will the ghetto-dweller find a psychiatrist to testify that she has a grave risk of emotional impairment if she is forced to give birth to her nth baby?" a leading criminologist asked.[141]

Poor persons also suffered when improvements in medical technology altered the balance between abortions granted for medical and nonmedi-cal indications. During the 1950s and 1960s, hospitals became increas-ingly able safely to bring to term pregnant women who formerly would have had medical indications for abortion. One prominent doctor in-formed the 1951 Congress of American College of Surgeons that "any-one who performs a therapeutic abortion is either ignorant of modern medical methods of treating the complications of pregnancy or is unwill-ing to take the time to use them."[142] These advances in medical technique sharply reduced the number of hospital abortions performed to save maternal life. The University of Virginia, for example, performed 128 abortions for medical indications between 1941 to 1950, but only 11 such abortions over the next five years. That institution's abortion rates for renal diseases, hypertensive diseases, and tuberculosis were cut in half, and abortions for cardiac and neuropsychiatric diseases were eliminated altogether.[143]

Despite the "shrinking medical indications for abortion,"[144] the number of abortions performed at many hospitals did not fall dramatically. Significant decreases in abortions granted for medical indications were partially offset at many medical institutions by substantial increases in the number of legal abortions granted for psychiatric and fetal indications. Thus from 1963 to 1968, the incidence of psychiatric indications for abortion increased sevenfold, from 0.57 to 3.61 per thousand live births. To take a particular example, the percentage of abortions performed for psychiatric indications in Buffalo hospitals went from 13 percent in 1943 to 87.5 percent in 1963. The percentage of abortions performed for psychiatric indications in that city did drop in 1964, but only because a rubella outbreak the same year caused a substantial increase in the number of abortions performed for fetal indications.[145]

These increases and decreases in abortions performed for different indications had a grossly disparate impact on women of different economic classes. Many physicians aborted any women whose pregnancy seriously endangered her health. Hence, ward patients and private patients were equally affected by reductions in medically necessary abortions. Poor women and women of color, however, rarely obtained abortions when their pregnancies did not threaten their physical health. As a result, only women able to afford the private service of voluntary or proprietary hospitals benefited from the increase in abortions for psychiatric or fetal indications.[146] In New York Hospital, for example, the abortion rate for private patients between 1941 and 1954 remained fairly steady as a substantial increase in abortions for psychiatric indications nearly compensated for contemporaneous decreases in medical indications for abortion. Ward patients at the same institution experienced a similar decrease in abortions performed for medical indications, but virtually no corresponding increase in abortions performed for psychiatric indications. Hence, the abortion rate for poor women at New York Hospital during those fourteen years dropped by two-thirds.[147]

The combination of abortion review boards, reform statutes, and fewer medical indications for abortion had a particularly devastating effect on abortion services at municipal hospitals. Obtaining an abortion at these medical institutions during the 1950s and 1960s proved nearly impossible for poorer women. Hospitals that "handled the majority of poor and minority group patients," pro-choice activist Lawrence Lader stated, "virtually eliminated abortion" in the years before *Roe*. By the middle of the twentieth century, some prominent municipal hospitals had abortion rates near or even less than one per 10,000 births. Abortion rates at Los

Angeles County Hospital, which admitted only clinic patients, went from one for every 106 births in 1931–35 to one for every 8,383 births in 1946–50.[148]

Thus, when the number of hospital abortions performed in the 1950s and early 1960s declined somewhat, poor women bore the brunt of that decrease. There were fewer circumstances under which less affluent women could procure medically necessary abortions, and hospitals rarely aborted ward patients for any other reason. By comparison, when in the late 1960s and early 1970s liberalized abortion policies permitted hospitals to perform more abortions, affluent women were the primary beneficiaries. Reform laws dramatically increased the number of abortions performed for psychiatric indications, and such abortions were almost always obtained by the paying customers. Dr. Kenneth Niswander's survey of changes in abortion practices at Buffalo hospitals clearly demonstrated the discriminatory effect of trends toward fewer medically necessary abortions and more abortions performed for psychiatric and fetal indications. "In the 1940's," he stated,

> when the majority of abortions were done for medical reasons, the incidence on the ward and private services were about the same. In the 1950's when medical reasons accounted for fewer abortions, the incidence on the private service rose to twice that of the ward service. In the 1960's when the number of abortions for psychiatric or fetal reasons rose dramatically, the incidence on the private service soared to better than twenty times greater than that of the clinic service.[149]

The disparity between white and nonwhite hospital abortion rates also increased sharply during the 1950s and 1960s. One study of abortions in New York City found that a 40 percent reduction in the number of hospital abortions granted to white women in this time period corresponded with a 65 and a 90 percent decrease for black and Puerto Rican women, respectively.[150] The disparities between black and white abortion mortality rates similarly soared immediately before *Roe* as safe abortions became relatively easier to procure for those with resources and connections. From 1933 to 1966, the national abortion mortality rate for black women increased from two to six times that of white women.[151] From 1960 to 1969, the black mortality rate in Georgia went from four to fourteen times the comparable rate for white women.[152]

"CRIMINAL" ABORTION

The distribution of safe unsanctioned abortions before *Roe* was also capricious and discriminatory. As Professor Herbert Packer noted, "the legal prohibition" on abortion "rais[ed the] risk and reward for the illegal practitioner and . . . depress[ed] the quality of the services offered."[153] "Criminal" abortionists were not subject to state regulation and inspection. Their abilities varied substantially, and information about the relative merits of different practitioners was difficult and expensive to procure.[154] Moreover, pregnant women had to locate abortionists quickly. Many women had little choice as to who would terminate their pregnancy. Lucky women had their abortions clandestinely terminated by licensed doctors in medical settings; unlucky women might find themselves aborted by a mechanic in the back of a car.[155]

The price for an illegal abortion was highly variable. Some criminal abortionists charged reasonable prices and even offered discounts to poorer persons. Others forced women to have sex as part of their fee.[156] More often than not, professional abortionists charged whatever they thought their patient would pay. Few women left "the abortionist's office with much above cab fare."[157] In these circumstances, chance played a substantial role in the price women paid for abortions and the quality of service they received. "Poor women," one study concluded, "sometimes put themselves deeply in debt to pay for expensive abortions, while wealthy women are sometimes unable to find the highly skilled practitioners they can afford to pay."[158]

Luck mattered, but financial resources clearly played a crucial role in securing access to an illegal abortion. Because prohibition raised the fees abortionists charged for their services, some women were priced out of the black and gray markets. Observers recognized, however, that "abortion remained readily available to women who could pay the financial and emotional cost of dealing with the underground." Garrett Hardin, a leading authority on population control, stated that "in California, it is safe to say that any knowledgeable woman with $500 in her pocket can secure an abortion."[159]

More significantly, in spite of many exceptions, wealth and race usually determined whether a woman received a competent (and sympathetic) abortion by an illegal practitioner. "The white and the affluent," Betty Sarvis and Hyman Rodman recognized, "had preferential access to illegal abortions, particularly to those carried out by physicians."[160] A New York social worker declared that, in her experience, "the safer, more reliable and expensive . . . methods are reserved for those can pay for them." "It was fairly easy for me to find a real doctor to do my abortion," a self-described "white middle-class" woman remembers. "He did a good job and I had no problems with it afterwards." Other (though certainly not all) privileged women had similarly positive experiences on the gray market.[161]

Most lower-class women were not as fortunate when they decided to terminate an unwanted pregnancy. Because they lacked the resources necessary to find and pay for adequate care, poor women were more likely to suffer and die from botched abortions.[162] "A large number of illegal abortions," persons familiar with pre-*Roe* practices emphasize, "were self-induced or performed by unskilled and untrained personnel working under dangerous septic conditions, unaccountable to professional guidelines and safeguards and unreached by ordinary government licensing procedures or other safeguards."[163] Women who lived to tell about their illegal abortions consistently highlight the unsanitary conditions under which their procedure was performed. "Kathleen's" abortion was performed in a place that "looked like a flophouse" by an abortionist who "smelled of booze" and "tried to kiss" her afterward.[164] A vice squad detective in the pre-*Roe* era remembers that

> the house was usually run-down. The room was dirty. The abortion was usually done on a bed or a kitchen table, sometimes on the floor. The instruments were wrapped in a newspaper. They weren't sterilized. They weren't even washed from one client to another. It was just filth.[165]

Several factors contributed to the superior service that wealthy Americans purchased on the black and gray markets. Black and gray markets are "wealth sensitive." Information about quality is usually expensive and frequently attainable only by affluent or lucky citizens.[166] Furthermore, doctors who were personally unwilling to perform abortions frequently referred their private patients to competent gray-market practitioners. One prominent physician-abortionist, G. Lotrell Timanus, received approximately 5,000 referrals from over 300 doctors during his thirty-five-year practice in Baltimore. The organizers of an abortion mill located in the affluent Murray Hill section of Park Avenue, New York, "associat[ed] themselves with physicians of spotless legal record who certif[ied] that each abortion is necessary to the life or health of the patient." A more squeamish physician "taped [a reliable] abortionist's phone number in a public phone booth in his office building" and then suggested "to abortion-seeking patients that they drop by." Some doctors reduced the chance of septic abortion by giving prescriptions for antibiotics to their private patients when referring them to unsanctioned abortionists.[167] Finally, the abortion underground in many regions of the United States was organized by and for middle- and upper-class citizens. As researchers at the Alan Guttmacher Institute point out, the "problem pregnancy consultation services" that clergy formed to "refe[r] women to competent, though illegal, practitioners, were used primarily by women of means."[168]

Racial prejudice played a role similar to wealth in the distribution of safe, illegal abortions. Because their business was nominally illegal, criminal abortionists were not subject to state or federal antidiscrimination laws. Women of color, particularly in the South, were rarely able to find competent abortionists willing to terminate their pregnancies. Minority women, Lader observed, "invariably ended up in the grasp of the hacks and butchers of the underworld."[169] From 1940 to 1970, the black mortality rate after "criminal" abortion was 2.4 to 9 times higher than that of white women.[170] Doctors at the Center for Disease Control (CDC) concluded in 1971 that "abortion mortality from nonhospital abortions in Georgia is becoming increasingly a black health problem."[171]

ABORTION TOURISM

Affluent women obviously enjoyed disproportionate access to abortions in foreign countries where the procedure was readily available (and presumably safe). Cuba (pre-Castro), Mexico, England (after 1968), Sweden, and Japan were particularly popular sites before *Roe* for wealthy persons who wished to terminate a pregnancy without legal or medical complications. English doctors in both 1969 and 1970 performed approximately 1,600 abortions for American women.[172] Many Americans flew to San Juan where abortions, while not legal, were easy to obtain. One prominent doctor admitted, "in my practice, if you are fairly rich you go to Puerto Rico and get a good abortion. If you are not very rich, you stay around here and get a crummy one, and if you are poor, you have an illegitimate child."[173] As with every other aspect of abortion before *Roe*, the experiences of women seeking abortions abroad varied dramatically. Many women found the process terrifying, intimidating, and humiliating, but a few took the expression "abortion tourism" literally, combining their abortion with a week of sightseeing.[174]

Privileged Americans effectively gained the right to abortion on demand in 1971 when the New York legislature repealed all state restrictions on abortion.[175] With the exception of a very minor incident in Massachusetts,[176] law enforcement officials never interfered with travel agents who arranged abortions in states where abortion was legal for women who lived in jurisdictions that banned the procedure.[177] In 1971 and 1972, as many Georgians had legal abortions in New York City as had legal abortions in Georgia.[178] Overall, nearly two-thirds of the women who had abortions in New York City in the two years after that state repealed its abortion law were nonresidents.[179] This option was only open to those who could journey to states where abortion was legal. "Out-of-state travel costs," one study notes, "prevented most poor minorities from using the new abortion broker arrangements." The clientele of Jane became overwhelming black and Hispanic in 1971, as their former white middle-class patrons began traveling to New York when faced with an unwanted pregnancy. Overall, 87 percent of the nonresidents who received abortions in New York City from 1971 to 1973 were white.[180]

Discrimination, Early Abortion Reformers, and Roe

In virtually every dimension, the system of abortion regulation in place immediately before *Roe* discriminated egregiously against poor women and women of color. "At all points of choice," persons familiar with abortion law in action asserted, "the middle-class white woman usually has more alternatives than the lower-class black woman."[181] Affluent women enjoyed disproportionate access to hospital abortions because state officials gave physicians the license to grant their private patients indulgences from the criminal law. Affluent women enjoyed disproportionate access to safe, illegal abortions because private doctors referred them to competent abortionists, because they could afford competent abortionists, and because the police ignored (and sometimes protected) competent abortionists. As B. James George of Michigan Law School noted,

> among women, married and unmarried, who become pregnant, a certain number will wish to be aborted. Those with money and connections will either find a compliant practitioner who will terminate the pregnancy safely, but not cheaply, or purchase a ticket to a country in which an abortion can be performed legally. For those without the means or the connections necessary to secure an abortion in that way, the choice is less satisfactory. The mother may have to carry the child to term. . . . She may have to find an unqualified quack who butchers his patients, or she may have to try to induce an abortion herself.[182]

The ways in which the exclusive gray market discriminated by wealth and race provided the main ammunition for early abortion rights activists.[183] Participants at the first major Planned Parenthood Conference on Abortion in 1958 issued a joint statement decrying the "inequality of availability of legal abortion" as "undemocratic." Harriet Pilpel bluntly stated that "even the denial of equal protection represented by segregated schools appears less heinous than this class and economic discrimination."[184] Pilpel and other early reformers consistently demanded that poor women and woman of color have the same access that wealthy white women had historically enjoyed to safe abortions. "Unenforceability," the historian James Mohr states, "might be one thing, but discriminatory enforcement was another." Dr. Guttmacher insisted that the law "should be made more lenient so as to at least grant legal sanction for all women to be legally aborted for those indications which many doctors now recognize for their individual private patients."[185]

Early proponents of abortion reform did not concoct a public health or law enforcement crisis to serve those ends that inspire contemporary pro-choice advocates. The public health professionals who led the attack on restrictive abortion policies during the 1950s and 1960s had little enthusiasm for the sexual revolution or equal rights for women. No one challenged Sophia Kleegman at the 1958 Planned Parenthood conference when she declared, "The ultimate fulfillment of a woman is the bearing and rearing of children, [and] there is no other experience in life on any level that will provide the same sense of fulfillment of happiness, of complete pervading contentment."[186] Kleegman and her associates were concerned with the social costs that restrictive abortion laws imposed on poor women and women of color, costs they witnessed daily in their professional capacity as doctors, social workers, and public health specialists.

Early constitutional attacks on abortion bans similarly emphasized the discriminatory application of such measures. The first academic defenses of legal abortion placed as much emphasis on how abortion law in action discriminated against poor persons as on how abortion bans violated the privacy rights of all Americans. "The poor," Professors Alan Charles and Susan Alexander declared in the 1971 *Hastings Law Journal*, "are being denied a service which is lawfully available to others; the service is of great importance to their lives and health; the denial is because of artificial barriers created by the state."[187] The amicus briefs submitted in *Roe* by Planned Parenthood, the State Communities Aid Association, and the National Legal Program on Health Problems of the Poor all claimed that malenforced abortion bans violated the equal protection rights of lower class citizens. Sarah Weddington, the attorney for "Jane Roe" (Norma McCorvey), spent much of her energy during oral argument in *Roe* condemning "the inability of 'the poor and disadvantaged' to obtain abortions in Texas."[188]

Anecdotal evidence supports the suggestion that whatever its ostensible rationale, *Roe* "grew out of a strong sense of equity."[189] A University of Texas law professor recalls being told by Justice Powell that *Roe* "provided opportunities for the less affluent to enjoy the rights their more affluent sisters were already exercising."[190] One lower federal court explicitly relied on the equal protection rights of poor persons when declaring malenforced restrictions on abortion unconstitutional. "It is legally proper and imperative," Judge Gerhard A. Gesell declared in *United States v. Vuitch*, "that uniform medical abortion services be provided all segments of the population, the poor as well as the rich."[191]

ABORTION PRESENT

Legislation and judicial decisions repealing pro-life policies dramatically changed abortion law on the books. Every state penal code in 1963 forbade abortion under most circumstances. By 1973, those laws were removed by legislative decree or voided by judicial order. Hawaii (1971),

New York (1971), Alaska (1970), and Washington (1971) enacted statutes that gave women the right to abortion on demand. Courts in California (1969, 1972), Georgia (1970), Texas (1970), Florida (1971), Connecticut (1972), Vermont (1972), New Jersey (1972), Illinois (1971), Wisconsin (1970), Kansas (1972), and Washington, D.C. (1970) declared unconstitutional all significant state restrictions on reproductive choice.[192] Finally, the Supreme Court of the United States in *Roe v. Wade* (1973) ruled that the "right of privacy" found in the Ninth or Fourteenth Amendments "is broad enough to encompass a woman's decision whether or not to terminate her pregnancy." Justice Harry Blackmun's majority opinion held that states could not interfere with first trimester abortions and could "regulate the abortion procedure in ways that are reasonably related to maternal health" only during or after the second trimester.[193] The Supreme Court did subsequently sustain laws limiting governmental funding for abortions or requiring short waiting periods, "informed" consent, and parental notice before an abortion can be performed.[194] From 1973 to the present, however, the justices have never let elected officials prevent a private physician from granting an abortion to a consenting adult.

Legislative and judicial repeals of all penal bans on abortion had a more complex effect on abortion law in action. Although pro-life activists repeatedly denounce *Roe*[195] for promoting the slaughter of the unborn, actual abortion rates increased only slightly after legalization. The changes after 1970 in abortion laws on the books had a much greater impact on the classification of most abortions than on the total number of abortions performed. From 1970 to 1977, "illegal abortion was almost entirely replaced by legal procedures in the United States."[196] Women who had "criminal" abortions in 1965 had "therapeutic" abortions in 1975. Poor women and women of color were the primary beneficiaries of this substitution, for after *Roe* their access to safe, legal, and relatively cheap abortions increased substantially. Much of the small increase in the total number of abortions that resulted from legalization occurred because lower-class women were finally able to afford safe abortions and because greater publicity made poor women and women of color aware that safe abortions were available.[197]

Post-*Roe* statutory efforts to limit access to legal abortion are not significantly influencing abortion law in action. When providers are nearby, funding bans and various state regulations do not reduce the procreative choices actually open to most women. To be sure, significant access problems remain: most medical institutions and physicians have no desire to exercise their legal right to perform abortions. Still, the present mildly regulated market in reproductive services makes safe abortions far more available to poor women and women of color than did the gray and black markets of the past.

The Scope of Abortion Present

Legalization had little impact on the total number of abortions performed in the United States. Although after 1970 (and 1973) some women had abortions who would otherwise have given birth, demographers found that "a far more significant effect of liberalization of the abortion law has been the replacement of dangerous, discriminatory, undignified and costly illegal abortions by legal abortions performed under medical auspices."[198] By a series of admittedly speculative extrapolations from various population trends,[199] Dr. Christopher Tietze estimates that 70 to 90 percent of all abortions performed after *Roe* merely replaced illegal abortions that previous pro-life measures on the books had not prevented. If these hypotheses are correct, then evidence that 1.5 to 1.6 million legal abortions are now performed annually in the United States supports estimates of at least one million illegal abortions each year during the 1950s and 1960s.[200]

The proportion of women giving birth did decrease in the early 1970s, but this decline was not related to legal abortion. Birth rates were already falling significantly as contraception improved and Americans began to want fewer children. A statistical analysis of maternity trends found that "no precipitous decline of birth rates appears to have followed the *Roe* decision."[201] Population experts believe that fertility and birth rates historically reflect broad social dynamics and are rarely influenced by the specific abortion practices in a society. "Declines in fertility," Professor Mary Ann Lamanna states, "are probably not dependent on using any one means such as abortion, but will tend to occur as a result of changing values regardless of access to abortion."[202]

The Bias of Abortion Present

IMPROVEMENTS

Legislative and judicial repeals of abortion laws on the books had a dramatic and immediate egalitarian impact on access to legal abortion services. "When abortions are readily available," public health authorities observe, "the groups that are lower in the scale of social stratification . . . are the groups that make the greatest use of abortion facilities."[203] After *Roe*, doctors could provide abortion services to all consenting women without risking prosecution. Enterprising entrepreneurs opened abortion clinics that offered relatively cheap abortions and frequently made a tidy profit.[204] Providers who refused to abort women of different races became subject to federal and state antidiscrimination laws.

Newly instituted pro-choice policies helped many poor women finance their abortions. By removing the criminal tariff and permitting the procedure to be done on an outpatient basis, legalization significantly reduced the cost of a simple abortion. Willard Cates of the CDC estimates that *Roe* lowered the price of an abortion from $500 to $150.[205] Prices dropped by 90 percent in some regions of the country when obtaining an abortion in a specialized clinic became a legal option.[206] Legalization permitted philanthropic organizations to subsidize abortion fees for those who could not otherwise afford to terminate a pregnancy. Many abortion clinics offer discounts and some waive payment entirely for indigent patients.[207]

These price reductions instantly increased legal abortion rates. In states and localities where only affluent families had enjoyed access to safe abortions, poor women and women of color immediately began procuring legal abortions as frequently as did more privileged women. Before New York repealed its restrictions on abortion, 94 percent of all legal abortions in that state were granted to white women. The year New York abandoned its pro-life measures, women of color obtained 56 percent of all legal abortions.[208]

Less fortunate women at present have much higher legal abortion rates than their more affluent counterparts. Rosalind Petchesky of Hunter College estimates that "Medicaid-eligible women, a disproportionate number of whom are women of color, have an abortion rate that is three times higher than that of the white, married, middle- or working-class majority."[209] The national abortion rate for women of color is significantly greater than the abortion rate for white women. Doctors at the CDC note that black women "use legal abortion at approximately twice the rate of their white counterparts." Black and white women in 1981 had 549 and 329 abortions, respectively, for every thousand births.[210]

Legalization has not completely eliminated economic and racial disparities in maternal mortality and morbidity rates.[211] Nevertheless, far fewer women of all races and classes presently suffer botched abortions. Dr. Tietze estimates that as of 1984, legalized abortion had saved 1,500 maternal lives and prevented "several tens of thousands . . . of life-threatening, but not fatal complications."[212] In California, legislation that permitted abortion on demand increased the abortion rate twenty-five-fold while decreasing hospital admissions for septic abortion to a seventh of pre-legalization rates.[213] Septic abortion after *Roe* went the way of malaria in the United States. "The experienced gynecologist," several practicing physicians recognize, "need only make rounds on the gynecology ward of any municipal hospital to recognize the difference that legal abortion has made."[214]

Roe not only improved maternal health by replacing unsafe, usually illegal, abortions with safer legal abortions, but legislative and judicial repeals of pro-life measures also set forces in motion that substantially improved the quality of legal abortions. Legalization helped many women have safer, earlier abortions, allowed states to regulate and inspect abortion providers, enabled doctors to improve their abortion techniques, and permitted researchers to develop safer methods of pregnancy termination.[215] Thus, the death rate from *legal* abortions between 1970 and 1980 fell sharply, from 18.6 to 0.5 per 100,000 procedures.[216]

As compared to the impact of simple legalization, the impact of federal and state laws restricting welfare payments for abortions has been relatively insignificant. Despite much legal and public hand-wringing,[217] the government funding cutoffs sustained in *Maher v. Roe*[218] and *Harris v. McRae*[219] had very little effect on abortion rates. Federally financed abortions fell from 300,000 to fewer than 3,000 per year following passage of the Hyde Amendment. Nevertheless, researchers at both the CDC and the Alan Guttmacher Institute (AGI) believe that 94 percent of the women financially eligible for Medicaid still obtain abortions. Approximately 200,000 of these women live in states that fund all abortions; the rest rely on various private sources for financing. Public health specialists estimate that only 15,000 women annually bear unwanted children as a result of the Hyde Amendment and only 3,000 turn to illegal abortions.[220] Local funding restrictions have had similarly insignificant effects on abortion rates. One study estimates that states that do not pay for the abortions of indigent patients only reduce abortion rates by one per thousand women.[221] "Women who do not desire to bear a child," surveys find, "will terminate the pregnancy, regardless of how small the amount of public funds available."[222]

Official bans on abortion funding do impose severe burdens on poor women, many of whom, when faced with unwanted pregnancies, must sacrifice necessities to finance their abortions.[223] Still, approximately sixteen times as many poor women have had legal abortions as a consequence of legalization (282,000) than have done without that procedure as a consequence of decisions denying federal Medicaid funds (18,000).[224] The CDC estimates that even if a "total funding cutoff" occurs throughout the United States, "only one in every five women" on Medicaid would "carry a pregnancy to delivery which might otherwise have been aborted."[225] Hence, claims that the Hyde Amendment and similar measures make abortions available only to the affluent are wild exaggerations, not responsible arguments. As one commentary correctly notes, although "funding an abortion can involve a considerable amount of hardship for poor families, it still is a far cry from the 'back alley' days when the cost in dollars and often in personal risk in exploitation were much higher."[226]

State laws regulating abortion have also had little impact on access to reproductive services. Many communities do not enforce the abortion regulations found in their penal code,[227] while regulations in other localities are enforced in ways that do not unduly burden women. For example, Massachusetts judges routinely grant abortions to minors who do not wish to notify their parents.[228] Most states permit women seeking abortion to satisfy legally mandated informed consent requirements through the mail or by phone. Mississippi alone requires women to make two trips to an abortion provider before terminating an unwanted pregnancy.[229] Restrictive policies that lower legal abortion rates within a state typically increase the legal abortion rate in bordering states with more liberal abortion policies. Massachusetts minors travel to Rhode Island and New Hampshire to evade parental consent requirements; Mississippi adults travel to Tennessee and Alabama to avoid statutory waiting periods.[230]

State regulations are not entirely toothless. One study concludes that laws requiring parental notification reduce the average legal abortion rate by five per thousand women, and laws imposing waiting periods reduce the average legal abortion rate by eight per thousand women.[231] A survey in Mississippi found residents procuring 10 percent fewer abortions after a law mandating a strict waiting period and informed consent took effect.[232] Those regulations, however, did not disproportionately burden poor women or women of color. Less privileged women apparently overcome so many obstacles when seeking an abortion that one more legal barrier does not significantly influence their abortion decision.[233] Humane considerations support minimizing the distinct burdens poor women seeking abortion face, but post-*Casey* regulations have not yet forced many less fortunate women to bear unwanted children or seek dangerous illegal abortions.

Conversely, no evidence suggests that present regulations on abortion serve any of their ostensible purposes. Most legal barriers merely delay the eventual abortion, thus increasing both the expense and risk of the procedure.[234] Few women find state-mandated information packets and waiting periods useful when they consider whether to abort an unwanted pregnancy. Ninety-three percent of the women surveyed by the AGI "were unable to name a single benefit they had experienced by being required to wait to have an abortion."[235] Parental notification laws lowered abortion rates slightly in Minnesota, but such policies did "not significantly increase the likelihood that a minor will speak to a parent." Researchers found a "catch-22 for the father: If he is absent, he is irrelevant and thus not informed; if he is compassionate and open, his daughter does not want to disappoint him."[236]

FAILURES

The present system of abortion regulation may be more egalitarian than its predecessor, but the hopes many reformers had that all Americans would enjoy equal access to abortion on demand have not been realized. Abortion laws on the books that offer women the right to terminate their pregnancies do not guarantee that women who want abortions will find a competent and willing provider. "Access to abortion," commentators recognize, "depends not only on a women's decision to terminate her pregnancy, but on her ability to locate a cooperative practitioner."[237] Everyone familiar with current abortion law in action admits that "as with access to medical services generally, those who are young, poor, and members of minority groups do not have equal access to legally induced abortions."[238] Researchers at the AGI estimate that more than 100,000 women a year forgo legal abortions because they cannot travel to the nearest sanctioned abortionist.[239]

Abortions remain scarce because, although hospitals are free to provide abortion services, many continue their restrictive pre-*Roe* practices. Gerald Rosenberg of the University of Chicago points out that "in response to the Court, hospitals did not change their policies to permit abortions."[240] Abortion rates in different hospitals vary as significantly today as they did before *Roe*. A recent survey found that less than one-fifth of all short-term hospitals and less than one-quarter of all private hospitals in the United States provide patients with abortions. A majority of American hospitals in 1986 had not yet performed their first abortion. Many hospitals that do offer abortion services terminate very few pregnancies and will not perform that procedure in the second trimester. Only eighty-three hospitals in the United States performed more than four hundred abortions in 1988.[241]

Legalization barely influenced the abortion practices of most obstetricians. Laws may permit doctors to terminate pregnancies, but most do not offer that service to the general public. Abortions in traditional medical settings are still frequently distributed on the basis of economic class. Many practitioners provide abortions only to their private patients, unless a stranger's pregnancy is life-threatening. "Private practice," the leading study of communal medical services reports, "continues to serve as the major barrier to a more equitable provision of abortion service."[242]

The proliferation of freestanding abortion clinics has partially compensated for the refusal of doctors in private practice to provide equal abortion services. As of 1992, abortion and other specialized clinics performed approximately 89 percent of all first trimester abortions in the United States.[243] Many women, however, cannot easily visit an abortion clinic. Clinics require economies of scale to pay for costs (and make a profit). For that reason, clinics are typically located only in metropolitan areas where they can perform the number of abortions necessary to stay open. "Abortion providers," commentators point out, are "limited for the most part to those counties where the need for abortion is large enough to support a specialized clinic."[244]

Few clinics or abortion services of any kind exist in less heavily populated regions of this country. In 1992, 84 percent of all counties in the United States lacked a single abortion provider. Rural counties are particularly in need of this service. Only 7 percent of all rural counties have an abortion provider and only 1 percent have a provider that performs more than four hundred abortions annually.[245] Women who live in jurisdictions without abortion providers must go on expensive journeys in order to terminate an unwanted pregnancy. One study found that "a decade after *Roe*, more than 10 percent of the women seeking abortions in twenty-two states still had to travel out of state."[246]

Access problems are worsening. Surveys reveal a steady decrease in the number of abortion providers and major abortion providers in the United States.[247] The siege conditions under which many clinics operate apparently deter all but the most committed pro-choice physicians from performing many abortions. Active abortion clinics routinely experience vandalism and threats of physical violence. Several doctors have been murdered.[248] Abortion clinics face other, less dramatic difficulties when hiring doctors. The work is not prestigious, the procedure is tedious, and the wages relatively low. Planned Parenthood of New York City has trouble finding physicians willing to perform abortions four days a week for $150,000 a year because gynecologists in private practice make twice that figure.[249]

This shortage of abortion providers significantly influences the distribution of legal abortions. "The local availability of abortion services," numerous contemporary studies conclude, "is the single most powerful determinant of variations in abortion rates in the United States."[250] For this reason, women who cannot afford to travel long distances are often unable to exercise their constitutional right to abortion on demand. Researchers in Georgia found that for every one hundred miles of distance from an abortion provider, white abortion rates were reduced by 62 per 1,000 women and black abortion rates were reduced by 78 per 1,000 women. Nationally, women are twice as likely to have a legal abortion if they live in a county that has a major abortion provider.[251]

Women who live in jurisdictions hostile to *Roe* are also frequently unable to exercise their constitutional right to abortion on demand. Although the Supreme Court has not permitted states to implement any significant restriction on abortion, legal abortion rates in various states differ dramatically. In 1988, 46 of every 1,000 women in California had a legal abortion, but only 5 of every 1,000 women in Wyoming exercised that constitutional right.[252] While the number of abortion providers in different states explains much of this disparity, official policies do exert some effects on legal abortion rates.[253] Moreover, the ghost of past abortion practices influences contemporary legal abortion rates from the grave. Even controlling for present legal policies, states that permitted abortion on demand before *Roe* have an average of about 18 more legal abortions per 1,000 women than states that had previously criminalized virtually all abortions. "States with pre-*Roe* laws allowing abortion with minor exceptions and states which were generally prohibitive," Professors Robin Wolpert and Gerald Rosenberg estimate, have on average 5 and 3 more legal abortions per 1,000 women respectively than states that were more restrictive.[254]

To conclude that *Roe* had little impact on abortion law in action, however, would be a serious mistake. Although abortions still are not equally available to all, legalization substantially improved the access poor women and women of color enjoy to abortion on demand. The best demographic estimates suggest that the number of pregnant women not having access to legal abortion has been reduced 90 percent, from the 1,000,000 women annually who procured illegal abortions in 1960s to the 100,000 women annually who lack access to legal abortion in the 1990s. Illegal abortion still creates health problems in some rural counties,[255] but most obstetricians trained after 1973 have never seen an actual case of septic abortion.

The nature of the main obstacle to more equal choice has changed since the judiciary declared abortion a constitutional right. Most disparities in access to abortion presently stem from perfectly lawful behavior. No statute or judicial decision requires doctors to provide free abortions or establish abortion clinics in rural areas. Before *Roe*, in contrast, most disparities in access to abortion stemmed from *illegal* behavior. Although most state penal codes prohibited abortion except when necessary to save the life of the pregnant women, law enforcement officials tolerated physicians who performed gray-market abortions for their affluent patients. In a capitalist market society, significant philosophical and constitutional differences exist between disparities that are consequences of free markets and disparities that result from capriciously enforced criminal laws.[256]

ABORTION FUTURE

Predicting the future is always hazardous. For every *The Emergence of a Conservative Majority*, presciently written by Kevin Phillips in 1968, there are the equivalent of at least three *Herald Tribune* polls proclaiming that Alf Landon will defeat Franklin Delano Roosevelt in the 1936 presidential election. Political prognosticators have had a particularly bad record divining the course of American reproductive politics. Pundits pronounced *Roe* dead immediately before *Casey*, then prematurely buried the pro-life movement after the 1992 election. Reproductive rights seemed durable when President Clinton first took office. But two years later, the Christian Coalition demonstrated renewed political strength and prominent Republican strategists began looking for opportunities to place the recriminalization of abortion back on the political agenda.[257]

Anticipating future developments in American abortion policies is particularly difficult because new contraceptive and abortifacient technologies are dramatically altering family planning practices.[258] Still, evidence from the recent past suggests two lessons for future policy makers. First, future American abortion laws in action will permit most abortions, no matter what language is used by future American abortion laws on the books. Second, laws that regulate all abortions offer better reproductive choices to poor women and women of color than laws that prohibit abortion in certain vaguely defined circumstances. A regulated market in abortion services is not identical in practice to a free or subsidized market. Nevertheless, the practical differences between free and regulated markets in abortion services are dwarfed by the practical differences between exclusive gray and regulated markets.

Proposed bans on abortion are advertised as measures designed to protect the unborn, but their passage will probably not substantially affect overall abortion rates. "Even if the legal situation were to revert to the *status quo ante Roe v. Wade*," students of public policy claim, "no evidence supports the assumption that the annual number of abortions performed on U.S. citizens would significantly decrease."[259] Throughout the twentieth century, the abortion rate in this country remained fairly steady as the actual mix of legal and illegal abortions adjusted to official policy. Should Americans in the near future desire approximately the same number of children and not change their contraceptive or sexual habits, new bans on abortion will primarily increase illegal abortions at the expense of legal abortions.

Recriminalizing abortion will not protect the unborn because pro-life laws on the books are nearly impossible to implement. Criminal measures succeed in practice only when the bulk of the community shares the sentiments embodied by the law. Because more Americans support abortion rights than in the past, localities that recriminalize abortion will experience even greater public pressure not to prosecute competent abortionists than we have seen historically. Fewer police officials will investigate or arrest competent abortionists, fewer jurors will convict them, and fewer judges will impose substantial sentences on them. Citizens and officials hostile to abortion rights will confront increasing numbers of pregnant women who can travel to jurisdictions where abortion is legal or can obtain such drugs as RU-486, a substance that promises relatively safe, self-induced abortions.[260] Significantly, no major pro-life official has announced a plan for preventing the rebirth of the abortion underground.[261]

Strong pro-choice advocates may condemn any modification of *Roe*,[262] but not all compromises have the same affect on access to abortion services. Studies of post-*Roe* and pre-*Roe* law in action indicate that compromises permitting states to regulate all abortions have far more equitable effects than compromises permitting states to prohibit some abortions. When abortion is legal and abortion providers available, women of all economic classes and races are usually able to terminate an unwanted pregnancy legally and safely.[263] Funding bans and legal regulations do little good, and they unnecessarily burden women seeking abortions. Nevertheless, funding bans have little impact on access to safe abortion services, and most legal regulations are not yet having a disproportionate impact on poor women and women of color.

Should the Supreme Court further modify or overrule the *Roe/Casey* regime, however, the bans on abortion most likely to be enacted and implemented will reproduce the worst discriminatory features of the exclusive gray market. Many observers maintain that, given judicial permission, most states should and will adopt policies that empower physicians to use their discretion when determining whether sufficient indications exist for abortion.[264] Such rules as those permitting abortions only when pregnant women demonstrate some generalized risk to their mental or physical health seem fair compromises in the abstract. But advocates of these bargains tend to forget that the precise wording of abortion laws on the books rarely describes abortion law in action. History suggests that access to abortion is most equal when the law either prohibits all abortions or allows abortion on demand. The more complex and subjective the standards for determining when an abortion is legal, the greater the disparities in abortion rates between favored and disfavored social groups. As Judge Guido Calabresi and Professor Phillip Bobbitt point out, "any rule which discriminates between some situations in which abortion will be allowed and some in which it is not gives greater access to the articulate and well-represented."[265] When the law on the books permits physicians to make subjective judgments, the law in action penalizes only those women who lack the resources and connections necessary to procure sympathetic medical testimony on their behalf.

Several features of future practice may exacerbate the inevitable discriminatory impact that recriminalization will have on legal abortion rates. Few women in the late twentieth and early twenty-first centuries will have legitimate medical indications for abortion. Advances in medical technique now enable doctors to bring to term many pregnancies that would have presented grave threats to maternal health in 1971. Drs. Kenneth

Niswander and Manuel Porto point out that at present, even patients with heart conditions can, with proper medication, be "delivered without complication."[266] By a process of elimination, therefore, a higher proportion of future abortions will be performed for psychiatric and other subjective indications. Abortion decisions in these circumstances will be medically complex and legally borderline, at best. Hence, most physicians will again run whatever legal risks abortion presents only when their affluent and overwhelmingly white private patients request that their pregnancies be terminated.

The existence of jurisdictional pockets where abortion on demand is legal will further aggravate disparities in class access to legal abortions. Should *Roe* be overruled, a number of states, particularly those in the Northeast and on the West Coast, will grant women a statutory or state constitutional right to terminate their pregnancies. Persons who are able to identify such states and to travel there will secure legal abortions. Such ventures will often be expensive. Still, the New York experience in 1971–72 demonstrates that the price will hardly inhibit affluent citizens and will be affordable to the middle class. Poorer Americans who live more than a short bus ride from a pro-choice state, however, will have to forgo abortion tourism.

Philosophers and law professors may regard abortion as a matter of life and death, but the policy alternatives facing late-twentieth-century Americans are less stark. No matter what the ultimate fate of *Roe*, a substantial number of pregnant women, perhaps a majority, will continue enjoying a de facto right to abortion on demand. These women will live in jurisdictions where abortion remains legal, be able to travel to jurisdictions where abortion remains legal, or have the resources and connections necessary to procure a safe, illegal abortion where they live. As Professor Luker observes, "the only real policy choice that confronts Americans is whether a significant portion of [unwanted] pregnancies will be ended legally or illegally."[267] Put differently, the relevant political and constitutional decision that citizens of this country must soon make is not whether everyone or no one will enjoy abortion rights, but whether everyone or only some persons will enjoy abortion rights.

CHAPTER III

Equal Choice

EQUAL JUSTICE UNDER LAW

The central premise of equal choice is simple. No state may make abortion policies that discriminate against poor persons or persons of color. Policies that intentionally distribute rights on the basis of economic class or race violate a venerated principle of Western civilization, *isonomia* or equality before the law. Pericles' funeral oration praises Athenian institutions for making every polity member "equal before the law," and the Torah extends this privilege to all persons: "You shall have one ordinance," Leviticus 24.22 commands, "for stranger and for citizen alike."[1] Legal equality is a sacred precept of the American creed as well. "Opposition to 'class legislation' and 'special legislation,'" intellectual historians point out, has "been part of Anglo-American political philosophy since long before the Declaration of Independence."[2] Americans inscribed the phrase "Equal Justice under Law" over the entrance to their highest court, and members of that tribunal must swear to do "equal right to the poor and to the rich."

Equality before the law is a fundamental constitutional principle. The persons responsible for the Fourteenth Amendment[3] intended to prohibit certain forms of race discrimination, and they regarded racially biased enforcement of the criminal law as the paradigmatic violation of the equal protection clause. Reconstruction Republicans also intended to prohibit certain kinds of discrimination against poor persons, and they regarded class-biased enforcement of the criminal law as an unconstitutional evil. Hence, government officials may not constitutionally help establish or maintain an exclusive gray market that provides affluent white women with de facto immunities from statutory bans on abortion. When privileged women in a community are free to terminate their pregnancies without substantial medical and legal complications, all women must be accorded the same formal liberty. States may reenact pro-life policies that contain additional precautions designed to prevent the rebirth of the exclusive gray market. Such safeguards, however, are conspicuously absent from all recent proposals to recriminalize abortion.

The Supreme Court has a special obligation to protect this right to equal choice. Members of the national judiciary normally presume that the people's elected representatives are making policies that reflect popu-

lar sentiment and respect constitutional rights. Nevertheless, federal justices must ensure that democratically chosen legislators govern by general
laws. This standard is violated whenever official decisions help establish or
maintain exclusive gray markets. Two distinct laws exist in practice when
the state penal code formally bans abortion. One law leaves most doctors
free to terminate pregnancies for their private patients, almost all of whom
are affluent and white. The other law prevents competent abortionists
from offering their services to the general public. A judiciary that declared
this double standard unconstitutional would not be substituting its considered judgment that abortion be legal for the legislature's considered
judgment that abortion be banned. Rather, justices who strike down
maladministered bans on abortion simply remedy the unconstitutional inequalities that result when governing officials fail in practice to choose
between pro-life and pro-choice policies.

Fears that systemic application of equal choice principles across the entire criminal law might require abandoning every provision in the penal
code overlook important distinctions between pre-*Roe* abortion law in
action and other maladministered statutes. Even if societies must tolerate
fairly high levels of discrimination in law enforcement practices, constitutional authorities should not sustain laws that most prominent persons
violate with impunity. Official policies that grant favored classes of citizens
indulgences from the penal code remove the most powerful democratic
safeguard against tyranny: governing officials can be trusted to protect
fundamental rights only when persons with the power to make the laws
know that they, their families, and their leading supporters remain subject
to whatever laws they make. Although the discriminatory enforcement of
any law is an unconstitutional evil, officials committed to democratic principles must make special efforts to ensure that no law remains on the
books that might be repealed immediately if uniformly enforced.

Constitutional, Legal, and Moral Arguments

Equal choice relies primarily on constitutional and legal arguments. The
constitutional arguments discuss the meaning of the due process and
equal protection clauses, while the legal arguments analyze how contemporary judicial decisions interpret those constitutional provisions. Legal
arguments are directed at judges, who prefer to follow precedent when
handing down constitutional decisions. Constitutional arguments, by
contrast, are directed at citizens committed to the American constitutional order. Although litigators arguing before the Supreme Court are
well advised to assume "the Constitution is what the judges say it is,"[4] in
the long run persuasive constitutional arguments have greater societal im-

pact than legal arguments. Should electoral majorities become convinced that equal choice claims are constitutionally sound, the justices subsequently appointed to the federal bench will make equal choice principles the law of the land.[5]

Constitutional principles and contemporary case law clearly support the major premise of the equal choice attack on statutes banning reproductive choice. State abortion practices that discriminate against poor women and women of color violate the Fourteenth Amendment and are inconsistent with authoritative legal precedents. Constitutional and present legal standards for determining what constitutes discriminatory state action, however, *may* differ. The traditional constitutional test for intentional discrimination is satisfied by equal choice arguments. State policies that cause substantial race and class disparities without serving any legitimate social purpose normally violate the equal protection clause, no matter what the subjective mental state of the persons responsible for their enactment or administration. Unfortunately, the Rehnquist Court is moving toward a tougher interpretation of discriminatory intent. A 5–4 majority recently ruled in *McCleskey v. Kemp*[6] that persons sentenced to death must prove that state officials discriminated against them personally. Should the Court apply *McCleskey* to all criminal cases, legal equal choice arguments will fail.

Sympathetic judges could uphold equal choice claims without actually overruling *McCleskey*. The precise holding of that case is still unclear. Some language in *McCleskey* does indicate that the justices will require all victims of racially biased law enforcement to prove they were personally discriminated against. Justice Powell's majority opinion, however, implies that the Court would find discriminatory state action when, as was the case with abortion before *Roe*, communities made no effort to reduce severe race and class disparities in the administration of their penal code.

More to the point, *McCleskey*, as discussed below, is a constitutional abomination that should not govern future cases. Common sense and the plain meaning of the equal protection clause suggest that when state actors cannot offer plausible justifications for practices that severely burden poor persons and persons of color, government officials must be hiding unconstitutional race and class discrimination. Many distinguished scholars and the American Bar Association point out that *McCleskey* violates basic canons of both constitutional interpretation and human decency. That decision rests on historically dubious foundations and threatens the practical abandonment of the central purpose underlying the post–Civil War amendments: equal racial and class justice under law.

Even if *McCleskey* is taken as sound constitutional law, that case does not vitiate the moral force of equal choice principles. The Constitution establishes minimum thresholds that elected officials are prohibited from

crossing, but policies that satisfy these constitutional norms may not necessarily satisfy broader egalitarian principles. Legislatures and citizens
committed to a more rigorous equality under law would not keep in their
penal code controversial and burdensome bans on abortion that affluent
white families easily evade. Indeed, a generous people committed to the
spirit as well as the letter of constitutional equality would fund abortions
for indigent women and abjure common state regulations of procreative
choice. The Hyde Amendment, parental consent laws, mandatory waiting
periods, and related measures save no money, prevent few abortions,
rarely improve communication between parents and pregnant minors,
and do not promote informed abortion decisions. Such policies in practice
do little more than erect spite fences that poor pregnant women seeking
abortions must uncomfortably scale.[7]

CONSTITUTIONAL EQUALITY

Race

Three hundred years of political struggle have finally established a national
consensus among Americans—in word if not in deed—that persons of
color must not be denied any right, privilege, or status possessed by any
other polity member. To remove all doubts as to whether persons of color
are entitled to equal justice under law, the American people in 1868 formally placed a ban on race discrimination in their national constitution.[8]
Anyone remotely familiar with the history of the United States knows that
"the one pervading purpose found in" the Thirteenth, Fourteenth, and
Fifteenth Amendments was "the freedom of the slave race, the security
and firm establishment of that freedom and the protection of the newly
made freeman and citizen from the oppression of those that formerly had
exercised unlimited dominion over him."[9] The central question of much
current equal protection jurisprudence is whether other victims of discrimination are entitled to the same constitutional protection that persons
of color enjoy.[10]

The persons responsible for the Fourteenth Amendment specifically intended to abolish racially biased enforcement of the criminal law.[11] Reconstruction Republicans vigorously condemned ex-Confederate states
for not punishing white persons who committed crimes against persons of
color and for punishing persons of color for conduct that was tolerated
when done by white persons. Angry Northerners demanded that the
Thirty-ninth Congress "ensure not only that state laws call for fair treatment of citizens" but also that state officers execute laws without "difference or partiality." Otherwise, one influential advocate pointed out, "the
most execrable tyranny may be practiced on one race, while the other

would be partially exempt."[12] Federal legislators investigating the treatment of persons of color in the postwar South heard numerous complaints about the discriminatory administration of local criminal laws. The War Department quickly responded to these injustices by forbidding "the prosecution of Negroes charged with offenses for which whites were not prosecuted or punished in the same manner or degree."[13]

Congress first attempted to prohibit disparate law enforcement by passing the Civil Rights Act of 1866. Persons of color, that statute declared, could not be "subjected . . . to any other different punishment, pains or penalties for the commission of any act . . . than are prescribed for white persons committing like acts."[14] When President Andrew Johnson questioned whether the federal government had the constitutional power to enact such measures, Republicans responded by proposing, framing, and ratifying the Fourteenth Amendment. Even conservative constitutional historians recognize that, at a minimum, the proponents of the Fourteenth Amendment intended to constitutionalize every provision in the Civil Rights Act of 1866.[15]

State practices that give white persons a practical immunity from statutory bans on abortion clearly violate the Civil Rights Act of 1866 and, hence, are unconstitutional. State officials who never arrest physicians who perform abortions for white women engage in the racially selective law enforcement practices that the Reconstruction Congress sought to abolish.[16] Moreover, the persons responsible for the Fourteenth Amendment specifically intended that persons of color be free to purchase any good or service readily available to white persons.[17] Thus, when white women are allowed by law or custom to purchase safe abortions, our constitutional commitment to "equal protection of the law" requires that women of color be afforded the same option for controlling their fertility.

Economic Class

Laws and policies that discriminate against poor persons also violate the Constitution. Americans used the phrase "equal protection of the law" and expressed concerns about class legislation long before they became committed to any form of racial equality.[18] The Revolutionary colonists demanded "equal laws, equally executed,"[19] and the nation they founded was "dedicated to the proposition that all men are created equal." The preamble to many state constitutions explicitly recognized that self-evident truth. Virginia's famed Declaration of Rights, for example, announced that "all men are by nature equally free and independent."[20] The forces unleashed by independence intensified this social commitment to equality. The theme "equal rights for all, special privileges for none," a noted authority on early American politics observes, "reappeared in [Jef-fersonian] Republican rhetoric in endlessly different forms like a Wagne-rian leitmotif."[21]

Early American jurists translated this public commitment to equality into the legal requirement that all laws be general. Daniel Webster's influ-ential argument in the *Dartmouth College* case maintained that the due process clauses in the federal and state constitutions guaranteed that "every citizen shall hold his life, liberty, property, and immunities, under the protection of the general rules which govern society."[22] Many local judges in antebellum America expressed the same sentiments when strik-ing down state laws that singled out specific individuals or groups for special treatment. In one widely cited case, future Supreme Court Justice John Catron demonstrated his dual commitment to equal rights and con-voluted syntax by ruling that "the idea of a people through their represen-tatives making laws whereby are swept away the life, liberty and property of one or a few citizens by which neither the representatives nor their other constituents are willing to be bound is too odious to be tolerated."[23]

Prominent Jacksonians relied heavily on egalitarian rhetoric when con-demning practices that allowed affluent citizens to enjoy special privileges. Andrew Jackson's influential veto in 1832 of the Bank Bill contended that government must "confine itself to *equal protection*, and, as Heaven does its rains, shower its favors alike on the high and the low, the rich and the poor."[24] Mid-nineteenth-century thinkers used similar phrases when censuring laws that gave exclusive rights to members of favored economic classes. After observing that "whenever an exception is made to the general law of the land, . . . it will always be found to be in favor of wealth," the influential Jacksonian editor and publicist William Leggett proclaimed that

> the sole reliance of the laboring classes . . . is a system of legislation which leaves all to the free exercise of their talents and industry within the limits of the general law and which, on no pretense of public good, bestows on any particular class of industry or any particular body of men rights or privileges not equally enjoyed by the great aggregate of the body politic.[25]

The Fourteenth Amendment constitutionalized the traditional American demand for general laws. Leading Reconstruction Republican politicians declared that their purpose in amending the Constitution was to make racial classifications as constitutionally obnoxious as wealth classifications. Senator Henry Wilson of Massachusetts stated that "by the equality of man we mean that the poorest man, be he black or white . . . is as much entitled to the protection of the law as the richest and proudest man." Thaddeus Stevens would "remodel all our institutions as to have freed them from every vestige of human oppression, of inequality of rights, of the recognized degradation of the poor, and of the superior caste of the rich."[26] At no point did any person responsible for the Fourteenth Amendment specifically declare that persons of color required special constitutional protection that poor persons could do without. Instead, after stating that section 1 "abolishes all class legislation in the States," Jacob Howard, the member of the Joint Committee on Reconstruction who explained the Fourteenth Amendment to the full Senate, declared that the measure would merely "*extend* to the black man . . . the poor privilege of equal protection of the laws" (emphasis added).[27]

For the next hundred years, American jurists consistently recognized that "property" cannot be "a pretext for unequal or exclusive civil rights."[28] Late-nineteenth- and early-twentieth-century constitutional commentators reminded their sizable audience that the equal protection clause prohibited all class-based legislation and not merely legislation that discriminated against racial minorities. Thomas Cooley, the most influential legal treatise writer of the Gilded Age, insisted that it was "a maxim in constitutional law" that "those who make the laws are to govern by promulgated, established laws, not to be varied in particular cases, but to have one rule for rich and poor, for the favorite at court and the countryman at plough."[29] Prominent conservative justices announced similar principles from the bench. "Our whole system of law," Chief Justice William Howard Taft proclaimed in 1921, "is predicated on the general fundamental principle of equality of application of the law."[30]

The Supreme Court reaffirmed the American commitment to equal justice under law on numerous occasions during the 1950s, 1960s, and 1970s. Anticipating and later participating to a limited degree in the War on Poverty, the federal judiciary frequently condemned statutes that conditioned the exercise of legal rights on a person's ability to pay. "Lines drawn on the basis of wealth and property, like those of race," Justice Douglas stated in an opinion declaring the poll tax unconstitutional, "are traditionally disfavored."[31] Although some justices disputed particular applications of the constitutional requirement that laws be general, the Court remained united on the principle that states could not grant special privileges to affluent citizens. The second Justice Harlan, who often dissented vigorously from Warren Court decisions finding equal protection clause violations, thought it obvious that state officials "are prohibited from discriminating between 'rich' and 'poor' as such in the formulation and application of their laws."[32]

Modern Supreme Court decisions protecting the rights of criminal suspects provide particularly strong precedents for equal choice claims. The constitutional aspiration for equal justice, the justices recognize, remains unfulfilled when individual rights to life, liberty, or property depend on whether persons have the financial resources to refute allegations against them. Both conservative and liberal jurists insist that wealth should not unduly influence the criminal process. The "noble ideal" that "every defendant stands equal before the law," a unanimous Court held in *Gideon v. Wainwright*, "cannot be realized if the poor man charged with crime has to face his accusers without a lawyer to assist him."[33]

If "there can be no equal justice where the kind of appeal [trial] a man gets depends on the amount of money he has,"[34] then there can be no equal justice when decisions to arrest and prosecute persons suspected of criminal offenses depend on how much money they have or, in the case of abortion, how much money their clientele has. *Gideon* and other entrenched judicial precedents establish that wealth must not buy special privileges at any stage of the criminal process, from crime control to sentencing. The United States—Jacksonian Democrats, Reconstruction Republicans, and contemporary jurists of all ideological stripes agree—is "dedicated to affording equal justice to all and special privileges to none in the administration of its criminal law."[35] Of course, "[a]bsolute equality is not required"[36] in a capitalist society. Nevertheless, state policies that enable affluent persons to enjoy substantial advantages in the criminal process, either because they can afford counsel or because they are not arrested when they transgress statutory norms, are inconsistent with the language of the equal protection clause, the intentions of those responsible for that provision, the traditional American demand for general laws, and a distinguished line of judicial precedents requiring state officials to "weig[h] the interests of rich and poor criminals in equal scale."[37]

Those academic lawyers and judges who question whether the Constitution protects the poor per se[38] are responding to a very different constitutional claim, the claim that the Fourteenth Amendment guarantees all persons the right to possess certain kinds of property. Many social democrats now speak of the "new property" and seek to "transform the widely held notion of welfare as a privilege into a right."[39] Frank Michelman of Harvard Law School, in particular, actively defends "constitutional rights to provision for certain basic ingredients of individual welfare, such as food, shelter, health care, and education." If persons cannot find adequate sustenance in the marketplace, Michelman and others assert, government has a constitutional obligation to provide them with the necessary goods and services.[40]

The equal choice argument for a free market in safe abortions is constitutionally distinct from the new property argument for a subsidized market in safe abortions. Proponents of equal justice under law claim that class legislation on the books or in action violates the acknowledged Fourteenth Amendment right to be treated as a legal equal, not the more controversial constitutional right to be provided with essential resources at the public's expense. Restrictions on abortion were unconstitutional as applied, equal choice maintains, because when state officials do not prevent doctors from providing abortion services to their affluent white private patients, the equal protection clause requires that state officials not prevent doctors from providing the same services to the general public. The exclusive gray market in safe abortion services violated the Fourteenth Amendment, in this view, by providing affluent white citizens with exactly the kind of special privileges Jacksonian Democrats and their Reconstruction descendants meant to abolish.

Whether the Constitution requires state officials to help poor persons finance abortions is an entirely different question, one on which proponents of equal choice may disagree. Elected officials respect equal choice principles when they allow market forces to determine who has access to abortion. Poor persons may not do very well in this free market even when allowed to participate.[41] Nevertheless, the establishment of an exclusive gray market prevents even the formal equality of opportunity demanded by any reasonable interpretation of the Fourteenth Amendment.

DISCRIMINATORY STATE ACTION

Pro-Life versus Equal Choice

Prominent opponents of *Roe* freely admit that state officials may not constitutionally exempt affluent white families from statutory bans on abortion or any other provision of the penal code. John Noonan, a leading pro-life theorist and federal judge, enthusiastically embraces "the principle . . . that the law should be equal law" as "a foundation stone of democracy."[42] Noonan and his occasional coauthor, David Louisell, even concede the existence of a gray market that primarily serviced the abortion needs of wealthier Americans.[43] But pro-life commentators who agree that government officials cannot make abortion policies that discriminate against poor persons and persons of color nevertheless maintain that government officials did not so discriminate before *Roe* when administering statutory bans on abortion. Opponents of reproductive choice treat the race and class biases of the exclusive gray market in safe abortions as the inevitable by-product of reasonable law enforcement practices in communities that lacked the resources necessary to identify and punish every criminal actor.

Pro-life attacks on equal choice arguments condemn that defense of *Roe* for failing to demonstrate state action and intentional discrimination, two essential elements of any valid equal protection claim. No *state*, we are told, denied equal choice to any person. Private physicians were the parties who offered gray-market abortions only to affluent white women. State policies that exacerbated the gray market's disparate impact on poor persons and persons of color did not violate constitutional norms, because governmental officials did not adopt them for discriminatory purposes. "The statutes regulating abortion do not intend to discriminate," Louisell and Noonan declare. Unfortunately, abortion is hard to detect because "its perpetration is secret."[44] In their view, the skill of the abortionist and the complicity of aborted women prevented law enforcement officials from learning or obtaining evidence that a criminal abortion had been committed.

Pro-life commentators insist that official failures to enforce bans on abortion are no different than official failures to prevent or punish other crimes. If *Roe* was correctly decided because most abortionists were never detected and punished, they argue, then persons would have a constitutional right to steal car batteries in New York City. Evidence that the police cannot apprehend the perpetrators of many illegal acts, however, does not transform a crime into a constitutional right. People, Louisell and Noonan correctly state, do not normally "argue from [the] enormous number of violations . . . that we should reform the law of larceny to accommodate the moral standards of those who steal from others."[45]

This pro-life vision of wily abortionists escaping official detection is a convenient fantasy. Affluent white women obtained safe abortions before *Roe* because law enforcement officials made *conscious* decisions not to arrest or punish doctors known to be providing abortion services to their elite friends and private patients. The law enforcement community in most jurisdictions deliberately ignored doctors who performed "criminal" abortions. Most competent abortionists terminated pregnancies discreetly, but not secretly. Indeed, some physicians were quite open about their illicit abortion practices. Doctors described their gray-market activities at national conferences and published statistics documenting their crimes. Police officers who were not regular readers of the *American Journal of Public Health* could examine the records of most major hospitals where the details of illegal abortions were meticulously kept. Nevertheless, the physicians who led the early movement for abortion reform were rarely arrested and police officers never seriously investigated the hospitals whose illegal practices those doctors exposed. By comparison, consider the increased rates of conviction that would result if persons who make their living by stealing car batteries began keeping detailed and accessible records about their successful heists, discussing their ongoing criminal activity at public conferences of professional gangsters, and publishing incriminating data in *Hot Cars Quarterly*.

Law enforcement officials who did not ignore illegal physician-abortionists were more likely to assist than arrest them. As we have seen, the underground abortion network could not have existed without official cooperation. The police occasionally protected illegal abortionists from blackmailers who threatened to "expose" their criminal activity. More often, physician-abortionists and elected officials negotiated informal treaties: the police prevented unsafe abortionists from selling their wares but allowed competent doctors to terminate pregnancies for their largely white and upper-class clientele. Physicians permitted by law enforcement officials to grant more fortunate citizens a de facto right to abortion on demand, however, were expected not to perform that procedure frequently enough so as to provide all persons in the community with the same practical immunity from the criminal law. The few legitimate doctors who got into legal trouble for terminating pregnancies typically offered abortion services to the general public.[46]

The official practices that helped establish and maintain the exclusive gray market were responsible for the race and class disparities in access to safe abortions. Contrary to pro-life (and pro-choice) speculations, laissez-faire medical policies are relatively egalitarian. The aftermath of *Roe* establishes that most poor persons and persons of color can terminate unwanted pregnancies safely and legally when given the opportunity to secure an abortion in a mildly regulated market.[47] The majority of less privileged women could not procure safe abortions before *Roe*, because law enforcement officials prevented those competent abortionists who performed abortions for affluent women from providing the same services to all abortion-seeking women.

Pre-*Roe* abortion policies had a disparate impact on poor women and women of color because legal restrictions on reproductive choice were selectively enforced, and not because market societies normally distribute superior goods and services to more affluent citizens. In the exclusive gray market, money did not buy a bigger supply of those goods and services money may lawfully purchase. Instead, with the implicit or explicit permission of state actors, wealth purchased indulgences from the criminal law. Contrary to pro-life assertions,[48] affluent women did not get better abortions before *Roe* for the same reason they bought better cars. Instead, they were more likely than average women to procure safe abortions throughout the first seventy years of the twentieth century for the same reason affluent Americans now get better cocaine and are more likely to have their speeding tickets fixed.

By incorrectly blaming the pathologies of restrictive abortion laws in action on the normal operation of black markets, Noonan, Louisell, and like-minded commentators obscure the actual gray-market forces that provided affluent citizens with a de facto right to abortion on demand before *Roe*. Accepted limits on the capacity of police officers were not responsible for the gross race and class inequalities in access to safe abortion services: these disparities existed because most communities did not want to prevent doctors from terminating pregnancies for privileged women. Americans have historically had the resources and the ability necessary to shut down the gray market in safe abortion services. Our society has simply lacked the necessary will.

Properly understood, the official acts that helped create and maintain the exclusive gray market satisfy quite conservative constitutional standards for discriminatory state action. History, well-settled legal precedents, and common sense all demonstrate that selective enforcement of the penal code constitutes state action for purposes of the Fourteenth Amendment. Pro-life advocates cannot save restrictions on abortion by claiming that state actors virtuously delegated their law enforcement powers to physicians who, admittedly, discriminated against poor persons and persons of color. Private persons deputized to administer statutory bans become state actors subject to all constitutional constraints. Moreover, judges usually presume discriminatory motives when facially neutral law enforcement policies that further no legitimate social purpose place unique and severe burdens on members of disfavored economic classes and racial castes. Law enforcement officials who let doctors perform gray-market abortions for their affluent white clientele unconstitutionally discriminated against poor persons and persons of color because those selective enforcement practices furthered no communal end that statutory bans on abortion might serve.

State Action

The Fourteenth Amendment declares that "no *State* shall . . . deny to any person within its jurisdiction the equal protection of the laws" (emphasis added). This language strongly suggests that private discrimination, however egregious, does not violate constitutional norms. Legal history supports this reading of the post–Civil War Constitution. From the inception of the Fourteenth Amendment to the present, the Supreme Court has consistently held that litigants must establish state action when making equal protection claims.[49] Many applications of state action are controversial.[50] Nevertheless, that doctrine is based on values most Americans share. Persons should have the right to make certain personal decisions free from official scrutiny. Thus government officials are not and should not be held responsible for my dating only Jewish women or never inviting a poor person to lunch. Indeed, related "zones of privacy" provide the constitutional foundations for the best-known liberal defense of legal abortion.[51]

Claims that equal choice arguments fail to establish state action, however, are easy to refute. An official decision not to enforce a law is and has always been recognized as state action. The persons responsible for the Fourteenth Amendment were specifically concerned with the evils that resulted when ex-Confederate states refused to protect persons of color from white criminals. The Joint Committee on Reconstruction condemned "this deep-seated prejudice against color [that] . . . leads to acts of cruelty, oppression, and murder, which the local authorities are at no pains to prevent or punish";[52] Congress subsequently proposed and the American people ratified a constitutional provision that forbids states from "deny[ing] to any person the equal protection of the laws." This language does not distinguish between state acts of commission and state acts of omission that deny some persons legal protections available to others.

Judicial tribunals recognize that state action is just as present when government officials do not enforce the law as when government officials enforce the law. A long line of cases holds that "selectivity in the enforcement of criminal laws is . . . subject to constitutional constraint."[53] The justices often reject selective enforcement claims on their merits, but no legal opinion or commentary seriously maintains that state action is absent when governmental officials do not enforce a law at all or only in particular cases. All official enforcement decisions must meet Fourteenth Amendment standards, even decisions to ignore violations of the criminal law.[54]

Intentional Discrimination

The requirement of intentional discrimination does not have as solid a foundation as state action in constitutional language. Many progressive jurists believe that state officials "deny . . . the equal protection of the laws" whenever official policies have practical consequences that perpetuate the subordination of traditionally disadvantaged groups.[55] The Supreme Court, however, has adopted a more conservative interpretation of intentional discrimination, one that emphasizes formal equality of opportunity rather than actual equality of result. The justices insist that state officials violate the equal protection clause only when official policies are designed to provide special benefits or to impose distinct burdens on the basis of race, class, or some other constitutionally illegitimate criterion. Proof that white persons perform better than persons of color on general intelligence tests, Justice White's majority opinion in *Washington v. Davis* ruled, did not establish an equal protection violation in the absence of evidence that the state employers who used those examinations intended to discriminate against persons of color.[56] *Washington v. Davis* has been severely criticized,[57] but that decision's demanding standard for intentional discrimination remains the law of the land.

This conservative constitutional test for proving intentional discrimination still allows persons making equal protection claims to present evidence of disproportionate impact. Justices who insist that disparate effects do not prove purposive discrimination nonetheless recognize that the disproportionate consequences of a policy under constitutional attack may establish a prima facie case that state actors are violating the Fourteenth Amendment. "Impact," Burger Court opinions repeatedly asserted, "provides an 'important starting point'" for determining whether a seemingly neutral policy has been adopted for unconstitutional reasons. Justice White in *Washington* explicitly stated that "an invidious discriminatory purpose may often be inferred from the totality of the relevant facts, including the fact, if it is true, that the law bears more heavily on one race than another."[58]

When persons claiming unconstitutional discrimination establish that a practice with the potential for abuse has resulted in race, class, or other suspicious disparities, the state must prove that the challenged practice advances legitimate public ends. Policies adversely affecting poor persons and persons of color, the justices have ruled, must "be plausibly explained on a neutral basis."[59] This rule constitutionalizes the commonsense position that persons normally intend the consequences of their actions, that authors who fire shots at hostile reviewers intend to maim their critics. Thus, officials who knowingly adopt measures that result in constitutionally suspicious disparities are presumed to have intended that result. Unless those officials offer some plausible justification for practices that severely burden members of disfavored races and economic classes, constitutional logic and common sense compel finding them guilty of intentional discrimination.[60]

The conservative constitutional test for invidious intent does not force persons making equal protection claims to present any evidence that directly implicates the mental state of the government actors they accuse of favoring or disfavoring a race or class. "It is unrealistic," committed proponents of the purposeful discrimination standard recognize, "to require the victim of alleged discrimination to uncover the actual subjective intent of the decisionmaker."[61] Thus, equal choice advocates may demonstrate invidious intent without proving that some prominent state officials actually thought or declared, "Let's help establish and maintain a gray market in abortion services that will provide a great service to affluent white women [or severely burden poor persons and persons of color]." "Officials," one observer notes, "now rarely express their prejudices openly, even when they seek self-consciously to harm a person or group."[62] Direct proof of unconstitutional attitudes is also next to impossible in selective enforcement cases because race and class disparities in those instances are the product of decisions made by thousands of relatively independent state actors.

Congress recently codified similar guidelines for establishing illegal discrimination. The crucial provision of the Civil Rights Act of 1991 declares that "an unlawful employment practice" exists when an employer "uses a particular employment practice that causes a disparate impact on the basis of race, color, religion, sex, or national origin," but "fails to demonstrate that the challenged practice is job related for the position in question and consistent with business necessity."[63] Although the Civil Rights Act regulates only employment practices, recent judicial decisions recognize that "the Fourteenth Amendment's mandate that race discrimination be eliminated from all official acts and proceedings of the State is most compelling in the judicial system."[64] Thus, police and prosecutors should, at a minimum, be subject to the antidiscrimination rules that presently govern private employers.[65]

The equal choice argument easily satisfies the conservative constitutional test for finding purposive discrimination. Law enforcement practices before *Roe* helped create a racially and economically exclusive gray market in safe abortion services. No legitimate law enforcement concern explains why police and prosecutors decided to ignore doctors who only performed abortions for their affluent white private patients. The lack of authentic purpose may not be as immediately obvious as in *Gomillion v. Lightfoot* (1960), a case that arose when the city boundaries of Tuskegee, Alabama, were changed from a square to "an uncouth twenty-eight-sided" figure in order to disenfranchise virtually all persons of color in the community. The incredible irregularity of the new borders, Justice Frankfurter observed, was "tantamount for all practical purposes to a mathematical demonstration" of discriminatory intent.[66] Geometric proof aside, however, American abortion policies before *Roe* seem incapable of being explained or justified by either the public ends of pro-life measures or any genuine law enforcement need.

Law enforcement policies before *Roe* were hardly designed to save fetal lives. Standard police and prosecutorial practices were indifferent, if not hostile, to the interests of embryos. In most communities, state officials ignored and sometimes protected competent abortionists; only abortionists who killed their clients were arrested.[67] This official toleration of the exclusive gray market in safe abortions was particularly destructive of fetal life because that market contained no natural deterrent to illegal abortion. Many persons undoubtedly hesitated before purchasing an abortion on the black market: women were almost always guaranteed substantial discomfort and risked permanent injuries, even death, when they purchased the services of a criminal abortionist. Gray-market physicians, by comparison, sold safe abortions at reasonable prices. In the absence of any serious threat of criminal sanction, women who had private doctors willing to terminate their pregnancies had only to confront whatever moral qualms they had about having an abortion or breaking the law before making their decision. These moral qualms undoubtedly caused some women to carry an unwanted pregnancy to term. Still, given the vast numbers of women whose soul-searching did not prevent them from procuring an illegal abortion, official toleration of the exclusive gray market in safe abortions cannot be described as part of a serious effort to save fetal lives.

Law enforcement policies that ignored competent abortionists were also not motivated by official concerns with dangerous medical practices. Police officers who thought they had a statutory mandate to protect maternal health would not have prevented physician-abortionists from offering their services to the general public. Even staunch pro-life theorists recognize that state officials "ac[t] irrationally" when they artificially restrict abortion services merely "to prevent maternal deaths."[68] Law enforcement practices that limited the scope of the gray market harmed and were known to harm pregnant women. Indeed, pre-*Roe* abortion law in action created a public health crisis by forcing poor women and women of color who were determined to terminate their pregnancies to risk life-threatening abortions on the black market.

Finally, official toleration of the exclusive gray market in safe abortion services cannot be explained by those law enforcement practices that often excuse official failures to enforce other penal provisions. Abortion was not considered a minor offense before *Roe*. Pro-life laws on the books often classified persons who terminated pregnancies as murderers and subjected them to long prison sentences. Nevertheless, no jurisdiction devoted the necessary resources to bring competent abortionists to justice, resources communities routinely brought to bear when attempting to apprehend criminals whose acts warranted similar statutory sanctions. Significantly, a community truly committed to preventing abortion would have had little difficulty destroying the gray market. Unlike drug dealers, doctors who performed abortions were easy to identify and apprehend. Reputable abortionists typically kept public records of their misdeeds, performed abortions at well-marked offices and hospitals, and did not violently resist arrest. Law enforcement officials, however, concentrated their limited efforts on black-market practitioners, who were far more difficult to identify and potentially more risky to arrest than gray-market practitioners.

Police officers rarely bothered physician-abortionists because American communities did not really wish to shut down the gray market. Even if a police officer arrested a competent abortionist, and many police officers were unwilling to do so, the physician generally escaped being punished to any significant degree.[69] Members of the executive branch would not prosecute competent abortionists, juries would not convict them, and judges would not sentence them. From the perspective of the police, arresting prominent physicians for performing abortions was no more rational than giving parking tickets to the community's mayor or leading employer. In neither case was identifying and apprehending a criminal suspect likely to result in any criminal sanction.

Despite this rational excuse for ignoring competent abortionists, these police officers still violated constitutional rights. The best explanation for official tolerance of the exclusive gray market in safe abortions is also the best explanation for racial injustices in the South after the Civil War. Many late-nineteenth-century prosecutors would not prosecute white persons who committed crimes against persons of color, juries would not convict them, and judges would not sentence them. Even if an intrepid late-nineteenth-century Southern police officer arrested a member of the Klan for injuring a person of color, and most police officers were unwilling to do so, the Klansman would probably escape being punished to any significant degree. Reconstruction Republicans were aware that discriminatory law enforcement has these many dimensions. They sought to ensure that men and women of all races and economic classes would be governed by general laws; they did not intend to abolish only one manifestation of existing discriminatory practices. Thus, the community's unwillingness to punish doctors who performed abortions on the gray market no more justifies selective enforcement policies in pre-*Roe* America than the community's unwillingness to punish white criminals who victimized persons of color justifies selective enforcement policies in the post–Civil War South.

McCLESKEY

In 1987, the Rehnquist Court announced that some persons making equal protection claims would have to satisfy a much tougher test for unconstitutional discrimination than the conservative standard laid down in *Washington v. Davis* and subsequent cases. By a 5–4 vote, the justices ruled that Georgia's death penalty law was being constitutionally administered, even though a sophisticated study of that state's capital sentencing process concluded that "defendants charged with killing white victims were 4.3 times as likely to receive a death penalty as defendants charged with killing blacks."[70] Justice Powell's opinion for the Court in *McCleskey v. Kemp* declared that general statistics were rarely relevant in death penalty cases. Persons making equal protection attacks on capital sentencing processes, the *McCleskey* majority decided, had to "prove that purposeful discrimination had a discriminatory impact on [them]."[71]

The Rehnquist Court's new test for establishing intentional discrimination in capital cases places a major precedential obstacle in the path of equal choice and other selective enforcement claims. The requirement that victims "prove decisionmakers in [their] case acted with discriminatory purpose"[72] is practically impossible to meet. Today's law enforcement officials never confess that they discriminate on the basis of race or economic class. Much legal discrimination now takes "the form of an un-conscious reaction to the race [or class] of the defendant or victim."[73] Remarkably, members of the *McCleskey* majority recognize that not all prejudices are overtly expressed. Justice White publicly declared in an-other case that "more subtle, less consciously held racial attitudes" may unconstitutionally "influence a juror's decision."[74] Yet when these sub-conscious racial or class prejudices are operating, the general surveys that *McCleskey* ruled inadmissible are often the only available means for deter-mining whether illegitimate factors are influencing official decisions. In a society that condemns explicit racial and class epithets, a judicial demand that victims of selective enforcement prove specific animus against them will leave most equal protection violations unidentified and unremedied.

Still, legal grounds exist for claiming that, initial appearances to the contrary, *McCleskey* actually supports equal choice claims. Although some passages in Justice Powell's opinion suggest the *McCleskey* test should be used whenever persons claim selective enforcement of any criminal law, other passages indicate that individualized proof of discrimination might be required only when persons challenge the outcomes of capital sentenc-ing processes.[75] Justice Powell placed great weight on the special proce-dures Georgia established to prevent the recurrence of past racial dispari-ties in the application of that state's death penalty law. Those procedures, he insisted, had substantially reduced arbitrary and capricious capital sen-tencing decisions. In his opinion, prosecutorial and jury decisions had successfully "sorted out cases where the sentencing of death is highly likely and highly unlikely, leaving [only] a midrange of cases where the imposition of the death penalty in any particular case is less predictable." Thus, the *McCleskey* majority concluded that "*in light of the safeguards designed to minimize racial bias in the process*" (emphasis added), oppo-nents of the death penalty did "not demonstrate a constitutionally signifi-cant risk of racial bias affecting the Georgia capital sentencing process."[76]

If "safeguards designed to minimize racial bias" played a crucial role in *McCleskey*, then that decision provides no doctrinal grounds for requiring persons making equal choice claims to present individualized evidence of discrimination. No state took any step to reduce the arbitrary and discrim-inatory enforcement of statutory bans on abortion, even though most of-ficials knew that affluent white women enjoyed de facto immunities from pro-life measures. Indeed, many state actors supported the racially and economically exclusive gray market in safe abortion services. More-over, in sharp contrast to Georgia's capital sentencing process, race and class disparities in access to safe abortions were not limited to legally bor-derline cases. The clearer the illegality of the abortion, the greater the race and class disparities in access to safe abortion services.[77] Thus, until pro-life measures include provisions that promise to foster more evenhanded enforcement of statutory bans on abortion, federal justices more concerned than the present Rehnquist Court majority with discriminatory law enforcement can champion equal choice without explicitly overruling *McCleskey*.[78]

The Constitution and constitutional community provide stronger reasons than legal precedent for not extending *McCleskey* beyond capital punishment. The American legal establishment has resoundingly criticized the Rehnquist Court's demand that prisoners sentenced to death prove that purposeful discrimination affected the outcome in their case. *McCleskey* was instantly condemned by the American Bar Association, an organization that takes no position on either abortion or capital punishment. Distinguished legal commentators describe the ruling as "a scandal" and "a miscarriage of justice."[79] Randall Kennedy of Harvard Law School, a proponent of capital punishment,[80] maintains that "the majority in *McCleskey* repressed the truth and validated racially oppressive official behavior." Judge Guido Calabresi lambasts *McCleskey* as "the ultimate failure of the Court to do its job." Even Justice Powell in retirement recanted his *McCleskey* opinion.[81]

These sharp attacks on *McCleskey* have solid foundations in constitutional history and tradition. Although Justice Powell claimed that the Court had only "accepted statistics as proof of intent to discriminate *in certain limited contexts*" (emphasis added),[82] *McCleskey* does not and could not cite one case in which the Court had previously rejected disparate impact as evidence of unconstitutional purpose.[83] Indeed, the *McCleskey* majority apparently forgot that "discriminatory enforcement of States' criminal laws was a matter of great concern for the drafters" of the Fourteenth Amendment.[84] The Reconstruction Congress (and judicial decisions prior to *McCleskey*) authorized constitutional authorities to void state practices that presented merely a significant risk of intentional discrimination in individual cases.[85] Those members of the Freedmen's Bureau who were committed to racial justice never required persons of color to "prove that purposive discrimination had a discriminatory impact on them."[86] One may wonder how many victims of selective law enforcement practices in 1868 would have been able to vindicate their Fourteenth Amendment rights had they been required to satisfy the *McCleskey* standard.

Those who maintain that individuals gain no rights because other members of their race or class have been discriminated against misconstrue the evils *McCleskey* condones. Warren McCleskey participated in a lottery in which the race of his victim greatly enhanced his chance of being selected for the death penalty. McCleskey might have been sentenced to death had he murdered a person of color, but, to the best of present knowledge, the race of his victim significantly increased the chances of his receiving that ultimate sanction. If *McCleskey* remains good law, members of the law enforcement community will be allowed to engage in practices that clearly discriminate against persons of color, as long as no individual person of color can clearly demonstrate that he or she was victimized by that practice.

A Note on Post-Casey Regulations

In sharp contrast to pre-*Roe* bans on abortion, post-*Casey* regulations of abortion are being implemented in ways that are constitutional under the conservative equal protection standard laid down in *Washington v. Davis*. No evidence suggests that police and prosecutors responsible for administering statutory waiting periods or funding bans are intentionally discriminating against poor women or women of color. Indeed, most post-*Casey* regulations have not even had a disproportionate impact on less fortunate Americans. With the significant exception of funding bans, regulations on abortion at present are not affecting the relative capacity of poor women and women of color to terminate their pregnancies safely and legally.[87] Thus, as long as the law enforcement community continues to require that the rich and poor alike pay cash, read state material on fetal development, and obtain spousal consent before terminating a pregnancy, state policies that discourage or even unduly burden abortion will not violate equal choice principles.[88]

Future abortion regulations, of course, might prevent most poor women from legally terminating an unwanted pregnancy. States could price less affluent women out of the market in safe abortions by requiring that all abortions be performed in hospitals or hospital-like settings.[89] Such policies would run afoul of contemporary equal protection standards only if the relevant legislative history clearly demonstrates that elected officials imposed hospitalization requirements for the purpose of burdening poor persons[90] or if the evidence unequivocally demonstrates that hospitalization does not in any way promote maternal health. If, however, as is most likely the case, the justices characterize hospitalization requirements as reasonable means for ensuring that pregnancies are terminated safely,[91] then such policies will be sustained as long as *Washington v. Davis* and the conservative test for intentional discrimination remain the law of the land.[92] Furthermore, even if the Supreme Court recognizes that mandatory hospitalization requirements in the vast majority of cases "offe[r] no advantages over ambulatory care,"[93] present equal protection law permits states to discourage abortion more directly by taxing the procedure. Steep taxes on gasoline, alcohol, and cigarettes have never been ruled unconstitutional, even though such policies disproportionately burden the poor.

Still, constitutionality is not the sole or even most important measure of the justice and wisdom of policies that in practice make abortions relatively unavailable to members of disadvantaged classes or castes. Given the impact of an unwanted child on any woman's future life, persons committed to a meaningful equality of opportunity should oppose legislation that in practice will force the poor and only the poor to carry their unwanted pregnancies to term. Moreover, equal choice provides an important political safeguard against oppressive abortion regulations. When reproductive policies are impartially administered, all women who want to terminate unwanted pregnancies are burdened by whatever regulations on abortion the local legislature enacts. Dubious hospitalization requirements (or taxes on abortions) may not prevent middle-class families from terminating unwanted pregnancies, but the increased costs of abortion services under such policies will motivate many citizens to vote against politicians who advocate measures that substantially increase the price of a simple abortion. It is perhaps significant that Illinois quickly abandoned its statutory requirement that abortion clinics resemble hospital operating rooms when, in the wake of *Webster*, most persons thought the Supreme Court would actually sustain that policy.[94]

JUDICIAL REVIEW
General Laws and Constitutional Democracy

The proper role of the federal judiciary seems the most hotly disputed issue in contemporary debates over abortion policy. Pro-choice advocates demand that the Supreme Court protect reproductive liberties from fundamentalist majorities bent on violating constitutional rights. Pro-life commentators condemn the *Roe* Court for basing judicial decisions on personal predilections rather than on constitutional principle. Yet closer examination of these claims reveals that proponents and opponents of *Roe* share a common theory of judicial review. All parties to the abortion controversy assume that federal courts must protect constitutional rights from governmental infringement. No prominent advocate of procreative choice claims that the judiciary should protect abortion rights even if such rights are not guaranteed by the Constitution; no supporter of restrictions on abortion claims that the judiciary should sustain pro-life policies even if abortion rights are protected by the Constitution. The debate over judicial review of bans on abortion is thus merely an extension of the debate over the constitutional status of reproductive choice. For this reason, constitutional defenses of legal abortion presently double as defenses of judicial solicitude for legal abortion. Should equal choice arguments convince previously ambivalent or anti-*Roe* citizens that pro-life policies in practice violate the Fourteenth Amendment, these new allies will automatically support judicial decisions declaring statutory bans on abortion unconstitutional.

Equal choice survives even stricter theories of judicial review than those held by most pro-life and pro-choice advocates, theories that significantly constrain the judicial power to strike down policies judges believe are unconstitutional. The best and best-known such theory of the judicial function calls on justices to scrutinize strictly only those constitutional violations that are consequences of particular deviations from ordinary and acceptable democratic practices. Democratic process models of the judicial power require that justices presume constitutional all policies that reflect intelligent majoritarian sentiment and respect equally the interests and good of all citizens.[95] This judicial presumption of constitutionality is not merited, however, when democratic processes fail to yield general laws. Justices in such circumstances must decide independently whether the discriminatory practice serves sufficiently weighty social purposes to pass constitutional muster.

The special judicial duty to condemn unconstitutional discrimination against less favored citizens has deep roots in the American political, judicial, and constitutional traditions. Mid-nineteenth-century state judges explicitly recognized that ordinary democratic safeguards often fail to prevent rights violations that are visited upon only a limited number of citizens. As the Pennsylvania Supreme Court declared in *Ervine's Appeal* (1851),

> when, in the exercise of proper legislative powers, general laws are enacted, which bear or may bear on the whole community, if they are unjust and against the spirit of the Constitution, the whole community will be interested to procure their repeal by a voice potential. And that is the great security for fair and just legislation.
>
> But when individuals are selected from the mass, and laws are enacted affecting their property, . . . who is to stand up for them, thus isolated from the mass, in injury and injustice, or where are they to seek relief from such acts of despotic power? They have no refuge but in the courts, the only secure place for determining conflicting rights by due course of law.[96]

The principle of *Ervine's Appeal* was steadily refined during the twentieth century. Chief Justice Harlan Fiske Stone proposed weakening "the presumption of constitutionality" in cases involving "prejudices against discrete and insular minorities." "The Court itself must step in," Stone's law clerk, Louis Lusky, later noted, "where dislike of minorities renders [democratic] processes ineffectual to accomplish their underlying purpose of holding out a real hope that unwise laws will be changed."[97] John Hart Ely and Judge Guido Calabresi have recently advanced similar theories, both emphasizing the particular judicial obligation to "guard" against "unjustified selective treatment." Calabresi points out that this concern is not simply with "how such laws are written; it is also a matter of how they are applied." "The ultimate question," he maintains, "must be: *in practice* do[es the law] burden all of us, or only those that do not carry any weight in the legislature."[98]

Basic principles of democratic governance support political process theories of judicial review. Proponents of popular government insist that average citizens are fairly intelligent and capable of identifying their rights. Robert Dahl, the preeminent democratic theorist in late-twentieth-century America, maintains that "democracy—rule by the people—can be justified only on the assumption that ordinary people are, in general, qualified to govern themselves."[99] Democracy is the form of government that best protects fundamental freedoms, in this view, because frequent elections provide responsible and thoughtful citizens with the opportunities necessary to overthrow any political coalition that is tyrannizing the general populace. "The majority," James Madison declared in *The Federalist Papers*, can always "defeat the sinister views" of the minority simply "by regular vote."[100]

If the people are the best judges of their interests, then federal justices should hesitate before striking down impartially administered pro-life measures that issue from fair political processes.[101] Such statutory bans on abortion do not on their face or as applied grant special privileges to any favored class of citizens. Unwanted children burden most parents and communities. Though women are more severely burdened than men before and (almost always) after birth, few men benefit individually or as a group from laws that force women to carry their pregnancies to term. Hence, when satisfactory democratic and administrative procedures result in severe limits on reproductive choice, the best explanation for that outcome is that most men and women hold a principled belief that abortion is wrong.[102] Perhaps the people are mistaken, but surely unelected justices ought to pause before cheerfully substituting their considered judgment of what rights have been retained in the Constitution by the people for the people's considered judgment of their constitutional liberties.

Democratic majorities can be trusted to protect fundamental freedoms, however, only when they govern by general laws, laws that give all persons the same rights and responsibilities. The assumptions of self-interest and rationality that justify democratic rule are unwarranted when the law on the books or in action tolerates exceptions for politically powerful groups. Such inequalities undermine democratic safeguards for essential liberties because citizens cannot be expected to respect the rights and interests of other persons to nearly the same degree that they respect their own good. Thus, contemporary democratic theorists insist that an "elementary principle of fairness" requires "that laws cannot rightfully be imposed on others by persons who are not themselves obliged to obey those laws."[103] This democratic failure is particular likely to occur when the individuals on the short end of the legal stick belong to marginal social groups. The ballot box and ordinary legislative processes do not offer sufficient opportunities for statutory reform when politically impotent citizens are denied benefits provided to more influential elites. "Legislatures," commentators recognize, "are uniquely inept at identifying instances in which they have burdened only those to whom they need not answer."[104]

For these reasons, federal justices must be especially suspicious when the law provides majorities or socially advantaged persons with legal rights and benefits not available to all. John Hart Ely correctly observes that when "the system is constructed so that 'people like us' run no realistic risk of . . . punishment, some nonpolitical check . . . is needed."[105] Legitimate public needs may explain why majorities or favored groups are entitled to benefits denied to less fortunate citizens. Still, Ely notes that "insofar as political officials ha[ve] chosen to provide or protect X for some people (generally people like themselves), they had better make sure that everyone was being similarly accommodated or be prepared to explain pretty convincingly why not."[106] When faced with apparent deviations from formal legal equality, courts should not automatically presume that majorities have made a considered and defensible judgment that only they should enjoy a particular liberty or benefit. Rather, disparate treatment typically reflects either unconstitutional favoritism toward elites or social hostility and indifference toward the disfavored groups.[107]

State policies that help distribute abortions on the basis of race or economic class manifest this unconstitutional official favoritism. No good reason exists for making abortions generally available only to affluent white women. Indeed, no advocate of restrictive policies has ever suggested a legitimate basis for such disparate treatment. Hence, the justices in *Roe* could not in good conscience describe the exclusive gray market in safe abortion services as a principled choice that reflected the considered judgment of popular majorities. The gray market existed because, in violation of the Constitution, state officials were indifferent, if not hostile, to those poor women and women of color who had the same need for abortion services as their more fortunate white sisters.[108]

The discriminatory state practices that fostered this exclusive gray market seriously obstructed political efforts to reform or repeal pro-life measures. Public opinion surveys and election returns suggest that affluent citizens who enjoyed a de facto right to abortion on demand before 1973 rarely placed great weight on reproductive policies when making voting decisions. The same has been true after *Roe*. Although support for pro-choice positions increases with income, support for pro-business, pro-life political candidates also increases with income, and at approximately the same rate. In recent presidential elections, for example, the candidate who most favored deregulating the economy and recriminalizing abortion has had much better success among more affluent than less affluent citizens.[109] Affluent Americans may have been willing to tolerate Reagan-Bush abortion policies in order to reap what they believed were the superior benefits of Reagan-Bush economic policies. Nevertheless, socially liberal Republican suburbanites might have fought much harder against the increasingly militant pro-life public stance of the GOP had these yuppies thought their reproductive choices were genuinely at stake.

The gray market also weakened pre-*Roe* support for legal abortion by artificially reducing the number of self-identified pro-choice supporters. Some citizens who knew that abortion services were readily available to them may have failed to support the repeal of abortion bans because they underestimated the actual costs those prohibitions imposed on women who could not enter the gray or, for that matter, black market. Many affluent Americans may have sincerely thought they favored pro-life policies, secure in the knowledge that a safe abortion was readily available should circumstances force them to change their minds. Significantly, pro-life women are as likely as other women to choose abortion when faced with an unwanted pregnancy. One study found that more than two-thirds of all women obtaining abortions were not clearly pro-choice prior to that experience. Some of these women thought abortion was justified in a few circumstances, but their abortions often did not satisfy those conditions.[110]

Although measuring latent support for reproductive choice before *Roe* is next to impossible, maladministered abortion bans clearly placed unconstitutional and undemocratic obstacles in the path of mid-twentieth-century abortion reformers. Dr. Alan Guttmacher thought that "the more strictly laws [against abortion] were enforced, the more likely it is that the body politic will rise up against them."[111] Guttmacher's conjecture became reality in 1967, when California quickly liberalized the state penal code after public authorities threatened private physicians who were performing abortions for fetal indications.[112] The surge in pro-choice voting and political contributions after *Webster v. Reproductive Health Services*[113] similarly indicates that many citizens publicly support pro-choice policies only when they believe their access to safe abortions is threatened.

For these reasons, judicial decisions striking down maladministered laws do not necessarily violate popular sovereignty or other basic democratic principles. American reproductive and political behavior suggest that the existence of selectively enforced pro-life measures before *Roe* is a very unreliable measure of the number of citizens and elected officials who actually believed and believe competent abortionists should be subject to

severe criminal sanctions. The significant number of formerly pro-life officials who suddenly converted to pro-choice positions when the Supreme
Court's decision in *Webster* permitted states to reenact substantial restriction on abortion[114] similarly indicates that judicial decisions protecting
abortion rights may have more accurately reflected public opinion than
did the legislation those decisions declared unconstitutional.

Remedies

Constitutional authorities seem to have two remedial choices when faced
with equal choice violations. The above discussion has assumed that the
Supreme Court should declare restrictions on abortion unconstitutional
when such policies are implemented in ways that discriminate against
poor persons and persons of color. Pro-life advocates, however, might
suggest an alternative. Perhaps the Supreme Court should require offending communities to enforce their pro-life policies more strictly or at least
offer state legislatures that option. Had the justices in *Roe* been inspired
by that version of equal choice, they would have ordered state police in all
American communities to arrest every active participant in the abortion
underground!

Pro-choice fears that equal choice principles would legitimate a draconian pro-life regime contain an important grain of truth: abortion policies
that are as restrictive in action as they are on the statutory books do treat
persons of all races and social classes as legal equals. Nevertheless, federal
justices are constitutionally obligated to void any unconstitutionally administered statute. Constitutional history and case law firmly demonstrate
that legal abortion is the only corrective the judiciary may order after finding that existing pro-life policies violate equal choice.

The framers of the post–Civil War Constitution explicitly made the
legal status of privileged citizens the standard by which the rights of all
other citizens would be determined. "All persons born in the United
States and not subject to any foreign power," the Civil Rights Act of 1866
decreed, "shall have the same right . . . to full and equal benefit of all laws
and proceedings for the security of person and property, *as is enjoyed by
white citizens*" (emphasis added).[115] As the debates over the Fourteenth
Amendment made clear, the proponents of the equal protection clause
also believed that "all persons . . . shall have the same right . . . to full
and equal benefit of all laws and proceedings for the security of person
and property, as is enjoyed by [*a particularly favored class* of] white
citizens."[116] Thus, constitutional authorities are not free to choose between "bottom-up" or "top-down" remedies when faced with equal protection violations. When a community treats affluent white women in a

certain way, all women have a constitutional right to receive the same treatment.[117]

The Supreme Court has consistently respected the framers' judgment that all persons be governed by the same rules, regulations, and practices that govern the most favored class of citizens in a community. Judicial decisions have unfailingly ruled that victims of past discrimination be provided with the previously denied benefit or liberty. The justices in *Missouri ex rel. Gaines v. Canada*[118] ordered that Lloyd Gaines be admitted to the state's previously all-white law school. Missouri was not permitted to shut down all public institutions of legal education. In *Frontiero v. Richardson*,[119] the Supreme Court ordered the navy to provide women officers with the same benefits that male officials were enjoying; the navy was not allowed to have male officers return stipends they would not have received had they been female. Thus, when poor persons and persons of color complain that state practices afford only white women a de facto right to abortion on demand, the Court must order the offending state to permit all women to terminate their pregnancies. The Constitution forbids judicial remedies that let communities determine for themselves how to cure their equal choice violations.

The federal judiciary is not, however, empowered to respond to equal choice violations by declaring that all persons shall henceforth enjoy a perpetual right to abortion on demand. Nothing in the equal protection clause forbids legislatures from denying some benefit to all citizens that was once unconstitutionally available to a select few. Thus, with the constitutional imprimatur of the Supreme Court, the citizens of Jackson, Mississippi, closed every public pool in their city after a federal court ordered local officials to allow all persons of color to use those formerly white-only facilities.[120] The mere requirement that courts void restrictions on abortion that are being unconstitutionally implemented seems, for this reason, to be of little import. Women apparently gain the right to reproductive choice only during the short interval between the favorable judicial order and unfavorable legislative action.

Nevertheless, states that seek to reinstitute pro-life measures face severe constitutional hurdles. The Supreme Court has never let communities reenact statutes that had previously been unconstitutionally implemented merely on the basis of bare official assurances that new measures will be enforced more equitably. When the justices ruled that states were capriciously enforcing their death penalty statutes,[121] they demanded that any new capital punishment scheme include comprehensive procedures that would prevent the recurrence of past discrimination.[122] The precise constitutional requirements of such an enforcement scheme are unclear and depend in practice on whether the justices continue supporting the original decision that declared unconstitutional the law in action.[123] Still, justices committed to equal choice would probably demand that local officials detail how they intended to police private hospitals, prevent doctors from disguising abortions as D & C's, force juries to convict popular abortionists, and discourage resident women from obtaining abortions in pro-choice jurisdictions. These invasive measures would, in turn, only heighten opposition to renewed pro-life policies in both the medical community and among affluent citizens accustomed to having access to abortion.[124]

More significantly for present purposes, no pro-life legislature, activist, or organization has proposed a plan that promises to prevent selective implementation of new restrictions on abortion. In the absence of such an enforcement scheme, justices and other constitutional authorities must presume that future statutory bans on abortion will be administered in the same discriminatory manner as such policies were administered in the past. The equal choice rights of poor women and women of color will again be violated repeatedly when law enforcement officials ignore doctors and hospitals that routinely abort pregnancies for their affluent white patients. Legislatures will not be able to diagnose or cure this constitutional ill because too many well-off Americans will lack sufficient motivation for engaging in the political action necessary to make abortion legal again. Until pro-life communities address these persistent discriminatory failings of abortion laws in action, equal choice advocates must continue supporting the result in *Roe*. Equal choice, at present, means pro-choice.

SLAUGHTERING THE COMPANY: THE PRUDENTIAL CASE AGAINST EQUAL CHOICE

At bottom, opposition to equal choice probably rests on the prohibitive cost of remedying all constitutional wrongs. Kantian philosophers may insist that justice be done no matter what the consequences,[125] but most citizens, elected officials, and judges think justice is only one of several important social virtues. Quests for justice are often abandoned when principled application of legal principles threatens the social order. The Fairy Queen in Gilbert and Sullivan's *Iolanthe* aptly summarizes this pragmatic rule when, after announcing that her minions have "all incurred death" by marrying mortals in violation of fairy laws, she confesses that she "cannot slaughter the whole company." Rigid adherence to legal and constitutional norms in this case and many others simply exacts too high a social price.

Equal choice principles similarly threaten to slaughter the whole company. Statutory bans on abortion discriminate in practice against poor persons and persons of color, but the same is true of most American laws.[126] "It is a sad and harsh probability," Louisell and Noonan point out, "that a large number of criminal laws bear with unequal severity in practice on the poor, who are more likely than the rich to be caught, to be prosecuted, to be unskillfully defended, to be convicted, and to be punished." Nevertheless, pro-life advocates insist, "these de facto defects" do not justify "selective invalidation" of pro-life measures.[127] Legal principles must be applied consistently, and hardly any provision in federal or state penal codes would survive constitutional scrutiny if justices struck down all imperfectly administered laws.[128] Blind fidelity to constitutional principle also does little to help victims of discriminatory law enforcement practices. Communities that remedy maladministered criminal statutes by abandoning laws against murder and other heinous offenses are far more likely to collapse than to achieve racial or class justice. Thus, whatever the constitutional and legal pedigree of equal choice, many people will sacrifice equality under law on the altar of law and order if a commitment to equal choice principles means that state officials will not punish most severe crimes.

This pragmatic limit on legal equality has little merit as a constitutional principle. The equal protection clause prohibits states from discriminating against poor persons or persons of color. Proof that state officials systemically violate that constitutional obligation does not excuse any individual constitutional infraction. No one argues *Brown* was wrongly decided by pointing out that every institution in the South was unconstitutionally segregated. Of course, Fourteenth Amendment law does permit legislatures to discriminate when doing so significantly advances the general welfare.[129] But the prudential defense of pro-life measures does not claim that law enforcement officials have legitimate reasons for favoring affluent white citizens; it simply maintains that principled adherence to equality under law would result in the practical abandonment of the penal code. For better or worse, critics of *Roe* suggest, judges must recognize that members of the law enforcement community in too many jurisdictions are incapable of scrupulously fulfilling their constitutional obligation to treat all citizens as legal equals.

That no society can remedy all race or class injustices, however, does not excuse social failures to remedy any racial or class injustice. Common sense suggests two grounds for distinguishing remedial from irremedial constitutional wrongs. First, societies committed to equality under law must take all reasonable steps to reduce discriminatory practices before tolerating any race or class injustice in the administration of the criminal law. State policies should not survive constitutional scrutiny when, as Justice White stated, "the risk" of "racial prejudice" is "unacceptable in light of the ease with which that risk could have been minimized."[130] Second, communities must make special efforts to prevent legal inequalities that differ in kind or in degree from the inequalities that inevitably plague the administration of most laws.[131] Even if no society can eliminate all discriminatory law enforcement practices, communities should remedy every equal protection wrong that violates other fundamental constitutional norms.

Restrictive abortion laws in action exhibited both these distinctive failings. State officials never attempted to reduce well-known constitutionally suspect disparities in access to safe abortion services, even though a few well-publicized arrests and convictions probably would have destroyed the exclusive gray market in most localities. Indeed, most law enforcement communities rarely made any sustained effort to enforce statutory bans on abortion.[132] These conscious failures to implement pro-life measures suggest that the communal interest in preventing abortion was not sufficiently weighty to justify any official practice that violated the equal protection clause. More significantly, the gray market in safe abortions perverted democratic processes in ways that most maladministered criminal laws do not. Persons denied access to gray-market abortions had good reason to think that abortion would have been legalized had the law enforcement community made a serious effort to ensure that all persons were equally subject to pro-life measures.

Equality under the law, fair democratic processes, and individual rights are closely related. Eighteenth-century Federalists maintained that the new national government would not violate fundamental rights, because, as Publius asserted, governing officials "can make no law which will not have its full operation on themselves and their friends, as well as on the great mass of society."[133] Early-nineteenth-century courts took this democratic obligation seriously. State judges declared laws that placed special burdens on select individuals unconstitutional when "a like general law affecting the whole community equally could not have been passed."[134] Twentieth-century constitutionalists express similar sentiments. "There is no more effective practical guarantee against arbitrary and unreasonable government," Justice Jackson declared in 1941, "than to require that the principles of law which officials impose upon a minority must be imposed generally."[135] State actors, these commentators agree, must not weaken political pressures to repeal controversial statutory bans by handing out to influential citizens practical indulgences from those laws.

The democratic relationships between equal justice and individual rights provide a vital distinction between pre-*Roe* abortion laws in action and other malenforced provisions in the penal code. Persons of color who commit felonies may be treated more severely than white felons by the legal system, but no one seriously maintains that homicide laws would be abolished if administered more evenhandedly. Affluent white Americans do not enjoy de facto immunities from the law against murder; the few elites who murder are usually punished severely, if not quite as severely as other citizens, and those found not guilty at trial typically pay exorbitant legal fees. Prominent Americans did, however, enjoy de facto immunities from laws against abortion. Many affluent citizens procured relatively cheap abortions without legal complications before *Roe* for themselves, their lovers, or members of their families. The physician-abortionists who terminated pregnancies for these upper-middle-class families recognized that "you could get away with [abortion] unquestionably, as long as you didn't do it as a business."[136] For these reasons, the gray market in safe abortion services significantly depressed public support for legal abortion. Americans who enjoyed this de facto right to abortion on demand were less likely to contribute to pro-choice causes or even to think of themselves as supporting pro-choice positions. No one knows whether pro-life laws would have remained in state penal codes if such measures have been more uniformly enforced.[137]

Just democratic societies do not tolerate laws that may remain on the books only because they are poorly administered. Ethical judgments must be universalizable. As Kant's categorical imperative states, persons should "act only according to that maxim by which they can at the same time will that it should become a universal law."[138] Thus, good citizens only advocate rules that they are willing to obey. A reluctance to slaughter the company may require Americans to accept inequities in the enforcement of laws that the vast majority of citizens support and respect. Nevertheless, citizens of a morally decent democracy must remove pro-life laws from the books when both enforcement practices and private behavior raise serious doubts that popular majorities have actually willed their reproductive choices to be limited.

THE SIMPLE JUSTICE OF GENERAL LAWS

An overly enthusiastic radio announcer once waxed eloquent on the rare ability of a young virtuoso to "play passages of substantial ease with the greatest of difficulty." Equal choice suffers from a similar infirmity. The equal choice defense of keeping abortion legal seemingly presents a simple idea in the most complicated fashion possible. The simple idea is that people should be governed by general laws. Poor persons and persons of color ought to possess the same legal rights and be subject to the same legal sanctions as members of more privileged economic classes and races. When communities permit affluent white women to purchase abortions or any other good, they are morally and constitutionally obligated to permit poor persons and persons of color to purchase the same services.

Complications occur when state officials make various excuses for their failure to achieve equality under the law—free markets distribute legal abortions unequally, some discretion is necessary when enforcing the criminal law, the police cannot prevent all illegal abortions from taking place, some private discrimination should be tolerated, physicians were primarily responsible for policing restrictions on abortion, all laws are unevenly enforced, and so on. Complications multiply because, although these excuses do not justify the ways in which restrictions on abortion were actually implemented, many are plausible in the abstract. Free markets do treat people as equals in a meaningful sense and offer important social benefits. Nevertheless, the merits of the invisible hand cannot justify pre-*Roe* abortion law in action, because Americans did not adopt laissez-faire reproductive policies before 1973. The long, sometimes tedious, process of sifting through other pro-life alibis similarly reveals no grounds that vindicate the discriminatory and arbitrary ways in which restrictions on abortion were implemented in the United States. No moral or constitutional excuse exists for law enforcement policies that establish and maintain a racially and economically exclusive gray market in safe abortion services.

Most persons sympathize with George Bush and Dan Quayle when these politicians acknowledge that they would be supportive should one of their children or grandchildren have an abortion. Equal choice only insists that all children and grandchildren enjoy the same opportunity. Americans have long debated what privileges scions of wealthy and politically influential families may legitimately enjoy. Immunity from the criminal law, however, has never been considered an advantage that money, power, or birth ought to secure. Few principles of justice are more basic than the idea that all persons are equal before the law: a person's legal rights must not depend on race, class, or social position.

A literal reading of "equal protection," the intentions of constitutional framers, American political traditions, and a long line of judicial precedents all support the principle that just societies do not have one law for the rich and another for the poor, one law for a master race and another for servile peoples. The persons responsible for the equal protection clause did not invent out of thin air a new right, but merely extended to persons of all races the law's traditional antipathy to class legislation. When for any reason, therefore, the law enforcement community grants members of identifiable social groups an immunity from statutory restrictions on abortion or any other action prohibited by penal law, that community constitutionally forfeits its right to punish anyone who engages in the same nominally forbidden activity.

CHAPTER IV

Rule by Law

BY THE LAW OF THE LAND

No two communities policed bans on abortion in the same fashion, and considerations other than racial or class prejudice influenced the administration of pro-life measures. Statutory prohibitions on abortion in some communities were enforced so infrequently as to preclude finding any pattern, discriminatory or otherwise, in their official administration.[1] Many officials implemented pro-life measures in ways that drove abortion underground, out of the sight of decent citizens. Abortion was frowned upon in public but winked at in private. Such policies did little to reduce abortion rates but did communicate a communal sense that abortion (or nonprocreative sexuality) violated societal mores.

No matter how enforcement practices before *Roe* are described, however, they did not pass constitutional muster. Restrictive abortion laws in action fell far short of the minimum standards that constitutional democracies must demand of the law enforcement community. Pro-life measures were never implemented in ways that furthered any constitutional purpose that might justify a legislative decision to ban abortion. Those statutory bans on abortion that were not selectively enforced were too arbitrarily administered to satisfy traditional due process proscriptions against statutory vagueness and unauthorized policy making by electorally unaccountable administrators.

Basic constitutional norms do not permit law enforcement communities to administer legal restrictions in any way they please. Constitutional democracy exists in name only when the persons responsible for executing legislative decrees are not constrained by the letter and spirit of those laws.[2] To prevent capricious law enforcement, the Fourteenth Amendment requires that the criminal law be enforced regularly and in a manner consistent with the public ends embodied in the penal code. Statutory bans on littering, for example, must be administered in ways that discourage littering, not some other behavior that individual officers of the law find undesirable. Thus, state officials violated our constitutional commitment to rule by law when they made conscious decisions to ignore the illegal practices of physician-abortionists or used their enforcement powers to further personal notions of good abortion policy not found in any duly authorized statute.

Judicial decisions striking down maladministered pro-life measures promote democratic government. Courts committed to the rule of law ensure that all exercises of public power reflect authoritative policy choices made by elected officials and not private whims of police officers, prosecutors, judges, and juries. Long-standing Supreme Court precedents condemn administrative practices that present the risk or reality of undue policy making by unelected officials. In particular, the justices refuse to sanction constitutionally borderline practices that a legislature did not expressly authorize.[3] These past decisions require, at a minimum, that elected officials clearly mandate any law enforcement practice that results in constitutionally suspect race or class disparities. The gray market in safe abortion services did not satisfy this judicial requirement. No law explicitly permitted law enforcement officials to tolerate or assist respected physicians who were performing illegal abortions for their private patients.

Rule by law and equal justice under law express different aspects of the general constitutional command that all criminal laws be uniformly administered. Victims of selective enforcement practices can demonstrate that law enforcement decisions were based on specific unconstitutional criteria. Victims of arbitrary or capricious enforcement, by comparison, cannot prove that law enforcement decisions were based on race, class, or any other particular unconstitutional criteria. The pattern of erratic enforcement in such circumstances, however, substantially rules out the possibility that police and prosecutorial decisions have any legitimate basis. Thus, when statutes are capriciously administered, a strong presumption exists that persons arrested and prosecuted for their violation have "been intentionally and purposefully singled out for prosecution on the basis of arbitrary or invidious criteria." Many cases, commentators point out, "are irresistibly suggestive of racial bias, and the invalidation of the laws involved often may plausibly be viewed as a prophylactic against such abuse."[4] Should arbitrarily enforced laws pass constitutional muster, state actors would be free to use race and other unconstitutional criteria when administering the criminal law, as long as they did not make a statistically significant number of arrests.

RULE BY LAW VERSUS RULE BY DISCRETION

Elected officials in constitutional democracies make the laws and establish the purposes that those laws serve. Government officials responsible for executing the laws must administer statutory provisions in ways that further the public goals established by the legislature. Law enforcement officials are not simply barred from deciding what conduct the law shall forbid—they have no independent authority to decide what societal values an existing criminal statute should advance. The rule of law breaks down when the police only arrest persons who officers of the law independently decide are troublemakers. Indeed, repressive regimes commonly use rarely enforced penal statutes to rid themselves of political dissidents or other undesirable citizens.[5]

Police officers and prosecutors who serve more humane political orders must, of course, exercise considerable discretion when determining the implementation strategy that best advances the purposes of the laws on the books. Still, members of the law enforcement community may not abuse that latitude by administering statutes in ways that serve different ends than those the legislature might plausibly have intended.[6] Arresting only persons who travel more than seventy in a sixty-five-miles-per-hour zone advances the goals of most speeding regulations; arresting only speeders who own foreign cars does not.

The Fourteenth Amendment furthers the rule of law by requiring rational administration of the criminal law. Constitutional commentators agree that the vague statute is unconstitutional because that measure "invites abusive and capricious enforcement, obscures discriminatory practices, and fosters individualization and irregularity in crime definition." Legislatures, a distinguished line of judicial precedents hold, are constitutionally obligated to "articulate [their] aims with a reasonable degree of clarity" in order to "reduc[e] the danger of caprice and discrimination in the administration of the laws."[7] Prominent pro-life commentators recognize these failings of vague laws in contexts other than abortion. When "there are no reasonably clear guidelines for the police and judges who have to enforce the law," a leading liberal opponent of *Roe* asserts, "the result is drumhead justice. Police and judges decide arbitrarily who gets taught a lesson."[8]

No matter how clear the law on the books, enforcement policies that are "unrelated to any specific determination made by the responsible policy-making organs of society" are also inconsistent with Fourteenth Amendment freedoms.[9] No significant constitutional distinction exists between the vague statute that presents the risk of unauthorized policy making by law enforcement officials and the maladministered statute that presents the reality of unauthorized policy making by law enforcement officials. Common sense refutes the perverse notion that the Constitution forbids the threat of an evil but not the evil itself. Police seizures of policy-making power in the guise of enforcing the penal code violate fundamental due process liberties.

That law enforcement officials may be making what would otherwise be constitutional, even highly desirable, policies does not suffice to save an unlawful official practice. Citizens who violate the law on the books may be punished only because they have violated that law, not because they are behaving in other ways that legal authorities find offensive. Thus, law enforcement officials may not give parking tickets only to students who misbehave in English class. Proof that most elected officials informally approve such police practices is constitutionally irrelevant. The law enforcement community may implement only the formal decrees passed by the people's elected representatives. In our society, legislatures determine what conduct shall be forbidden and they "may not so abdicate their responsibility for setting the standard of the criminal law."[10]

The present Supreme Court recognizes that fundamental due process rights require that persons suffer official sanctions only when those sanctions reflect the faithful implementation of policy choices made by elected officials. One reason why "government [must] articulate its aims with a reasonable degree of clarity," Justice O'Connor notes, is to "ensur[e] that state power will be exercised on behalf of policies reflecting an authoritative choice among competing values." Her fellow justices similarly maintain that when "the legislature fails to provide minimum guidelines," the unconstitutional danger exists that "policemen, prosecutors and juries" will "pursue their personal predilections" instead of fulfilling their official duty to implement the settlements reached by the people's elected representatives.[11] In a series of decisions, moderate and conservative justices have ruled that the due process clause forbids state actors from prosecuting or sentencing criminal suspects for an established illegal act more severely than similarly situated offenders solely because the alleged criminal also engaged in lawful conduct that the police or prosecutors find objectionable. "The decision to prosecute," Justice Powell points out, "may not be deliberately based upon an unjustifiable standard such as . . . the exercise of protected statutory and constitutional rights," even in cases in which the suspect has admitted committing a crime.[12] Talk aside, the Rehnquist Court has shown little enthusiasm for actually restricting police or prosecutorial discretion. Still, contemporary judicial opinions do contain much language that justices more committed to rule by law could use to provide solid precedential support for judicial decisions limiting lawless administration of the penal code.

This due process right to rule by law constrains official efforts to administer pro-life measures. Statutory bans on abortion do not license officers of the law to implement abortion policies in ways that serve purposes other than those embodied in duly authorized statutes. When legislatures explicitly declare that no person shall abort a fetus of twelve weeks or older, police officers cannot decide that they will arrest a woman who wants a late abortion because having a child will interfere with her career, but not a woman who wants a late abortion because her family is already too large. Nothing in the flat prohibition on second trimester abortions suggests that elected officials regard some grounds for having an abortion as better than others. Although such state action nominally takes place under color of law, law enforcement officials are making rather than administering policy. Some women are being prevented from terminating their pregnancies even though their reasons for seeking that procedure are as lawful as the reasons given by other women whom state officials allow to have abortions.

The constitutional ban on law enforcement practices that revise legislative policies in the guise of administering them provides the most basic grounds for condemning pre-*Roe* American abortion laws in action. Even if the state officials responsible for administering pro-life measures did not unconstitutionally discriminate against poor persons and persons of color, their enforcement policies were not designed to further any goal that restrictions on abortion might be thought to serve. As noted in chapter III, police officers and prosecutors did not make a serious effort to protect maternal health or fetal life when implementing statutory bans on abortion. Moreover, no legislature ever authorized the creation of a gray market in safe abortion services or indicated in any way that respectable citizens, physicians, and hospitals should be allowed to determine for themselves when an abortion was necessary.

At best, law enforcement officials before *Roe* can be said to have adopted a policy to "somewhat permit, but really discourage" abortions, a policy that fostered a limited gray market in safe abortion services. Doctors were allowed to perform a "reasonable number" of abortions each year, as long as they did not publicly advertise their willingness to terminate pregnancies. Such measures might have barely passed constitutional muster had they been authorized by a state legislature. Nevertheless, the constitutional defense of such legislative abortion policies cannot legitimate a similar "somewhat permit, but really discourage" policy that is independently established by unelected police officers and prosecutors. The due process right to rule by law prohibits the law enforcement community from implementing abortion policies that elected officials have the constitutional power to adopt when those policies were not, in fact, adopted by the local legislature.

No state ever passed abortion bans that could plausibly be characterized as licensing a limited gray market or favoring "somewhat permit, but really discourage" policies. State laws on the books at the time of *Roe* typically declared that women had a legal right to an abortion only in certain specified circumstances. Those laws neither recognized a permissible number of "illegal" abortions nor an impermissible number of legal abortions. Hence, no statutory mandate allowed law enforcement officials to tolerate competent doctors who discreetly performed a limited number of abortions for any reason. No matter how many abortions fell within a statutory exception to pro-life laws, all abortions and only those abortions that met the statutory requirements were legal.

Restrictions on abortion were usually classified with homicide laws or "offenses against the person,"[13] and the ban on violent felonies does not reflect a "somewhat permit, but really discourage" policy. Statutes that authorized justices to sentence illegal abortionists to long prison terms clearly expressed the legislative intention that abortion be prohibited and not merely stigmatized. To the extent that history provides any criteria other than maternal health for distinguishing among women seeking abortions, state actors should have ensured that affluent white women brought their pregnancies to term.[14] Instead, in direct contradiction of this implied legislative mandate, law enforcement officials helped create and maintain a gray market in abortions that catered almost exclusively to well-off Americans.

These details of restrictive American abortion policies in action turn standard anti-*Roe* claims against their espousers. Armies of constitutional commentators have fought under banners declaring "Elected Officials Should Make Abortion Policy." Had Bork, Ely, and other officers in that militia more carefully surveyed the political terrain, they would have noticed that elected officials lost control of abortion policy making long before *Roe* was decided. The constitutional problem was not simply that elected officials paralyzed by conflicting political pressures would neither repeal nor enforce restrictions on abortion. As recent debates over national health care suggest, legislators quite frequently find themselves unable to reaffirm or reject policy decisions that were previously enacted into law, and this failure does not normally create a valid due process attack on existing policy.[15] American abortion policies before *Roe* violated the due process right to rule by law not because of legislative inaction but because the administrative actions responsible for the gray market did not reflect any authoritative decision made by any state legislature at any time. Whether a competent doctor was allowed to perform an abortion without interference in 1970 depended almost entirely on the policy preferences of local police officers and prosecutors. However one describes the ways in which pro-life measures were implemented before *Roe*, abortion law in action was insufficiently and, thus, unconstitutionally related to any responsible choice made by those elected officials authorized to make law in the United States.

JUDICIAL RULE BY LAW

The legislative failure before *Roe* to control reproductive policy supports judicial decisions striking down statutory bans on abortion. The democratic assumptions that normally justify judicial deference to elected officials do not justify judicial deference to unelected law enforcement agents. If anything, democratic theory requires very strict scrutiny of police and prosecutorial practices. Fair democratic and legislative processes produce self-government only when the law enforcement community carries out the commands of the people's elected representatives. "There can be little point in worrying about the distribution of the franchise and other personal political rights," Ely notes, "unless the important policy choices are being made by elected officials."[16]

Pre-*Roe* abortion law in action did not reflect any authoritative legislative decision. Although the law on the books declared that some reasons for abortion were more acceptable than others, the law enforcement community rarely expressed any interest in the different circumstances that led women to seek abortion. Competent abortionists who serviced affluent white women were allowed to terminate pregnancies for any reason, as long as they did not do so too visibly or too often. In the absence of any legislation that mandated this selective administration of statutory bans on abortion, no reliable evidence exists that electoral or legislative majorities before *Roe* supported the actual implementation of pro-life policies. Thus, the gray market in safe abortion services that *Roe* eliminated lacked any democratic authorization, unless one believes that democracies vest law enforcement officials with the power to administer the penal code in any way they please.

Pre-*Roe* abortion laws in action warranted especially strict judicial scrutiny because the persons responsible for administering the law in a constitutional democracy must avoid constitutionally borderline practices not clearly sanctioned by the people's elected representatives. Close constitutional calls should be made by democratically chosen officers, not by relatively unaccountable members of the law enforcement community. "The more fundamental the issue," Alexander Bickel insisted, "the more important it is that it be decided in the first instance by the legislature." Thus, judicial tribunals must not presume that elected officials have authorized law enforcement practices that many citizens believe violate constitutional liberties. "Judges," prominent legal commentators agree, "should not attribute to the legislature an intention to impinge fundamental rights unless the legislature has carefully considered the issue and clearly expressed its intention."[17]

Several important legal precedents condemn dubious constitutional

practices that might have been sustained had they been expressly authorized by elected officials. During the McCarthy era, the Supreme Court
refused to let congressional committees question citizens about their political activities and prohibited state department agents from denying pass-
ports to suspected Communists, because no statute plainly permitted
those inquisitors and bureaucrats to tread so closely to constitutionally
protected freedoms. "Explicit action," the justices insisted,

> especially in areas of doubtful constitutionality, requires careful and pur-
> posive consideration by those responsible for enacting and implementing
> our laws. Without explicit action by lawmakers, decisions of great constitu-
> tional import and effect would be relegated by default to administrators
> who, under our system of government, are not endowed with authority to
> decide them.[18]

American abortion law in action did not satisfy this demand for "explicit action by lawmakers." No legislature ever specifically authorized the
creation of an exclusive gray market or "somewhat permit, but really discourage" policies. Such policies were the consequences of numerous decisions made by unelected law officials, many of whom were hostile to, indifferent to, or unaware of the public ends that pro-life measures were
supposed to promote. Because these administrators were not "endowed
with the authority" to make "doubtful constitutional decisions," the federal judiciary had an obligation to strike down pre-*Roe* abortion policies,
even if those policies might have passed constitutional muster had they
been unambiguously commissioned by a legislature.

LAW ENFORCEMENT IN A DEMOCRACY

Taken together, abortion law in action, widely held views on political justice, basic constitutional principles, and established legal precedents demonstrate that bans on reproductive choice were implemented in ways that
violated the equal protection rights of poor persons and persons of color.
Without any statutory authorization, police officers and prosecutors
"somewhat permitted" affluent women to terminate their pregnancies
safely, while "really discouraging" others in the same circumstances from
exercising the same rights. Reproductive policies in many communities
also violated due process rights. Members of the law enforcement community flouted statutory commands when they arbitrarily determined
who would have access to safe abortions. Most significantly, whether "selective enforcement," "capricious enforcement," or "permit somewhat,
but really discourage" best describes their administration, abortion policies before *Roe* had, at most, a distant relationship to the goals expressed

in legislative measures. As such, restrictive American reproductive policies violated our society's commitment to rule by law.

These failings are hardly unique to pre-*Roe* abortion laws. As Prohibition and statutory bans on popular expressions of human sexuality demonstrate, democratic societies cannot fairly enforce laws against behaviors that too many prominent persons believe do not merit legal sanctions. When such laws are allowed to remain in the penal code, the inevitable result is arbitrary and capricious law enforcement. Herbert Packer, a leading criminologist, points out that "the enforcement ratio of private consensual sex offenses must show incredibly heavy odds against arrest—perhaps one in ten million?" "The scanty available evidence," he notes further, "suggests that enforcement takes place mainly in a context in which other mores, not reinforced by law, are being flouted, as, for example, where the partners are of different races."[19] The experience of Jack Johnson, the first person of color to win the prestigious heavyweight boxing championship, provides a disturbing illustration of who gets punished when most respectable citizens enjoy practical immunities from restrictive sex laws on the books. Though Johnson was convicted after he violated the Mann Act's ban on crossing state lines with a female companion for immoral purposes, his real crimes were knocking out white men and sleeping with white women.[20]

The constitutional rights of criminal suspects is another area that would benefit from more emphasis on how constitutionally controversial policies are administered. The Fourteenth Amendment requires that the police demonstrate "probable cause" before arresting a criminal suspect, and judicial decisions allow officers of the law to conduct a stop-and-frisk when they have "a reasonable suspicion" that criminal activity is imminent.[21] Most studies, however, find that in practice "police use race as an independently significant, if not determinative, factor in deciding whom to follow, detain, search or arrest."[22] Whether the police stop a person carrying a television set across an urban street typically depends on whether that person is white or black and whether he or she looks rich or poor.[23] Thus, rather than develop objective criteria for determining what constitutes "probable cause" or "reasonable suspicion," constitutional commentators and authorities might follow the Civil Rights Act of 1866 and make the standard for measuring the Fourteenth Amendment rights of all citizens those conditions under which police arrest or search affluent white citizens.

Communities would probably sharply curtail stop-and-frisk practices and repeal laws banning certain forms of consensual sex if such policies were fully and fairly administered. A war on crime may seem less attractive when one cannot window shop or jog through an affluent white neighborhood without risking an unpleasant and occasionally abusive police encounter. Deviant sex may seem less deviant when friends and neighbors are imprisoned for engaging in sodomy.[24] The precise degree of arbitrariness necessary to strike down maladministered laws can be debated, but democratic societies must draw the line somewhere. In communities that vest law enforcement officials with absolute discretion, the only decision of lasting importance that elected officials make is their appointment of the police chief.

Capricious law enforcement practices can be prevented only when citizens, legislators, and judges committed to rule by law fight to repeal those laws on the books that their community lacks the will to enforce uniformly and regularly. Persons who fear the consequences of "handcuffing the police" forget that democratic processes are supposed to constrain law enforcement officials. In constitutional democracies, persons are governed only by the laws and policies made by their duly elected officials or set out in their constitution. Persons governed by official discretion live in a police state, no matter how well-intentioned or beneficent the police.

Realizing Equal Choice

PERSUASION AND POLITICS

Any fair-minded person should recognize the impeccable credentials of equal choice. Unlike pro-choice arguments, which rely heavily on controversial moral claims and interpretive theories, equal choice arguments follow naturally from political values and legal precepts that most Americans regard as axiomatic. Policies that grant affluent white women practical indulgences from the criminal law are inconsistent with widely held principles of justice as well as the plain, original, and historical meanings of the equal protection clause. Hence, repeating the arguments of chapters III and IV at appropriate moments may be the only political strategy necessary for keeping abortion legal. Once Americans are fully exposed to the philosophical and constitutional case for equal choice, legislators and executives will stop regulating abortion, voters will elect large pro-choice majorities, justices will continue (or resume) treating *Roe* as an authoritative constitutional decision, and opponents of legal abortion will refrain from proposing new bans until their pro-life policies have some reasonable chance of being fairly administered.

Still, some fair-minded persons will not find equal choice arguments so compelling. Critics may insist that my chapter II overestimates the inequalities that result when our society bans abortion or underestimates the number of fetal lives that pro-life policies save. Others may claim that the few fetal lives that bans on abortion save still outweigh the substantial race and economic inequalities that result when such policies are implemented. Anti-*Roe* commentators may argue that the equal protection clause does not protect equal choice rights or that state officials were not constitutionally responsible for the racial and class biases of the gray market. I think these and similar criticisms are wrong, but intelligent persons often disagree. For these reasons, even if equal choice arguments prove more persuasive than pro-choice arguments, they will not be the final word: no scholarly analysis can bring about the social consensus necessary to end the abortion controversy.

The inevitable contestability of all abortion policies compels advocates of reproductive choice to think politically in one last sense. They must consider the resources and strategies necessary to ensure that government officials keep abortion legal. To win the battle for procreative autonomy, equal choice (or pro-choice) advocates must first identify those persons and institutions most likely to endorse equal choice policies. They must devise tactics that maintain and expand that political support. Proponents of legal abortion must accurately assess the potential resources at their disposal and learn how to deploy those resources most effectively. Finally, persons who favor equal choice must spend their resources fighting against pro-life policies; they must not invest their limited political capital in other social struggles.

Unfortunately, few theorists think pragmatically about the political strategies necessary to secure and improve access to legal abortion. Many pro-choice tactics, like many pro-choice arguments, are based on abstract conjectures and convenient myths about late-twentieth-century American politics. The same fictions that serve as faulty constitutional foundations for defenses of *Roe* are used to justify political strategies that may not maintain *Roe* in the long run. Relying too often on simplistic conceptions of American party politics, advocates of abortion on demand ignore potential costs of their preferred methods for realizing reproductive choice. Obsessed with winning great victories in legislatures or courts, proponents of *Roe* have overlooked a subtle political tactic that might substantially improve their chance of keeping abortion legal.

Many proponents of abortion on demand once maintained that an independent judiciary could protect abortion rights even when voters consistently elected pro-life officials. The Rehnquist Court gave this proposition such a beating that by the late 1980s even some prominent pro-choice litigators recognized that abortion would not remain legal for long if committed proponents of recriminalization continued to dominate electoral and legislative processes.[1] Chastened by a series of judicial defeats, prominent members of Planned Parenthood, the National Abortion and Reproductive Rights Action League (NARAL), and like-minded organizations began assembling a durable pro-choice electoral majority. As presently conceptualized, however, this strategy is derived from a popular fallacy. Many abortion rights advocates assume that political demands for pro-choice policies will mobilize previously uninvolved women, poor persons, and persons of color into a reenergized progressive party. In fact, calls for legal abortion appeal most strongly to affluent suburbanites who have little interest in joining some version of Jesse Jackson's Rainbow Coalition. Moreover, strategies that concentrate proponents of legal abortion in one party enable opponents of legal abortion to gain or stay in power whenever voters become dissatisfied with the economic accomplishments of the pro-choice coalition. The substantial rise in the misery index during the late 1970s and the economic boom of the mid-1980s played a much greater role in the elections of Ronald Reagan and George Bush than did any increase in public support for bans on abortion.

Purposive efforts to depoliticize the abortion controversy offer a more realistic strategy for keeping abortion legal. Late-twentieth-century proponents of abortion on demand need not struggle to gain the legislative support necessary to pass pro-choice statutes: abortion will remain legal as long as legislatures are dominated by representatives who would rather avoid making any abortion policy. The greater the number of legislators who do not want to decide when women should be allowed to terminate a pregnancy, the more difficulty opponents of equal choice will have forcing legislatures even to consider passing new bans on abortion. Thus, abortion rights activists should at present fight harder to defeat pro-life candidates than to elect candidates committed to legal abortion. Instead of forging a pro-choice coalition, proponents of legal abortion must prevent pro-life forces from capturing a political party. When both political parties have the same proportion of pro-life and pro-choice advocates or are controlled by those lacking commitment to any abortion policy, opponents of *Roe* cannot gain power by riding the coattails of the Republican Party when the GOP enjoys electoral landslides because of voters' economic concerns.

Whenever abortion is removed from the political agenda, proponents of legal abortion can expect favorable decisions from the Supreme Court. When no explicit litmus test regarding *Roe* is used, justices appointed to the federal bench usually hold the highly favorable attitudes toward legal abortion typical of most American elites. Elite jurists who do not find pro-or equal choice rights in the Constitution may nevertheless lack the stomach for overruling legal precedents protecting reproductive freedoms. For this reason, abortion rights activists need not win decisive victories at the polls to ensure continued judicial support for *Roe*. An electoral standoff that prevents either side from enforcing litmus tests when staffing the federal judiciary favors the cause of reproductive choice. As long as pro-life forces are prevented from obtaining the political power necessary to pack the Supreme Court with anti-*Roe* jurists, *Roe* will remain the law of the land.

Keeping abortion off the political agenda admittedly will not improve the prospects for policies that enable all women to terminate an unwanted pregnancy. Poor women enjoy equal access to abortion in practice only when abortion providers are available and subsidized in all American counties. Such policies do not necessarily follow from equal choice principles and cannot be achieved in the absence of durable pro-choice legislative majorities. Nevertheless, under present political circumstances, committed pro-choice activists should still seriously consider adopting those strategies best designed to secure equal choice. For all of *Roe*'s practical failings, simple decriminalization increased legal abortion rates among poor women and women of color much more dramatically than any other policy likely to be adopted in the near future.

THE CRITIQUE OF PURE LITIGATION

Redress for Success

Throughout the 1960s, 1970s, and 1980s, supporters of abortion on demand relied primarily on federal and state judges to protect reproductive freedoms. Lawyers and law professors, in particular, touted litigation as the proper and best political strategy for ensuring that abortion became and remained legal. The status of abortion rights in the United States, leading jurists insisted, was "a legal question about the correct interpretation of the Constitution which in our political system *must* be settled one way or the other judicially, by the Supreme Court, rather than politically."[2] In order to secure this fundamental liberty, a generation of liberal and feminist lawyers spent their creative energies fashioning constitutional arguments that would convince judicial tribunals to declare unconstitutional every significant restriction on reproductive choice.[3]

Litigation never fully exhausted the tactics pro-choice advocates used. NARAL, Planned Parenthood, and other organizations lobbied elected officials extensively and conducted media campaigns publicizing the evils associated with illegal abortion. Radical feminist groups occasionally disrupted legislative hearings.[4] With few exceptions,[5] however, pro-choice activists emphasized efforts to have justices declare pro-life measures unconstitutional. A founder of NARAL bluntly stated that "the main attack [should] be through the courts" because "experience shows that getting a bill through a state legislature to repeal all laws is an agonizing and possibly fruitless procedure." Prominent abortion rights advocates warned local activists that state referenda on abortion were "highly dangerous," because failure "could seriously jeopardize the entire court action."[6]

Proponents of reproductive rights made several crucial choices that demonstrated their commitment to litigation. Pro-choice groups invested substantially more time and money fighting against such anti-*Roe* judicial nominees as Robert Bork than campaigning for such pro-choice presidential candidates as Michael Dukakis.[7] After 1973, proponents of abortion on demand adopted legislative strategies that assumed the Supreme Court would strike down important pro-life policies. Pro-choice activists and elected representatives did not fight as hard as they might have against the

Hyde Amendment, because they were confident that a litigation campaign would successfully restore Medicaid funding for abortion.[8]

This emphasis on litigation was initially a necessary consequence of the limited resources available to the pro-choice movement. Early proponents of legal abortion lacked the popular support and financial wherewithal to forge pro-choice majorities in the state and federal legislatures.[9] Litigation was the only affordable strategy that offered pro-choice forces some hope of achieving a nationwide repeal of all pro-life measures. Bringing cases before the Supreme Court is hardly inexpensive, but litigation is significantly cheaper than engaging in national lobbying or electoral campaigns. A few volunteer lawyers, several wealthy benefactors, and support from relatively small organizations provided the resources necessary for placing abortion on the agenda of the federal judiciary and achieving an extraordinary victory in *Roe v. Wade*.[10]

Pro-choice activists also relied on litigation because they thought judges would respond more favorably than legislators to appeals for legal abortion. The Supreme Court in the 1950s and 1960s frequently upheld claims of constitutional right that elected officials had previously rejected or ignored. *Brown v. Board of Education*[11] demonstrated that the federal judiciary would demand dramatic changes in American life when presented with the appropriate case. Judicial decisions in the 1960s and early 1970s indicated that the justices were similarly willing to transform American family and reproductive practices. By 1972, the Court had declared that all citizens had constitutional rights to marry, to use contraception, and, most significantly, "to be free from unwarranted governmental intrusion into matters so fundamentally affecting a person as the decision whether to bear or beget a child." Pro-choice lawyers confidently anticipated that the justices would regard finding a constitutional right to abortion only a small extension of these existing precedents.[12]

Roe v. Wade confirmed these predictions and hopes that the Supreme Court would be more willing than Congress or state legislatures to legalize abortion. In *Roe*, the justices declared unconstitutional the abortion bans on the books of at least forty-six states. Despite repeated state efforts to impose new restrictions on reproductive rights and despite landslides in the 1980, 1984, and 1988 presidential elections by candidates on record as favoring pro-life policies, *Roe* remained an authoritative constitutional precedent. Indeed, from 1973 to 1986 the Supreme Court generally extended judicial protection of constitutional abortion rights, striking down various consent provisions, waiting periods, and medical procedures that served little purpose other than to burden women who wished to terminate their pregnancies.[13]

Still, the pro-choice movement's continued commitment to litigation, at bottom, is probably best explained by the widely held belief in the

United States that persons with just causes eventually triumph in the judiciary. This faith in courts stems from our societal commitment to constitutional limits on democratic governance. Many Americans—lawyers in particular—insist that fundamental human liberties must not be subject to the vagaries of electoral or legislative processes. Justice Robert Jackson's often-cited opinion declaring mandatory flag saluting unconstitutional eloquently articulated the view that constitutional rights must remain above the political fray. "The very purpose of a Bill of Rights," Jackson declared,

> was to withdraw certain subjects from the vicissitudes of political controversy, to place them beyond the reach of majorities and officials and to establish them as legal principles to be applied by the courts. One's right to life, liberty, and property, to free speech, a free press, freedom of worship and assembly, and other fundamental rights may not be submitted to vote; they depend on the outcome of no elections.[14]

Even quite conservative devotees of judicial restraint echo this catechism. Robert Bork, for example, maintains that "the Constitution . . . was designed to remove a number of subjects from democratic control," most notably "the freedoms guaranteed by the Bill of Rights."[15]

Pro-choice activists zealously celebrate the perceived independence of constitutional liberties from political processes. Abortion, liberal academic lawyers proclaim, is one of the rights whose protection should "depend on the outcome of no elections." Proponents of *Roe* insist that reproductive freedoms not "be included in the list of interests that are subject to ordinary logrolling and electoral politics," and they praise the Supreme Court for withdrawing "the abortion decision . . . from the vicissitudes of political controversy."[16] "An unqualified argument favoring democracy," Ruth Colker of the University of Pittsburgh Law School declares, "is insensitive to the need for courts to safeguard equal protection of the law." NARAL crusader Lawrence Lader similarly maintains that what is "right constitutionally and morally should not be voted on."[17]

From their theoretical claim that electoral "politics *should* not dictate constitutional rights"[18] (emphasis added), many proponents of legal abortion deduce the empirical claim that electoral politics *do* not dictate constitutional rights. The Supreme Court, leading pro-choice scholars maintain, is institutionally capable of resisting hostile governing majorities. In their view, Article III will stymie elected officials who attempt to pack the Supreme Court with pro-life activists. Life tenure and the judicial commitment to decision by constitutional standards ensure that pro-choice lawyers will receive an impartial hearing in "the forum of principle"[19] and triumph when their cause is constitutionally just. "A primary reason for granting federal judges life tenure, and entrusting them with the interpretation of broad constitutional principles," one leading feminist scholar proclaims, "is to ensure some protection for evolving principles of liberty and equality." An article in the *Harvard Law Review* recognizes that "the possibility of and benefits from an independent judiciary could easily be overestimated." Nevertheless, its author concludes, given how the "institutional setting of the federal courts" enabled "many federal justices [to play] courageous and honorable roles in the early days of school segregation," pro-choice advocates "should not underestimate the possible value of a prestigious court made up of Justices who enjoy life tenure."[20]

Hopeful that independent justices would recognize the clear constitutional force of pro-choice arguments, proponents of abortion on demand thought the sky would not necessarily fall when candidates who explicitly promised to limit reproductive freedoms consistently won state and national elections. Pro-life legislatures might pass new restrictions on abortion and pro-life executives might attempt to pack the judiciary with anti-*Roe* justices. Nevertheless, abortion rights activists believed, pro-choice constitutional principles could prevail over pro-life electoral politics. In their view, when conservative Supreme Court justices were faced with compelling pro-choice constitutional arguments, those jurists might disappoint their pro-life political sponsors.

Backlash

For many years, litigation seemed the best means for achieving pro-choice policies. Although pro-life forces enjoyed many political successes from 1973 until 1988, particularly in presidential elections, the Supreme Court's faithful allegiance to *Roe* kept abortion legal, and abortion became increasingly available as a realistic reproductive option for many women. The number of legal abortions in the United States increased nearly threefold, from 586,800 the year before *Roe* to 1,588,600 in 1985.[21] Legalization shattered the exclusive gray market, dramatically reduced the price of abortion, and substantially improved maternal health. For the first time in American history, most poor women and women of color enjoyed significant, if still imperfect, access to safe abortions.[22]

Suggestions that the legal abortion rate might have reached present levels had pro-choice activists eschewed litigation[23] overlook several features of late-twentieth-century reproductive politics. Although the number of legal abortions increased rapidly before *Roe*, from 8,000 in 1966 to 586,800 in 1972, much of that increase took place after state and lower federal courts struck down local abortion bans. The number of legal abortions increased by over 100,000 annually after California judges ruled that the state's ban on abortion was unconstitutionally vague.[24] Furthermore, partisan efforts to have state legislatures repeal restrictions on abortion had lost steam by 1973. Pro-choice forces were poorly positioned to achieve further legislative gains and were a governor's veto away from seeing New York recriminalize abortion.[25] Finally, judicial rulings can be credited with keeping abortion rates fairly constant in the late 1970s and 1980s despite significant electoral victories by pro-life forces. We will never know what would have happened had *Roe* been decided differently. The best evidence, however, suggests that judicial decisions helped secure safe legal abortions for many women.[26]

But although litigation accomplished much good, that political strategy proved a problematic method for maintaining procreative choice. The high priority accorded to constitutional adjudication imposed significant costs on the pro-choice movement, even when the Supreme Court was striking down most restrictions on abortion. To begin with, litigation failed to achieve all the goals of the pro-choice movement. In particular, pro-choice lawyers could not secure the positive assistance from the state that some women need in order to obtain a legal abortion. The legal campaign for subsidized abortion collapsed in 1977 and 1980 when the Burger Court ruled that the federal and state governments had no constitutional obligation to finance abortions for women who could not otherwise terminate a pregnancy.[27] The justices never considered whether states must establish abortion services for all citizens, but no reason exists for thinking the Burger or Rehnquist Courts would have had any sympathy for such claims.[28]

More significantly, *Roe* set in motion a chain of events that crippled the pro-choice movement's ability to secure legislation to protect and expand reproductive freedoms. In the years immediately following *Roe*, opponents of abortion on demand seized the legislative initiative. Newly mobilized advocates of recriminalizing abortion helped elect numerous pro-life candidates to state and national office. Pro-life elected representatives passed measures that placed various obstacles in the path of women seeking to terminate their pregnancies. These new restrictions did not immediately reduce the total number of abortions performed in the United States[29] and many were declared unconstitutional shortly after passage. Still, the pro-life revival forced proponents of legal abortion to defend existing gains rather than propose new measures that might have improved access to the procedure. Bills requiring all counties to provide abortion services were not on the legislative agenda in most states during the 1970s and 1980s.[30] Moreover, politically influential social conservatives, energized by such decisions as *Roe*, thwarted other goals of the pro-choice movement. Religious fundamentalists blocked efforts to pass the Equal Rights Amendment, prevented broad distribution of contraception, and limited sex education in the public schools.[31]

Blaming *Roe* for creating the pro-life movement, however, misconstrues the decision's real impact on American politics. Success in the abortion conflict always has "the unintended effect of aiding the opposition organizationally" no matter how and in what forum such victories are achieved.[32] Pro-life voters mobilized whenever pro-choice activists made serious attempts to repeal all restrictions on abortion. In the year before *Roe* was decided, opponents of abortion on demand in Michigan and North Dakota conducted intense and bitter campaigns that defeated state referenda calling for legal abortion.[33] State judicial decisions declaring bans on abortion unconstitutional produced no greater backlash than did state statutes or referenda repealing previous pro-life statutes. New York was a pro-choice state when *Roe* was decided only because Governor Nelson Rockefeller vetoed legislation reinstituting the restrictions on abortion that state representatives had repealed in 1971.[34] Should *Roe* be overruled, pro-life political activism surely will continue. Members of Operation Rescue do not and will not distinguish abortion clinics that remain open by judicial decree from abortion clinics sanctioned by local legislation.

Roe weakened the relative power of the pro-choice movement because, in addition to inspiring the pro-life movement, judicial decisions protecting abortion rights demobilized potential supporters of reproductive freedom. The pro-choice movement may not "have fallen into a deep and fateful sleep . . . after *Roe*,"[35] but some groups did disband. More significantly, many potential supporters of reproductive liberties chose not to spend their scarce political resources counteracting the political tactics of the pro-life movement.[36]

The slogan "I'm pro-choice and I vote" obscured an important phenomenon in American politics during the 1970s and 1980s. The well-paid, highly educated persons who tended to support pro-choice policies were much more likely to vote than average citizens.[37] However, these pro-choice elites often voted against pro-choice candidates. Confident that the judiciary would protect abortion rights (and aware that whatever regulations slipped by the Court would not affect them), many affluent citizens supported pro-life candidates who promised to lower taxes.[38] Citizens with incomes above $50,000 during the 1980s were the strongest proponents of legal abortion and the strongest supporters of Ronald Reagan and George Bush, presidential nominees who ran on platforms promising to outlaw most abortions.[39] Thus, as long as affluent voters trusted courts to maintain legal abortion, they could make electoral decisions without having to choose between their economic conservatism and their social liberalism.

This artificial increase in electoral and legislative support for pro-life measures eventually undermined continued judicial adherence to *Roe*. The Reagan Justice Department conducted unprecedented investigations to ensure that their judicial appointees supported the anti-abortion policies of the administration. After 1986, pro-choice forces were strong enough to block confirmation of nominees on record as demanding that *Roe* be overruled. Nevertheless, proponents of legal abortion could not prevent Presidents Reagan and Bush from placing on the bench justices whose conservative record and philosophy strongly suggested that they opposed judicial solicitude for reproductive rights. Judge Clarence Thomas may have been the only American lawyer alive in 1991 who had never thought about *Roe*. He had, however, condemned most instances of liberal judicial activism and given speeches to conservative think tanks praising pro-life writings.

The Reagan and Bush administrations' effort to pack the judiciary with politically and socially conservative justices was relatively successful. The Supreme Court refused to recognize a constitutional right to engage in private homosexual acts and federal courts became significantly less sympathetic to most civil liberties claimants.[40] Nevertheless, pro-choice lawyers and law professors continued to count on judicial independence to preserve their cherished reproductive liberties. Shortly before the *Webster* decision was handed down, Ronald Dworkin urged the justices not to abandon their principled defense of abortion rights. The Supreme Court, his essay in the *New York Review of Books* implored, must "refuse to nourish the cynical view . . . that constitutional law is only a matter of which presidents appointed the last few justices."[41] Such pleas were not heeded.

Judicial solicitude for abortion rights ground to an abrupt halt in 1989 when the Supreme Court sustained a Missouri statute that mandated stringent abortion procedures and forbade abortions at any institution receiving state funds. Chief Justice Rehnquist's plurality opinion in *Webster v. Reproductive Health Services* bluntly admitted that "our holding today will allow some governmental regulation of abortion that would have been prohibited under the language of [earlier] cases."[42] The next year, the justices broadened the circumstances under which states could require minors to obtain parental consent for abortion. Three years after *Webster*, in *Planned Parenthood v. Casey*, all six justices appointed by Presidents Reagan or Bush (plus Justice White) sustained a law requiring the kind of mandatory waiting period and informed consent that did not withstand judicial scrutiny as late as 1986.[43]

The resignations of Justices William Brennan and Thurgood Marshall, and their replacement on the bench by Justices David Souter and Clarence Thomas, accelerated the Court's anti-*Roe* trend. No longer content to weaken judicial protection for abortion rights, the justices began engaging in pro-life policy making. A 5–4 majority in 1991 held that President Bush could deny federal funds to any organization that even mentioned abortion as a reproductive option. As the dissenting opinions in *Rust v.*

Sullivan[44] pointed out, the Rehnquist Court would not have had to affirm *Roe* to find fault with the "gag" rule. A tribunal truly neutral between pro-choice and pro-life policies might have noted that the president acted with dubious statutory authority. Neither the text nor the legislative history of the Public Health Services Act clearly supported President Bush's claim that he was statutorily empowered to limit the advice that federally funded family planning agencies could give their clientele.[45] Prior to *Rust*, past precedents and traditional judicial practice maintained that "[f]ederal statutes are to be so construed as to avoid serious doubts of their constitutionality." In their eagerness to promote pro-life policies or executive power, members of the Rehnquist Court ignored this accepted canon of judicial self-restraint.[46]

Judicial Independence Revisited

The very hope that the Supreme Court would provide substantial protection for abortion rights after that tribunal had been packed with anti-*Roe* jurists is based on a mistaken and unrealistic conception of judicial independence. Basic rules of legal ethics mandate that judicial rulings not be influenced by personal feelings toward or relationships between the parties before the court.[47] The Canons of Judicial Conduct do not, however, forbid justices from being influenced by personal beliefs about the legal principles at stake in a given case. No one thinks former Justice Thurgood Marshall violated judicial ethics by invariably supporting the claims made by his previous associates at the NAACP Legal Defense Fund. Marshall performed "the duties of the office impartially"[48] because his votes reflected his principles, principles that, not coincidentally, were almost always those being advocated by the NAACP. Having life tenure freed Marshall to rethink his judicial philosophy without fear of reprisal from his former political allies. Nevertheless, persons of the age and experience necessary to sit on the Supreme Court rarely alter their fundamental beliefs while on the bench. A justice who has held strong pro-life opinions for twenty years before being appointed to the federal judiciary will almost certainly hold strong pro-life opinions for the next twenty years. Even the most open-minded judicial critic of *Roe* is not likely to be convinced at oral argument by legal claims the justice has heard at least a hundred times previously.

United States v. Nixon,[49] the Watergate tapes case, illustrates how judges are and are not independent of their political sponsors. The Supreme Court in that case sealed President Nixon's doom by requiring him to turn over incriminating tape recordings to the special prosecutor. Legal commentators were particularly pleased that Nixon's four judicial appointees all voted against the president's claim of executive privilege. This, in their view, established that the Burger Court would not simply do the president's bidding. But according to a different analysis, the Burger Court in *Nixon* did nothing but the president's bidding. During his campaign for the presidency, Nixon emphasized the need for jurists who would "strengthen the peace forces as against the criminal forces of our land."[50] When judicial vacancies occurred, Nixon scrutinized prospective appointees for their willingness to support claims made by state and federal prosecutors. In *Nixon*, the justices faithfully carried out these wishes. That case held that when a prosecutor demands evidence necessary to convict criminal defendants, the president cannot refuse merely by relying on a generalized claim of executive privilege. The Supreme Court advanced Nixon's announced principles but failed to serve his interests only because of Nixon's own oversight: he never anticipated that in a case that would decide his political future, he would be on the side of those he had deemed "the criminal forces of our land."[51]

The Supreme Court's willingness to rule against the president in *Nixon* suggests that an independent judiciary will, if anything, be a boon for pro-life activists in the near future. A bench packed with anti-*Roe* jurists may not change direction when such policies no longer serve the personal or professional interests of key Republican elites. Justice Scalia might not be sympathetic to an anguished plea from George Bush that his fourteen-year-old granddaughter be allowed to have an abortion even though one of her natural parents refuses to consent. Nor might the Rehnquist Court start making pro-choice policies should the Republicans decide that the abortion issue in electoral politics slightly favors Democrats.[52] Having been appointed to the Supreme Court in part for the purpose of narrowing or overruling *Roe*, Chief Justice Rehnquist, Justice Scalia, and Justice Thomas are likely to continue expressing the opinions that helped secure their high positions.

Proponents of legal abortion have little reason to hope that other jurists appointed on the basis of their presumed anti-*Roe* beliefs will turn out to be clandestine pro-choice supporters or become converted to pro-choice beliefs while on the bench. Although such "mistakes" in the appointment process occasionally occur, two hundred years of judicial practice highlight their infrequency. History suggests that proponents of reproductive choice who call on Merlin the magician to change anti-*Roe* justices into frogs are being as realistic as those pro-choice advocates who hope that pro-life presidents will consistently be surprised when their carefully considered judicial appointments refuse to strike down most restrictions on abortion.

Very few justices frustrate their presidential sponsors. Of 111 persons who have served on the supreme bench, only Joseph Story (1811–45),

Oliver Wendell Holmes Jr. (1902–32), James C. McReynolds (1914–41), Earl Warren (1953–69), William J. Brennan Jr. (1956–90), and perhaps David Souter (1990–) opposed important policies preferred by the president who nominated them.[53] Justices who disappoint their former political allies often do so on very few issues. Holmes is sometimes classified as a presidential mistake because in *Northern Securities Co. v. United States*[54] he failed to support Theodore Roosevelt's antitrust policy.[55] Still, in virtually every other case Holmes decided during his thirty-year tenure on the bench, he voted as Roosevelt had hoped, in favor of those economic policies made by the people's elected officials. Justices are particularly unlikely to disappoint their sponsor on issues that were foremost on the president's mind when the justice was appointed. Nixon's appointees were more liberal than Nixon on women's issues, but no evidence suggests that Nixon was particularly concerned with gender rights when he selected his justices. Nixon was most interested in questions of law and order, and, as he discovered, on these matters his appointees expressed his philosophy all too well.

Pro-choice activists have some reason to hope that *Roe* might survive if pro-life executives only have the opportunity to fill five or six Supreme Court vacancies. Presidents make judicial appointments for various reasons, and future pro-life executives may confront a Senate unwilling to confirm an appointee clearly committed to overruling *Roe*. Some Reagan/Bush justices selected primarily because they supported laissez-faire economic policies seem amenable to supporting laissez-faire abortion policies.[56] Justices Kennedy and Souter have not been as willing as Justices Scalia and Thomas to abandon past precedents supporting legal abortion. If, however, pro-life executives are able to fill seven or eight Supreme Court vacancies and if overruling *Roe* is their major priority, no litigation strategy is likely to preserve abortion rights in the long run.

Legal Principles and Political Preferences

The continued pro-choice emphasis on litigation and judicial independence rests on a kind of philosophical arrogance. The Supreme Court can be counted on to sustain *Roe*, proponents of legal abortion consistently imply, because persons of moderate intelligence and moral decency recognize that the case was decided correctly. Politicians may yield to base instincts when courting pro-life voters, and law professors may wish to curry favor with socially conservative superiors. Nevertheless, once competent jurists are placed in a position where they can decide abortion issues solely on principle, *Roe*'s defenders are confident that such persons will rule that the Constitution protects abortion rights.

Opponents of *Roe* display the same imperious certitude. In their view, no principled jurist could possibly find abortion rights in the Constitution. Oblivious to numerous scholars who maintain otherwise, Robert Bork claims that "there is no room for argument about the conclusion that the [*Roe*] decision was the assumption of illegitimate judicial power." In his opinion, the result in that case could be supported only by persons who have "contempt for the limits of respectable politics."[57] One can easily imagine, in a slightly different universe, Bork or citizen Antonin Scalia, after a series of Democratic presidential landslides, imploring Justice Ronald Dworkin and his fellow liberals to overrule *Roe* and "refuse to nourish the cynical view . . . that constitutional law is only a matter of which presidents appointed the last few justices."

When political activists recognize, however grudgingly, that principled justices can, on reflection, disagree over whether abortion rights are protected by the Constitution, the case for using litigation as the sole means for securing legal abortion collapses. When opponents of abortion on demand are allowed to dominate electoral politics, pro-life officials are elected and they appoint to the federal bench justices who have principled and well-thought-out objections to *Roe v. Wade*. Appealing to Justice Scalia's principles is not a particularly promising strategy for protecting abortion rights. Rather, equal choice activists must engage in the political maneuvers necessary to prevent such persons as Antonin Scalia from sitting on the federal bench. Indeed, as many proponents of legal abortion are finally learning, should the public elect officials who will appoint and confirm to the Supreme Court such defenders of *Roe* as Ronald Dworkin, a future Dworkin Court might not have to protect abortion rights.

THE MYTH OF THE PRO-CHOICE MAJORITY

From the Supreme Court to the White House

In the wake of *Webster*, *Rust*, and the imbroglio over Clarence Thomas's nomination to the Supreme Court, proponents of legal abortion slowly abandoned their commitment to litigation in favor of political strategies aimed at creating a permanent pro-choice legislative majority. Armed with substantially increased membership rolls and financial resources, pro-choice organizations participated with much greater frequency and intensity in electoral and legislative processes. NARAL, Planned Parenthood, and allied groups worked diligently to recruit and support candidates dedicated to reproductive freedoms. Contributions by pro-choice political action committees increased from $640,000 in the 1987–88 election cycle to nearly $3,000,000 in the 1989–90 cycle. Most significantly, pro-choice activists drafted and pro-choice legislators in Congress introduced the

Freedom of Choice Act (FCA). This bill would give all women a right under federal law to terminate an unwanted pregnancy. Should the FCA be enacted, abortion would remain legal in all fifty states even if the Supreme Court overruled *Roe v. Wade*.[58]

This new enthusiasm for legislative and electoral processes was not simply one consequence of pro-choice advocates finally learning that a judiciary packed by Ronald Reagan and George Bush would not protect abortion rights. In the aftermath of *Webster*, abortion became an important issue to more voters, and many of those voters preferred pro-choice candidates.[59] Inspired by some election results, particularly in the 1989 Virginia and New Jersey gubernatorial races,[60] proponents of abortion on demand now believe that most Americans will vote pro-choice when winning elections is the only way to keep abortion legal.

Proponents of legal abortion were particularly encouraged by the substantial effect that surges in pro-choice voting had on the balance of power in the federal and state governments. Just as judicial decisions protecting abortion rights had given pro-life forces the legislative momentum, so judicial decisions threatening to abandon that protection handed the legislative initiative back to the pro-choice movement.[61] Increasing numbers of representatives committed to reproductive freedom were elected to public office during the late 1980s and early 1990s. Prominent politicians who had opposed abortion on demand quickly announced after *Webster* that they now thought abortion should remain legal. Between 1988 and 1989, twenty-seven members of Congress abandoned their earlier stance and endorsed federal funding for some abortions.[62] Numerous state officials experienced similar changes of heart. Local legislatures that once routinely passed restrictions on abortion that were subsequently declared unconstitutional by the courts were suddenly unable to enact identical restrictions that would have survived the new lower standard of judicial scrutiny.[63]

Much conventional wisdom in the spring of 1992 held that overruling *Roe* was the best gift the Rehnquist Court could give the political left. If weakened judicial support for legal abortion significantly strengthened pro-choice forces, then total repudiation might be the sole trigger needed to establish a durable pro-choice majority. Many liberal Democrats predicted that the demise of *Roe* would produce a pro-choice electoral backlash and foster grassroots efforts to advance a broader progressive agenda. "The withdrawal of the Court . . . from abortion," one prominent pro-choice legal academic confidently asserted, "appears to be fueling democratic engagement . . . in ways that will have more substantial healthy long-term implications for social reform than anything that could be expected from a Warren Court successor."[64]

Leading pro-choice activists acted on this vision of a world without

Roe. During oral argument in *Planned Parenthood v. Casey,* Kathryn Kolbert, the lawyer for Planned Parenthood, virtually begged the Supreme Court to stop protecting abortion rights in time to make reproductive policy a major issue in that fall's presidential election. When Justices Kennedy and O'Connor indicated that, although they would not uphold *Roe* in its entirety, they might offer some constitutional protection for abortion rights, Kolbert rejected their suggestions. "To abandon strict scrutiny for a less protective standard," she bluntly declared, "would be the same as overruling *Roe.*"[65]

Nothing beats winning elections as a means for realizing one's vision of social and constitutional justice. Nevertheless, present efforts to forge a national pro-choice legislative majority are beset with as many unrealistic assumptions about American politics as previous attempts to maintain a national pro-choice judicial majority. A pro-choice majority would keep abortion legal and improve access to that procedure, although probably not as much as abortion rights activists hope.[66] The more serious problem is that proponents of legal abortion seem unaware that two-party systems have a limited capacity for absorbing issues. Thus, pro-choice activists who fight to place reproductive issues on legislative agendas more often hinder than help political efforts to bring about other progressive reforms. As the Democratic Party becomes a better vehicle for pursuing the liberal abortion policies favored by most affluent Americans, that party has become a worse vehicle for pursuing the liberal redistributive policies favored by less affluent Americans. Moreover, the pro-choice forces in one party can be strengthened only by means that augment the strength of pro-life forces in the other party. In a society whose citizens generally vote their pocketbooks, the major consequence of making abortion a partisan issue has been to hold reproductive policies hostage to the condition of the national economy.

Pro-Choice Dreams

Winning elections matters. Political movements that conduct successful electoral campaigns are much better positioned than political movements that conduct successful litigation campaigns to realize their preferred goals. Lacking both "the purse and the sword," members of the "least dangerous branch" must hope that elected officials and citizens feel duty bound to implement judicial decrees.[67] Elected officials, by comparison, control important resources that can be used to secure compliance with legislative mandates or executive orders. Localities that oppose the will of the dominant national coalition may find their federal funds cut off. Recalcitrant officials and citizens may be arrested. In sharp contrast to litigation, electoral and legislative campaigns must mobilize large numbers of supporters if they are to be successful. Once advocates succeed in their initial policy-making endeavors, they have the necessary political resources already in place to resist the inevitable backlash that occurs after their first victories. Finally, durable electoral majorities need not worry in the long run about hostile judicial officials. The persons who control the legislative and executive branches of government consistently appoint justices to the federal bench who believe the dominant coalition's policies pass constitutional muster.[68] Franklin Delano Roosevelt, for example, so packed the Supreme Court that by 1941 the justices were unanimously upholding legislation that the Court had declared unconstitutional in 1936.[69]

For these reasons, proponents of legal abortion will most likely achieve their preferred policies by successfully forging durable legislative majorities in the national government and in all fifty states. Controlling both the purse and the sword, pro-choice elected majorities would have the power necessary to eliminate legal and the more significant practical barriers to abortion on demand. Every pro-choice physician in the nation would no longer be on call to handle the emergency that might occur should a Supreme Court justice who supports *Roe* fall seriously ill. Just consider the possible state of American abortion policies in the year 2012, after the United States has been governed for sixteen years by a pro-choice coalition led by Presidents Mario Cuomo, the former governor of New York, and Patricia Schroeder, a feminist representative from Colorado.[70]

In this utopia (or dystopia), the Freedom of Choice Act occupies a hallowed place in the United States Code. Legislation and executive orders guarantee government funding for any person who cannot afford to terminate a pregnancy and mandate that abortion providers are available throughout the United States. The Abortion Access Act of 1998 requires all medical institutions or practitioners accepting federal funds to perform abortions on demand as a condition of receiving that largesse. All agencies that receive federal funding are also required, when relevant, to inform women that abortion is a legitimate reproductive option. Attorney General Janet Benshoof [currently chief counsel for the Reproduction Rights Project] makes sure that pro-choice laws are strictly enforced. The Supreme Court, now headed by Chief Justice Ruth Bader Ginsburg, regards all these measures as constitutional.

In addition to guaranteeing all women access to abortion on demand, this imaginary pro-choice majority makes policies that reflect broader pro-choice visions of gender roles and sex. The Cuomo-Schroeder administrations and their legislative allies ratify the ERA, toughen federal and state laws prohibiting gender bias and sexual harassment, establish mandatory day care and parental leave programs for working parents, guarantee access to contraception, repeal all laws prohibiting sexual acts between consenting adults, and require that all schools provide sex education. Children are taught that women have the right to participate as equals in public life, that all persons have the right to control their sexuality, and that abortion is a fundamental human right. *Webster* and the pro-life movement are discussed in the same way as *Dred Scott v. Sanford*[71] and the pro-slavery movement. This school curriculum ensures that the next generation of voters is no more able to desire a United States without abortion rights than a United States with slavery. The few remaining pro-life advocates are confined to the lunatic fringes of American politics.

This futuristic vision illustrates just how secure legal abortion would be had proponents of reproductive choice conducted successful electoral campaigns as well as successful litigation campaigns. Given the extraordinary benefits listed above, few of which could be achieved by litigation, forging a nationwide pro-choice coalition seems the best strategy for securing legal abortion. American history demonstrates how a string of electoral victories may settle hotly disputed constitutional questions. Before 1932, respectable scholars, politicians, and justices advocated the "night watchman state" and maintained that the due process clause of the Fourteenth Amendment prohibited many state efforts to regulate the economy. Within in a few years, FDR's smashing political triumphs sent those doctrines into political and intellectual oblivion. New Deal Democrats so dominated the government from 1932 until 1980 that in order to remain competitive, the Republican Party accepted basic New Deal principles and argued that the GOP could do a better job managing the emerging welfare state.[72] Should the equal choice or pro-choice movement garner a victory along the dimensions of 1936, legal abortion would be guaranteed for at least a generation.

Proponents of legal abortion appeared to secure that victory in 1992. Democrats nominated a candidate publicly committed to pro-choice policies and would not even allow pro-life spokespersons to address their party's national convention. In contrast, pro-life speech dominated the Republican national convention. Unfortunately for George Bush, the strident rhetoric of Pat Buchanan and Pat Robertson drove prominent GOP women into the arms of the Clinton and Perot campaigns.[73] Less than a week after taking office, Clinton issued executive orders that rescinded the gag rule, permitted abortions in military hospitals overseas, and allowed the importation of the abortifacient RU-486.[74] Inspired by the president's example, congressional Democrats quickly moved to pass the Freedom of Choice Act. Pro-life hopes that the federal judiciary might overrule *Roe* faded when Clinton nominated Judge Ruth Bader Ginsburg to replace the retiring Justice White. The strategy of building a pro-choice majority seemed well on the way to fruition.

Pro-Choice Realities

Intoxicated by their apparent successes, proponents of legal abortion did not notice that the 1992 political season highlighted several sobering problems that plague efforts to establish a pro-choice majority. The "New Democrat" who campaigned more strongly for legal abortion than any previous nominee of his party offered much weaker support for progressive economic policies than any Democratic party presidential candidate in recent history. Indeed, Clinton publicly distanced himself from Jesse Jackson and the Rainbow Coalition by attacking the rap singer Sister Souljah and promising to get tough on welfare recipients. Moreover, increased pro-choice sentiment in the Democratic Party corresponded with hardened pro-life sentiment in the GOP. George Bush and Dan Quayle expressed stronger opposition to legal abortion in the 1992 campaign than they had articulated previously. Finally, despite their different positions on abortion, the race between George Bush and Bill Clinton did not revolve around whether proponents or opponents of legal abortion could turn out more voters. The result of the election, as well as the ebbs and flows of the campaign, depended almost entirely on whether voters trusted Governor Clinton or rejected trickle-down economics.[75]

PRO-CHOICE MAJORITIES AND PROGRESSIVE POLITICS

Prominent advocates of reproductive choice see the reemergence of the abortion issue in politics as having desirable "long-term implications for social reform."[76] Liberal activists and professors proclaim that reproductive freedoms neatly dovetail with the progressive economic and social reforms advocated by such movements as the Rainbow Coalition. Candidates strongly committed to legal abortion, in this view, bring increasing numbers of women, poor persons, and persons of color into the political process. By mobilizing these citizens, pro-choice politicians will help move the Democratic Party and overall political spectrum significantly to the left. Thus, the campaign for legal abortion is a means for achieving more radical social change as well as an end in itself. Leading social democrats expect that placing abortion on the political agenda will promote both reproductive policies that enable more poor women and women of color to terminate an unwanted pregnancy and redistributive policies that substantially improve the life prospects of less fortunate Americans.

When women, poor persons, and persons of color are mobilized, however, they are more likely to support restrictions on abortion than abortion on demand. Pro-life activists are typically poorer, less educated, and more religious than their pro-choice counterparts. More women than men oppose legal abortion, and persons of color have not been very concerned up to this point with the status of *Roe*.[77] As a result, abortion is less likely to mobilize a "rainbow coalition" than to distract or splinter such movements. Many lower-class citizens are quite willing to abandon the party of liberal economic policies for the party of conservative family values.

When pro-choice candidates succeed in *general* elections, they typically do so by appealing to suburban Republicans—suburban Republican women in particular. Such citizens are occasionally willing to abandon the party of laissez-faire economic policies for the party of laissez-faire family policies. GOP moderates do not, however, support pro-choice candidates who call for radical economic and social reforms. Thus, in order to woo economically conservative supporters of legal abortion, such politicians as Douglas Wilder, Ann Richards, Bill Clinton, and Paul Tsongas either muted or abandoned concerns for the poor and labor during their campaigns. As a result, their pro-choice victories did not further, but came at the expense of, more traditional progressive concerns. Abortion, in other words, only enters American politics when other issues get left out, issues that may be of pressing concern to many liberal pro-choice activists.

HOW TO CREATE AND EMPOWER A PRO-LIFE MINORITY/MAJORITY

The Democratic Party's transformation into a committed vehicle for advancing reproductive choice has had a second unanticipated cost, one that directly threatens legal abortion. Placing abortion on the political agenda does increase the benefits of victory. At the same time, however, that political strategy enhances the probability and magnitude of defeat. NARAL's relatively successful effort to influence the Democratic Party inadvertently helped solidify pro-life control over the Republican Party. The resulting partisan division has created unique opportunities for opponents of legal abortion to win control of the national government despite the absence of a popular anti-*Roe* consensus.

Activists bent on controlling one political party in a two-party state invariably help their rivals capture the other party. As one major coalition comes under the influence of persons who strongly support a particular policy, the other coalition becomes a haven for committed opponents of that policy. Late-twentieth-century abortion politics illustrate the workings of this third law of political motion. The Democratic Party adopted much stronger pro-choice positions during the 1980s than during the 1970s. As a result, that coalition lost the allegiance of some strongly pro-life New Dealers, but it attracted some strongly pro-choice voters who formerly had supported GOP candidates. The Republican coalition, by comparison, experienced an infusion of new pro-life voters and a corresponding exodus of older pro-choice voters. As a result, the GOP adopted much stronger pro-life positions during the 1980s than during the 1970s.[78] Many pro-choice and pro-life advocates retained their traditional partisan loyalties, thus causing significant internal debates within both parties over abortion policy.[79] Nevertheless, by the mid-1980s, the national Democratic and Republican Parties offered voters a clear choice on abortion: the Democratic platform called for legal abortion, while the Republican platform demanded that most abortions be recriminalized.

Were abortion the only issue on the political agenda, proponents of legal abortion might regard the division of the American political universe into rival pro-choice and pro-life factions as an unambiguous blessing. If public opinion presently favors legal abortion, then pro-choice candidates should win most national, state, and local elections. The vast majority of voters, however, consider other issues more important than abortion when casting their ballots. Thus, pro-choice candidates lose elections not only when more voters in their district support pro-life policies but also when pro-life candidates advocate other programs of greater interest to most voters.

Pro-choice commitments do not significantly help (or harm) most candidates because "only a small minority of the public sees abortion as one of its central concerns."[80] Study and after study concludes that, with the exception of the 1991–92 election cycle,[81] abortion has had very little effect on the overwhelming majority of elections. Fewer than one in one thousand voters in the 1976 election regarded abortion as one of the three most important problems facing the country. A study of the 1984 election found that of eight major issues, attitudes toward abortion had the least influence on actual votes for president or senator. Interviews with persons active in particular campaigns confirm the low political salience of the abortion controversy. Only two of the six hundred campaign managers surveyed after the 1978 House elections regarded abortion as an important issue in their district, and none thought the matter was the most important issue.[82]

Many citizens do not even know what candidates in their district think about abortion. Voter ignorance remains high even when the issue is highly publicized. Despite intense media coverage and efforts by political activists to emphasize abortion during the 1989 gubernatorial elections in Virginia and New Jersey, almost two-thirds of all New Jersey voters and more than half of all Virginia voters did not know the candidates' views on reproductive choice. Only one out of every seven voters in those states could correctly identify the abortion positions of candidates running for the state legislature in their district.[83] "Given the low level of information," a study of those elections concludes, "the mere fact that someone has been elected is not necessarily a mandate on the abortion issue."[84]

The political priorities of American voters thus confound efforts to convert popular support for legal abortion into permanent electoral and legislative majorities. When presented with a clear choice between pro-life and pro-choice candidates, most citizens cast their ballot for the politician they believe will make better economic or foreign policy decisions. Abortion issues are salient only when no major issue captures the public's attention.[85] Thus, whether proponents of legal abortion win or lose elections rarely has anything to do with abortion per se. The electoral successes that pro-life forces enjoyed in the 1978 and 1980 elections, for example, are generally acknowledged to have been "incidental consequences of the shift toward conservatives at that time."[86]

The low significance of abortion in most general elections explains why the national Republican Party did not abandon its pro-life platform when pro-choice candidates began doing better in important elections. Abortion issues are most salient in primary elections,[87] and the primary electorate of the GOP is now heavily pro-life. Republican presidential aspirants and other candidates seeking the GOP's nomination in many (though not all) localities must strongly oppose abortion on demand. When campaigning in general elections, these candidates may feel that they will lose fewer votes by sticking to their guns on abortion than by earning a reputation for waffling after partially repudiating their recently proclaimed pro-life views.

Because few voters emphasize abortion, the present fate of reproductive choice depends almost entirely on the broader forces that determine the fate of candidates and parties. Politicians who support unpopular abortion policies still gain public office when they champion popular tax cuts or run against an opponent tainted by scandal. Moreover, whenever the public perceives the pro-choice party as significantly less able to manage the economy or new world order than the pro-life party, the citizenry supports the pro-life party, even when the majority of voters actually favor reproductive choice. Bipartisan efforts to secure legal abortion are immune to such shifts in American partisan politics. At present, however, pro-choice forces lack the political support necessary to capture both major parties.

The events responsible for the presidencies of Ronald Reagan and George Bush demonstrate the risk that attends political strategies aimed at creating a pro-choice majority. During the 1950s and 1960s, the major parties did not take fundamentally different stands on issues of gender roles and sexuality. Public opinion polls showed a slow, steady increase in public support for contraception and abortion, but these increases were distributed equally among members of the major parties and major party elites.[88] Thus, when the New Deal Democratic presidential coalition was permanently destroyed in 1968, the change in the executive branch had no immediate effect on abortion policies. To the extent the Nixon administration did anything on reproductive issues other than make a little pro-life noise, its policies continued the gradual liberalization of the Johnson administration.[89] Nixon's judicial appointees were generally moderate Republicans who, with the sole exception of William Rehnquist, supported *Roe*.

This partisan balance changed during the 1970s. Democrats became perceived as the party of acid, abortion, amnesty, and George McGovern as Republicans began making self-conscious appeals to social conservatives. These appeals initially emphasized such racial questions as school busing. By the end of 1970s, however, pro-life voters were being actively courted by and moving to the GOP. The resulting partisan shifts did not directly affect national elections; the massive Republican gains in the 1978 and 1980 elections had little to do with abortion and everything to do with the state of the economy and the hostages in Iran.[90] Nevertheless, the increasing division of the parties along social issues meant that when the GOP returned to power for economic reasons, the leadership of that party would be publicly committed to banning abortion. American abortion politics do not explain why George Bush was elected to the vice presidency and presidency in the 1980s. The splintering of the parties on abortion lines, however, helps explain why a mainstream Republican politician who had been mildly pro-choice in 1970[91] turned rabidly pro-life by the time he became president in 1989.

The pro-life movement also piggybacked on economic issues in the 1994 congressional elections. Popular frustration with President Clinton and various middle-class fears enabled the Republican Party to gain control of both houses of the national legislature for the first time in forty years. Abortion played no role in this GOP triumph. Still, the very fact that Republicans won a landslide victory meant that the pro-life movement won a landslide victory. Anti-abortion forces may have gained as many as forty seats in the House and six in the Senate. As a result, the 104th Congress will not pass the Freedom of Choice Act or include abortion in any foreseeable health care plan.[92]

Pro-life forces are triumphing for similar reasons in local elections. Proponents of legal abortion celebrated in 1989 when Representative James Florio was elected governor of New Jersey by a landslide vote. Florio campaigned extensively on a pro-choice platform, and exit polls found that this support for *Roe* attracted many voters.[93] Once in office, however, Governor Florio antagonized New Jersey voters by enacting a series of tax increases that proved extraordinarily unpopular. The result was a statewide Democratic debacle. In the 1991 state elections, Republicans captured both the state senate and the state legislature. Liberal Democrats, in particular, fell victim to enraged taxpayers. Abortion was not an issue in that election. Yet because significantly more Democrats than Republicans supported legal abortion, the Democratic rout over taxes had the side effect of weakening the political forces supporting legal abortion. Surveys taken by New Jersey NARAL reveal that what was once a strongly pro-choice legislature is no longer so.[94]

These election results suggest that proponents of legal abortion should consider Stephen Sondheim's advice in *Into the Woods* and "be careful what [they] wish for, for wishes may come true." Abortion has become a partisan issue in American politics because, particularly at the national level, one party generally nominates candidates who favor legal abortion while the other party nominates candidates who favor restricting abortion. This division may give a slight advantage to pro-choice forces, although election returns are still unclear.[95] However, few elections are substantially influenced by abortion. When the economy is expanding, incumbents are elected; in downturns, voters turn to the party out of power. These electoral tendencies benefit pro-choice forces when, as was the case in 1992, the public rejected a pro-life executive who presided over a stalled economy. But in the preceding years, opponents of legal abortion were able to dominate the national executive because the public blamed the more pro-choice candidate for economic hard times and credited pro-life executives with engineering economic booms.

The Pro-Choice Dilemma

Proponents of legal abortion seem stuck with a limited and unsatisfactory set of strategic alternatives for realizing reproductive choice. They cannot rely solely on litigation, because abandoning the political process to pro-life forces will eventually result in a federal judiciary hostile to *Roe*. Forging a pro-choice political majority seems more promising, but in most elections too few citizens think abortion an important issue when deciding which candidates to support. As a result, when in contemporary American politics the party dedicated to abortion on demand battles the party committed to banning abortion, the fate of reproductive freedoms winds up inexorably bound to the unemployment and inflation rates. Women are free to terminate their pregnancies only when the pro-life coalition mismanages domestic affairs or the pro-choice coalition "grows the economy."

Of course, all political strategies have potential costs. Political efforts to replace people who think like George Bush and Antonin Scalia with people who think like Bill Clinton and Ronald Dworkin are more realistic than legal efforts to make Antonin Scalia think more like Ronald Dworkin. Bewitched by the vision of what a pro-choice majority could accomplish in theory, however, proponents of legal abortion fail to perceive that their longed-for pro-choice majority is likely to do much less in practice. More significantly, concentrating proponents of legal abortion in one party both removes other important issues from the political agenda and increases the possibility of a pro-life majority taking power. The question remains, does some other strategy promise more?

RETHINKING ABORTION POLITICS

Union Failures, Equal Choice Opportunities

Skilled political strategists know the strengths and weaknesses of their forces and those of their rivals. Movements seeking social change, candidates seeking political office, and generals seeking military victory must fully understand what resources they will and will not be able to bring to bear against their opponents. The long run of defeats suffered by the Army of the Potomac during the Civil War neatly illustrates how commanders who misconceive their side's relative assets and liabilities may ruin any campaign. From 1861 until 1864, Lincoln's generals made no headway in the Eastern theater of the war because, misled by wildly exaggerated reports of Southern forces, they did not adopt tactics that best took advantage of their enormous advantages in manpower and weaponry.[96] Success came only when Northern leaders recognized the true circumstances of each side. Ulysses Grant was no tactical genius, particularly in comparison with his counterpart, Robert E. Lee, but he was well aware of his army's superior numbers and armaments. Hence, he fought a war of attrition that eventually destroyed the Confederacy.

NARAL, Planned Parenthood, and allied organizations have made errors similar to those made by many Union commanders. Echoing the ill-fated General George McClellan, pro-choice advocates regard themselves as fighting against "vastly superior odds."[97] Convinced they are battling for the victims of American society against their powerful oppressors, proponents of legal abortion see their main strategic problems as first identifying the institution most likely to favor the politically disadvantaged and then obtaining the resources necessary to mobilize women, the poor, and racial minorities into a pro-choice majority coalition. In fact, the persons who most strongly favor legal abortion are the traditional winners of American politics: males, whites, and persons of high socioeconomic status. These pro-choice citizens have at their disposal the most sophisticated weaponry of modern politics: money, media, campaign technology, and control of prestigious institutions. The central strategic problem abortion rights advocates actually face is how to convince most affluent Americans to use their resources to further their pro-choice preferences.

Persons committed to equal choice will best use the support of fickle elites by striving to keep abortion off the political agenda. This strategy requires that pro-choice advocates eschew efforts to achieve overwhelming political triumphs and concentrate on a more modest goal: not losing legislative and electoral struggles. Proponents of legal abortion should fight to make the two major parties indistinguishable on abortion and place a higher priority on defeating pro-life candidates than on supporting pro-choice candidates. Affluent pro-choice citizens should support political efforts to depoliticize abortion,[98] because neither progressive nor fiscally conservative elites want reproductive issues to supplant economic distribution as the main battleground of American politics.

Defensive maneuvers aimed at not losing to pro-life forces will maintain a favorable political climate for legal abortion. As long as abortion is legal—and legal abortion will still be the status quo in every state should *Roe* be overruled—a strategy that prevents legislatures from making any reproductive policy ensures that abortion remains legal. Moreover, when elected officials refuse to make abortion policy and do not consider abortion when selecting federal justices, courts are staffed by elite lawyers, most of whom believe that women should be allowed to terminate unwanted pregnancies. Such jurists are unlikely to overrule *Roe*, even if they might not have supported abortion rights when the issue first came before the Supreme Court. These strategies—"defeat pro-life" and "depoliticize abortion"—will not make abortion equally accessible in practice to all women. Equal choice's emphasis on keeping abortion legal, however, promises to improve access to safe abortion services almost as much as would the more difficult and riskier alternative of forging a pro-choice majority.

Resources

Proponents of reproductive freedoms see themselves as championing the rights of underprivileged citizens. Knowing that legal abortion offers significant benefits to poor women and women of color, abortion rights advocates naturally conclude that women, the poor, and persons of color are the strongest supporters of abortion on demand. Litigation seems a promising strategy for decriminalizing abortion because judges in our society are thought to "enjoy a situational advantage over the people at large in listening for voices from the margins." "Courts," much conventional wisdom proclaims, "stand against any winds that blow as havens of refuge for those who might otherwise suffer because they are helpless, weak, outnumbered, or because they are non-conforming victims of prejudice and public excitement."[99] Grassroots efforts to mobilize a pro-choice majority seem a wise use of the potential political advantages in numbers that abortion rights advocates believe they enjoy. When united, women, poor persons, and persons of color constitute a majority of eligible voters in our society. Thus, many proponents of legal abortion assumed that an aroused Rainbow Coalition of these traditional losers in American politics would keep abortion legal.

The Rainbow Coalition's main grassroots constituency, however, is not committed to legal abortion: the less fortunate persons whom that movement mobilizes tend to support pro-life policies.[100] Moreover, most lower-middle- and lower-class citizens hold conservative attitudes toward gender roles and sexuality that are closely associated with opposition to the full spectrum of reproductive liberties, from sex education to abortion to demand, favored by pro-choice advocates. That opponents of legal abortion are poorer and less educated than their pro-choice counterparts may be surprising in light of uncontested evidence that bans on abortion primarily burden less affluent citizens. Nevertheless, studies uniformly conclude that "the same individuals who presumably incur the heaviest costs when abortion is legally prohibited also express the strongest verbal disapproval of legalized abortion."[101]

Until the characteristics of most proponents of legal abortion change, neither NARAL nor the Rainbow Coalition will prosper by joining forces. While mobilizing women, poor persons, and persons of color is a valuable political project, such efforts do not increase support for reproductive freedoms. When organizers of poor people's movements proclaim their fierce devotion to abortion on demand, they frequently antagonize less fortunate, socially conservative voters and drive them into the arms of the party espousing pro-business, socially conservative policies.

Proponents of reproductive freedom must recognize that pro-choice supporters and activists are disproportionately drawn from the ranks of well-educated, well-paid, and elite professionals. These affluent Americans typically hold liberal views on secularism, feminism, and sexuality that are closely associated with favorable attitudes toward reproductive choice.[102] For this reason, wealthy individuals are far more inclined to support the full spectrum of reproductive liberties favored by pro-choice advocates. "Abortion," a leading discussion of public opinion polls concludes, "is part of a larger cultural conflict between certain strata of the upper-middle class—the highly educated professionals, scientists, and intellectuals—and the mass of Americans who compose the working and lower-middle classes."[103]

The strength of pro-choice sentiments among elites is particularly startling. A survey of nearly 2,000 leaders of various professions found that two of every three high-status Americans strongly believe that women should have the right to terminate a pregnancy for any reason. Not only do self-labeled liberals and prominent persons employed in such relatively liberal strongholds as the mass media and academia overwhelmingly support abortion on demand, but clear majorities of other elites also favor legal abortion. "Half of the military elite, 62 percent of America's business leaders and almost three in four corporate lawyers" that responded to the questionnaire firmly oppose restrictions on abortion. Indeed, more than half of the "self-labeled conservatives" who participated in that study favor abortion on demand.[104]

Litigation is a promising means for realizing elite desires for legal abortion because the judiciary is the branch of government most dominated by well-paid and highly educated Americans. Today's Supreme Court justices typically have degrees from the best undergraduate and law schools. They usually occupy the highest status positions in the high-status legal profession, and their net wealth often places them among the top 5 percent of all citizens. Personal relationships may also incline federal justices toward elite pro-choice positions. Many know doctors familiar with the horrors of illegal abortion and some have friends and family members who are vocal proponents of reproductive choice.[105] Judicial decisions frequently reflect the justices' privileged status and connections. On matters ranging from school busing and affirmative action to school prayer and flag burning, Supreme Court justices typically make those policies favored by similarly advantaged elites.[106] Given the overwhelming pro-choice sentiments of most privileged citizens, Americans should not have been surprised when the Supreme Court found reproductive rights in the Constitution almost immediately after the American Bar Association voted to support the repeal of pro-life measures.[107]

Elite behavior also explains the electoral victories pro-choice forces enjoyed in the wake of *Webster*. The threatened overruling of *Roe* did not bring forth a surge of new voters into the electoral system. Turnout had been slowly declining in American elections and the reinsertion of abortion into political campaigns did little to reverse this trend.[108] Rather, in response to perceptions that the judiciary might completely abandon abortion rights, some elites—particularly elite women—became more willing to vote their pro-choice preferences in both general elections and party primaries.[109] *Webster* did little to empower the Rainbow Coalition, but that decision does appear responsible for the growing strength and visibility of Republicans for Choice, an affluent organization that champions both laissez-faire economics and laissez-faire abortion policies.[110]

Given their strong support among economic, educational, and political elites, proponents of legal abortion should never suffer electoral defeat. Persons of high socioeconomic status have, on average, greater influence in the selection of candidates and in policy making than other Americans. Affluent Americans control politically valuable resources, they participate in politics more frequently and efficaciously than their fellow citizens, and they even vote more often than less fortunate citizens.[111] Hence, when leading citizens are fairly united on a matter that sharply divides the rest of the populace, elite values should consistently be converted into the law of the land. The modern tradition of nominating only prestigious lawyers to the Supreme Court provides pro-choice forces with another substantial political advantage. Should policy-making responsibility for abortion devolve on a judiciary chosen without an abortion litmus test, the justices will almost certainly favor the liberal reproductive policies that elites prefer.

Abortion rights advocates could not expect to triumph completely during the 1960s and early 1970s, when support for reproductive choice had not yet fully diffused among affluent citizens. Yet something must be amiss for legal abortion to be so shaky twenty years after *Roe*. Pro-life leaders will no doubt claim that real Americans committed to moral values stood up to "cultural elites." Perhaps, but those cultural elites never put up much of a fight. Obsessed with mobilizing the dispossessed, many of whom are pro-life, proponents of legal abortion have not recognized that their fundamental strategic problem is getting affluent Americans who support reproductive choice to convert those policy preferences into political actions.

Tactics

If strong support among elites is the greatest political asset possessed by proponents of legal abortion, then the mercurial nature of that support is their greatest liability. Well-off voters support candidates who favor reproductive choice when no other issues are at stake. Unfortunately, most affluent Americans—and voters in general—are more concerned with matters other than abortion. Although American elites usually favor reproductive choice, their more fundamental commitment to lower taxes played a crucial role in the gradual weakening of abortion rights that took place during the 1980s. When faced with the tantalizing prospect of reducing the capital gains tax, many prosperous, socially liberal citizens seemed willing to risk having abortion recriminalized. In election after election, the vast majority of wealthy citizens favored Republican pro-business candidates who also campaigned on pro-life platforms. Once in office, these pro-business, pro-life officials sponsored new restrictions on abortion and they appointed jurists to the bench who were publicly opposed to *Roe* or who had very conservative judicial philosophies.[112]

This pattern of elite political behavior cannot be easily changed. Appeals to self-interest are probably futile. Affluent citizens suffered the least when abortion was nominally illegal and will suffer the least should abortion be recriminalized. Most wealthy women who live in states that might ban abortion know they will be able to terminate an unwanted pregnancy in states where abortion remains legal. Similarly, many commonly proposed restrictions on abortion have little effect on elites: affluent citizens certainly have little personal incentive to invest their political resources fighting for state policies that subsidize abortion.

Fortunate Americans would consistently vote for candidates who favored reproductive choice if the two major parties differed only on abortion policy. Such matters as the economy, redistributive policies, urban renewal, the environment, agriculture, foreign policy, education, race, drugs, and crime, however, cannot be removed from the political agenda. Indeed, most elites prefer that electoral and legislative battles be fought over the economy and related matters. Socially liberal suburbanites will not support efforts to limit political debate to abortion and other social issues unless assured that the government will make the commercial policies they favor. To some extent, this book is a flagrant attempt to shame affluent Americans into supporting legal abortion. As long as we are able to evade abortion laws, how dare we prevent other citizens from exercising the same reproductive choices![113] Nevertheless, one should not underestimate the power of hypocrisy or denial in American politics, particularly in light of evidence that many citizens firmly (and erroneously) believe that they would not seek an abortion or so counsel a loved one when faced with an unwanted pregnancy.[114]

To enlist the elite support necessary to keep abortion legal, equal choice advocates ought to take political steps that remove reproductive issues from the political agenda. This strategy should be enthusiastically endorsed by most affluent Americans. Members of Republicans for Choice suffer when forced to choose between candidates who will deregulate business and candidates who will deregulate abortion; liberal elites suffer when disagreements over abortion inhibit the mobilization of the Rainbow Coalition. Equal choice efforts to depoliticize abortion will surely be welcomed by those elected officials who did their best over the past twenty years to avoid taking political responsibility for making any abortion policy.[115] Most significantly, removing abortion from electoral politics will keep abortion legal. Contrary to accepted wisdom, the fate of reproductive freedom does not depend on abortion rights activists securing the political power necessary to elect either legislative majorities committed to passing the Freedom of Choice Act or presidents who make self-conscious efforts to appoint pro-choice jurists to the federal bench. Although pro-life forces will achieve their policy objectives only by winning enormous political victories, pro-choice forces will successfully keep abortion legal as long as they avoid major political losses.

Even if *Roe v. Wade* is overruled in the near future, abortion will remain legal in virtually every state. The onus of changing the status quo in a post-*Roe* world will fall heavily on opponents of reproductive choice. That burden, as early proponents of legal abortion know, is exceptionally difficult to overcome. In order to recriminalize abortion, pro-life forces must convince legislative majorities to vote for and, more significantly, *vote on* new restrictions. This preliminary effort to place pro-life policies on the legislative agenda will be vigorously opposed by pro-choice representatives and quietly opposed by those numerous elected officials who would rather not make any abortion policy. The latter, who make up majorities in most legislatures, will maneuver to keep most pro-life bills bottled up in legislative committees.[116] Hence, although pro-choice majorities were needed to repeal previous bans on abortion, proponents of legal abortion need not elect majorities to defeat proposals for new restrictions on abortion. When abortion is legal, abortion remains legal as long as legislative majorities want to avoid abortion issues at all cost.[117]

The elite composition of the judiciary places similarly high burdens on the pro-life movement. Politicians who want *Roe* overruled must take deliberate steps to ensure that new judicial appointees are hostile to abortion rights. Following the practices of the Reagan and Bush administrations, pro-life executives must search for justices who have articulated firm opposition to *Roe* or who have opposed virtually every modern exercise of the judicial power. Equal choice activists need not require such a firm litmus test. Legal elites who have never publicly expressed their views on reproductive policy probably hold pro-choice opinions or hold liberal attitudes on sex and gender roles that are closely associated with pro-choice opinions. Thus, a Court filled with randomly selected justices—justices selected on grounds other than their attitude toward *Roe*—will be almost as supportive of abortion rights as a court that was packed to be so.

Consider the following selection criteria that members of the executive and legislative branches might agree on to avoid the appearance of stacking the federal judiciary with judges predisposed either to support or to oppose the result in *Roe*.

> **1.** Prospective nominees must not have previously expressed clear opinions on whether the judiciary should protect abortion rights.
>
> **2.** Prospective nominees must not be closely affiliated with movements or politicians who either strongly oppose or strongly support judicial protection for abortion rights.
>
> **3.** Prospective nominees must not have a well-defined theory of constitutional interpretation or of the judicial function that clearly entails support for or opposition to judicial protection for abortion rights.

These criteria seem perfectly fair. A president who relied on these standards could not be accused of packing the judiciary with either pro-life or pro-choice jurists. The above guidelines would probably result in the appointment of many prestigious corporate lawyers whose fundamental legal commitments lie in such areas as federal jurisdiction, antitrust, or securities law. Three out of every four elite corporate lawyers, however, strongly favor legal abortion.[118] Thus, a judiciary staffed on the basis of the "neutral" standards listed above would most likely divide 7–2 in favor of sustaining *Roe*. This, not coincidentally, is the precise division of the *Roe* Court, no member of which was appointed because of a previous or supposed position on reproductive issues (or, for that matter, on gender rights). The real lesson of *Roe*, this analysis suggests, is that presidents honestly uninterested in abortion usually appoint justices who uphold abortion rights.[119]

With most legislators unwilling to make abortion policy and the overwhelming majority of lawyers qualified to sit on the Supreme Court favoring legal abortion, proponents of reproductive freedoms need not invest their scarce resources maximizing the number of strong pro-choice representatives elected to public office. Abortion will remain legal and the judiciary will continue adhering to *Roe* as long as equal choice advocates prevent strong pro-life representatives from winning elections or legislative struggles. Thus President Ford, who exhibited little interest in abortion throughout his political career, made as significant a contribution to reproductive choice as many officials who campaigned on pro-choice platforms. While in office, Ford never pushed pro-life legislation with any enthusiasm. When Justice William O. Douglas resigned, Ford appointed Justice John Paul Stevens to the Supreme Court. Stevens, a card-carrying member of the Republican elite, turned out to be a firm supporter of *Roe*. What abortion rights advocates cannot afford is the election of a Ronald Reagan or a George Bush, politicians committed to seeking pro-life political support. Such candidates and only such candidates will, if elected, make self-conscious efforts to regulate abortion and place anti-*Roe* justices on the federal bench.

If, at present, strongly pro-choice officials do little good and indifferent officials do little harm, then proponents of legal abortion should concentrate their political energies on defeating strongly pro-life officials. Equal choice advocates must teach candidates who actively support restrictions on abortion or actively court socially conservative voters that opponents of *Roe* will face well-funded opposition in both their party primaries and in general elections. The primary process may prove a particularly good forum for punishing politicians who oppose legal abortion. Republican elites might not be willing to support a pro-labor, pro-choice Democrat against a pro-business, pro-life Republican in a general election. Such voters, however, should support pro-business, pro-choice Republicans who run against pro-business, pro-life Republicans in GOP primaries.[120]

Proponents of *Roe* should leave alone politicians who, while on the campaign trail and in office, leave the abortion issue alone. The publicly indifferent candidate in many cases may be privately pro-choice. Those who vaguely murmur about too many abortions and who fail to make perfect scores on NARAL quizzes may be reflecting campaign needs rather than expressing heartfelt pro-life values. Whatever the case, proponents of legal abortion must remember that the difference between what a committed pro-life and an indifferent politician will accomplish in the near future is much greater than the corresponding difference between a committed pro-choice and indifferent politician .[121] Hence, not only should equal choice advocates target pro-life officials for electoral defeat, but when considering possible challengers they should be more willing to support a strong candidate who is indifferent on abortion rights than an indifferent candidate who is strong on abortion rights.

Proponents of legal abortion must prevent the two major parties from advocating fundamentally different reproductive policies. When Democrats and Republicans offer voters the same platforms and the same range of pro-choice and pro-life candidates running for public office, dramatic changes in the division of the partisan vote between the two parties on economic or other grounds do not have systemic consequences for abortion policies. The example of 1994 is instructive: many economically liberal pro-choice Democrats were replaced by many economically conservative pro-life Republicans because GOP candidates promised voters tax cuts and stronger measures against crime. Were proponents of legal abortion scattered equally over the political spectrum, that pro-choice debacle would not have occurred. When the public mood turned against the welfare state, pro-life, indifferent, and pro-choice economic conservatives would have replaced, respectively, pro-life, indifferent, and pro-choice economic liberals. Thus, when major parties are no longer useful vehicles for making abortion policy in this indirect fashion, the pro-life movement can win substantial electoral victories only by convincing the public to vote for pro-life policies. Opponents of legal abortion would not be able to piggyback their cause onto economic and foreign policy discontent, as they largely did during the 1980s and in 1994.

Under present conditions, proponents of legal abortion must tolerate a status quo in which the national parties and most state parties take no clear stand on abortion issues. When proponents of legal abortion wish to recruit and support strong pro-choice candidates, they should invest more time and money promoting pro-choice Republicans than pro-choice Democrats. Every effort should be made to strengthen such groups as Republicans for Choice while diminishing the role of such groups as NARAL in the Democratic Party. Of course, when Republicans run pro-life candidates, members of Republicans for Choice should support their opponents. Nevertheless, such persons must stay in the Republican Party where, by preventing the GOP from becoming clearly identified as the pro-life party, pro-choice Republicans do more to further legal abortion than they could do by defecting to the Democrats.

Future efforts to realize equal choice or pro-choice policies should be bipartisan efforts, established in ways that prevent the public from identifying either a pro-life or pro-choice party. Unlike a partisan pro-choice majority coalition, bipartisan pro-choice coalitions do not collapse when the major party that supports reproductive liberty suffers an electoral defeat for reasons having nothing to do with abortion. Pro-life forces can destroy a bipartisan pro-choice majority only by relying on the power of pro-life issues, and these issues have never proven sufficiently compelling for most voters to produce a national majority.

Efforts to keep abortion off the political agenda do not require that activists, candidates, and elected officials tone down their rhetoric in the least. The more citizens who are persuaded that abortion should remain legal, the greater the chance that any pro-choice or equal choice strategy will succeed. Naturally, the cause of reproductive choice would be greatly furthered if a philanthropic multimillionaire should give NARAL the money necessary to ensure that all citizens understand the basic arguments for legal abortion. Still, when proponents of legal abortion are considering how to invest scarce time and money in *electoral and legislative* campaigns, their resources will be best spent in defeating pro-life policies and candidates rather than in advancing pro-choice policies and candidates.

Priorities

Political efforts to depoliticize abortion seem the best means for keeping abortion legal in the near future. When the two major parties are not suitable vehicles for debating abortion policy, legislatures usually bury proposals to ban abortion in committee, and federal courts tend to be staffed by elite jurists who favor legal abortion. Keeping abortion off the political agenda, however, will not make abortion equally accessible to all women. Legislation is needed to fund abortion and, more important, to make abortion providers available in areas where none exist at present. A legislature controlled by representatives committed to making no abortion policy will not pass or even consider such measures. A "neutral" court might find a constitutional obligation to fund abortions, but such policies do little to increase access to abortion, although they do alleviate much misery. No foreseeable tribunal is likely to order states to provide the abortion facilities necessary for all women to be able to terminate an unwanted pregnancy. Hence, political strategies aimed at depoliticizing the abortion debate cannot fully realize some goals of the pro-choice movement.

Nevertheless, pro-choice advocates should seriously consider depoliticizing abortion. Efforts to forge the more powerful coalitions necessary to achieve every goal of the pro-choice movement risk creating and empowering the strong pro-life coalitions that present the greatest threats to the continued vitality of *Roe*. Moreover, legislative and judicial policies that merely keep abortion legal do substantially more to make that procedure available to less fortunate citizens than all other pro-choice measures combined. When abortion is legal, access increases dramatically: legalization substantially lowers the price of terminating a pregnancy and enables philanthropic organizations to assist impoverished women. Millions of poor women and women of color have had safe legal abortions because of *Roe v. Wade*. By contrast, laws denying funding or requiring either parental or spousal consent do not prevent more than one hundred thousand women annually from procuring abortions.

Efforts to remove abortion from the contemporary political agenda do not foreclose other means of making abortion more accessible. When abortion is legal, pro-choice supporters and activists may establish foundations that further defray the costs of abortions. Pro-choice physicians may provide abortion services where they are presently unavailable. Should abortion rights become more secure than at present, NARAL and allied organizations might channel some funds currently spent on electoral, legislative, and judicial campaigns aimed at keeping abortion legal into various efforts to provide abortion services for the needy.

Time favors pro-choice and equal choice advocates. Rights are typically more difficult to grant than to protect. The longer abortion remains legal, the more Americans will adopt ways of living in which abortion plays a crucial backup role. Young men and women who have grown up in a world in which abortion was legal now routinely make choices about career and family based on the assumption that they will be able to control their fertility. These new professionals no longer consider abortion a dirty little secret that cannot be mentioned or advocated in public. As a result, the new generation will fight harder to keep their reproductive freedoms than their parents did to establish those liberties.[122]

Several trends in popular attitudes and actions are strengthening the public's commitment to legal abortion. An increasing number of Americans support the gender roles and sexual behaviors that foster pro-choice attitudes. Pro-choice supporters are fashioned every time a parent encourages a daughter to become a doctor as well as or instead of a mommy, every time a couple decides that they would benefit if both were full-time workers, and every time consenting adults decide they have a right to express themselves sexually in any way they choose. Indeed, movements for legal abortion might ultimately be more successful if, instead of straightforwardly espousing reproductive choice, activists advocated those policies that create the kind of citizens who tend to hold pro-choice values.

PRO-CHOICE STRATEGY AND THE
NEW DEAL PARTY SYSTEM

The abortion controversy takes place against the background of a decaying New Deal party system.[123] The two major partisan coalitions that dominated American politics after World War II were structured to fight over economic issues. Democrats generally favored increased welfare spending; Republicans generally preferred limiting government regulation of economic life. Such sociocultural issues as abortion, by comparison, were rarely on electoral or legislative agendas from the 1930s until the early 1970s. Politicians aspiring for national office took no positions on abortion. Pro-life and pro-choice coalitions did not exist.

The low political salience of reproductive policy proved a mixed blessing for emerging proponents of legal abortion. Most elected officials, committed to taking no responsibility for abortion policy, consistently refused to repeal or to enforce the statutory bans that had been on the books since the late nineteenth century. No president considered abortion when selecting prestigious jurists for judicial appointments. This lack of partisan concern furthered the litigation campaign for abortion rights. When elites in both parties began favoring legal abortion, the elite justices on the Supreme Court proved quite sympathetic to claims that women had a constitutional right to terminate an unwanted pregnancy.

Much to the surprise of many commentators,[124] *Roe* did not settle the abortion controversy. Instead, the decision forced many politicians to take firmer stands on reproductive policy. The resulting infusion of the issue into electoral and legislative politics disrupted the older New Deal order. Pro-life activists with limited interest in laissez-faire economics took partial control of the Republican Party; pro-choice activists with limited interest in economic redistribution took partial control of the Democratic Party. Powerful pockets of resistance remain in both parties. Nevertheless, by the 1992 election, national Democratic officials were committed to making pro-choice policies and national Republican officials were committed to making pro-life policies.

The central strategic question that proponents of legal abortion must at present consider is whether they wish to further or fight the continuing decomposition of the New Deal party system. According to one view, equal choice advocates must continue modifying the New Deal party system in order to bring about an alignment in which one party wholeheartedly supports legal abortion (and the other party wholeheartedly opposes legal abortion). According to another view, equal choice advocates must restore the traditional New Deal partisan coalitions, neither of which articulated clear abortion policies.

Most pro-choice activists prefer the first alternative. Many feminists and social democrats are working to establish a new majoritarian party composed of women, poor persons, persons of color, and a few progressive white males. Once in power, they believe, that coalition will legalize abortion and substantially redistribute economic resources. Liberal reformers committed to building pro-choice majorities, however, fail to recognize that women, poor persons, and persons of color tend, if anything, to favor pro-life policies. Hence, before abortion can mobilize any kind of rainbow coalition, abortion rights activists must persuade less fortunate citizens that they ought to support reproductive liberties. Such efforts may not be quixotic fantasies: much of this book lays out political and constitutional arguments in favor of legal abortion that average citizens might find more convincing than conventional liberal or feminist appeals. Nevertheless, activists must remember that their sincere belief that some policy substantially improves the lot of any group does not necessarily mean that most of the persons in that group support that policy. Until more evidence suggests that less fortunate Americans are the leading proponents of abortion on demand, pro-choice and equal choice advocates must consider other strategies for keeping abortion legal.

Some more conservative members of the Democratic Party have devised an alternative approach. In their view, Democratic candidates might win the crucial votes of suburban Republicans by de-emphasizing that party's traditional commitment to economic redistribution and emphasizing its present commitment to legal abortion. The relative success of some "New Democrats" and, in a different sense, Ross Perot, suggests that pro-choice, pro-business platforms do appeal to economically conservative, socially liberal voters. Nevertheless, other proponents of legal abortion find this strategy unsatisfactory. Given their broader commitment to progressive reform, the leaders of many abortion rights groups will not voluntarily abandon their hopes for social and economic justice merely to secure the foundations for abortion rights.

Both liberal and conservative efforts to forge pro-choice majorities are also problematic because these strategies unwittingly assist pro-life forces. Opponents of legal abortion must capture a political party and place the reversal of *Roe* on the political agenda if they are to reregulate abortion. Pro-life activists must control the executive branch of government in order to pack the federal judiciary with anti-*Roe* jurists; they must control Congress and state legislatures in order to have the power necessary to vote on and vote for measures that ban abortion. Too few voters, however, think abortion an important enough issue when making electoral decisions to provide either proponents or opponents of legal abortion with clear control over these institutions. Therefore, pro-life activists can achieve their goals only by attaching their star to an existing party, gaining enough control in primary elections over that coalition to ensure that most of its candidates are pro-life, and then winning general elections when those candidates attract voters for reasons other than their position on abortion policy. Pro-choice efforts to capture one party facilitate this pro-life effort to capture the other party. Efforts to forge a pro-choice majority siphon proponents of legal abortion from the increasingly pro-life coalition and encourage those who oppose legal abortion to leave the increasingly pro-choice coalition. Then when the economy goes sour while the party of legal abortion is in power, the pro-life party takes office.

If pro-life activists must align the two parties on the basis of abortion to achieve their preferred policies, then pro-choice strategists should keep the parties evenly balanced on abortion. Rather than forge a pro-choice majority, proponents of legal abortion should prevent the establishment of a pro-life coalition. Thus, equal choice advocates must fight to strengthen a New Deal party system in which the major coalitions would rather fight over taxes than abortion. New Deal Democrats and Republicans have no desire to make any abortion policy. As a result, these traditional party politicians can be trusted to keep both pro-life and pro-choice proposals safely bottled up in legislative committees. In 1970, preserving the status quo meant that abortion remained illegal. In the 1990s, however, preserving the status quo means that abortion remains legal.

Federal judges in a strengthened New Deal system are unlikely to overrule *Roe*. Politicians who do not want responsibility for making reproductive policy will not appoint or confirm jurists known to oppose judicial solicitude for abortion rights. Instead, prestigious lawyers with no known opinions on reproductive choice will sit on the federal bench. The vast majority of these jurists will favor abortion on demand and be disinclined to abandon precedents granting all women the constitutional right to terminate a pregnancy.

Keeping abortion off the political agenda is a way to realize the pro-choice demand that abortion rights "should depend on the outcome of no elections." Too often, unfortunately, that expression is used as a pious slogan rather than as a blueprint for political action. Ritual chants that fundamental rights should not depend on a majoritarian decision do not make that so. Legal abortion will indeed be best secured when reproductive choice depends on the outcome of no election. Nevertheless, much hard political work remains to be done and tough political choices will have to be made for abortion policies to regain their immunity to shifts in American partisan politics.

The Allure of Pro-Life

PRO-LIFE ARGUMENTS are philosophically alluring. Revolutionary patriots cry "Give me liberty or give me death," but most citizens think life is a more fundamental right than freedom or choice. Communities punish murderers more severely than kidnappers. Federal justices recognize "the penalty of death is qualitatively different from a sentence of imprisonment, however long."[1] Basic notions of culpability also support pro-life policies. The unborn are not morally responsible for interfering with their would-be mother's liberty. In contrast, most adults can in theory control their fertility simply by controlling their behavior. Hence, imposing the costs of unwanted pregnancies on the persons whose sexual activity was responsible for conception places the burden of abortion on the parties best able to avoid that tragic choice between fetal life and procreative liberty. The case against *Roe* seems even stronger than the case against legal abortion. The Constitution does not explicitly protect abortion rights, and Americans have not historically thought that abortion is a fundamental liberty.[2]

Nevertheless, citizens need a strong reality check before they sign up to lobby against the Freedom of Choice Act or join Operation Rescue. Pro-life arguments retain their seductive power only when detached from their contemporary political and social moorings. The case for overruling *Roe* and recriminalizing abortion becomes far less enticing when citizens start comparing the probable consequences of actual reproductive policies. Contrary to much academic writing and partisan rhetoric, the current abortion debate does not present a stark choice between fetal life and procreative liberty. Statutory bans on abortion do not prevent many women from terminating unwanted pregnancies, and pro-life laws in action violate our constitutional commitment to equal justice and rule by law. Official failures to enforce pro-life measures also warp democratic processes. Citizens who enjoy practical immunities from laws banning abortion have little personal incentive to express their pro-choice convictions when voting or making other political decisions. Finally, and perhaps most important, the ability of most privileged families to evade restrictions on abortion distorts public debate over whether persons are able and ought to be required to make the significant sacrifices that pro-life commitments entail.

Americans committed to pro-life values should at present fight harder for policies that prevent women from having unwanted pregnancies than for policies that prevent women from terminating unwanted pregnancies. Statutory bans on abortion rarely affect reproductive choices. Women tend to abort a significant percentage of their unwanted pregnancies no matter what the law on the books says. However, many men and women respond favorably to sex education and contraceptive programs that help sexually active persons control their fertility. Heterosexual citizens living in the 1990s may be unwilling to abandon the pleasures of lovemaking, but most want to reduce their chances of conceiving a new life. Socially conservative voters who believe that procreation is the primary purpose of human sexuality may object to government programs that help couples engage in sex "without consequences." Those who claim that "life is an almost absolute value in history,"[3] however, cannot be deterred by such considerations. If better sex education and contraceptive distribution are the best ways to reduce abortions,[4] then better sex education and contraceptive distribution must be the first priority of a committed *pro-life* movement.

Statutory bans on abortion have been a particularly poor means for protecting the unborn because such measures are consistently administered in ways that intentionally discriminate against poor persons and persons of color. American law enforcement officials made a mockery of the Fourteenth Amendment's promise that all persons will be equal under the law by consciously ignoring private physicians who openly flouted abortion laws on the books. The racially and economically exclusive gray market that numerous government authorities helped establish and maintain enabled affluent citizens to satisfy their demand for safe abortions while leaving less fortunate Americans with an unhappy choice: bear an unwanted child or hazard a potentially dangerous black-market procedure. Rule by discretion replaced rule by law when police and prosecutors administering pro-life measures were unconstrained either by the purposes that statutory bans on abortion might serve or by the legitimate limitations of law enforcement. No reason exists for thinking that new bans on abortion will be better enforced. If communities are allowed to recriminalize abortion, wealth and whim will again determine who has access to safe abortions.

These selective and arbitrary legal practices are undemocratic. Majorities, democratic theorists generally agree, can be trusted to protect fundamental rights only when they govern themselves. Thus, elected officials and influential citizens who realize their private family planning practices will at most be inconvenienced by whatever statutory bans the legislature passes do not actually engage in self-government when they regulate abortion. The existence of abortion bans on the books may seem grounded in a societal consensus that abortion is wrong, but such rules apparently remain in state penal codes only because they do not sufficiently burden committed or potential pro-choice citizens.

The rhetorical power of anti-*Roe* arguments against judicial solicitude for abortion rights also fades in the light of social and political conditions. The phrase "unelected judges ought not second-guess the policy choices made by elected officials" has a nice ring. In practice, however, most elected representatives do everything in their power to avoid making abortion policy. As a result, abortion law in action bears very little relationship to the language of abortion law on the books or to the purposes that originally animated the passage of pro-life measures. For these reasons, the substantially underenforced pro-life laws that *Roe* declared unconstitutional did not reflect any authoritative legislative choice or present public condemnation of reproductive freedom.

This communal failure to enforce statutory bans on abortion contaminates public deliberation over reproductive policies. Pro-life positions may seem alluring only because persons advocating such positions can announce their willingness to accept the onerous burdens associated with bearing and raising an additional child while in fact retaining the power to back out of that commitment when the crucial point of decision is at hand. The numerous pro-life advocates who procure abortions are not insincere. Rather, like other Americans, they simply overestimate their capacity for selfless action when the possibility of sacrifice seems remote.[5]

Other citizens may be more steadfast, but I am painfully aware that my weak philosophical opposition to abortion is infected by my family's de facto immunity from proposed bans on reproductive choice. I think of myself as the sort of person who would make the significant personal sacrifices necessary to raise another child should my wife or one of my daughters experience an unwanted pregnancy. "Let the law ban abortion!" I tell myself. "I am sufficiently altruistic/heroic to bear any burdens that may result." In more self-reflective moments, however, I realize I cannot be certain what I would do should that fateful day arrive. Is there any reason for believing I am somehow different from other persons who erroneously thought they would have the courage of their convictions and parent every child they conceived? I might be relieved if my strongly pro-choice physician-spouse discreetly arranged a safe abortion for, say, my fifteen-year-old pregnant daughter. Perhaps my belief that abortion is a moral wrong simply bolsters my unrealistic self-image. I do resent insinuations that my philosophical instincts are pro-life only because, as a man, I am somehow incapable of sympathizing with the burden an unwanted pregnancy would place on my wife and daughters. Nevertheless, I cannot say with the confidence necessary to support new restrictions on abortion that

I would be pro-life if I really knew that, in our circumstances, pro-life really meant no choice.

My circumstances are not unique. No one who enjoys the status necessary to influence reproductive policy need fear that their procreative choices will depend on the next election or judicial decision. This simple truth structures and perverts late-twentieth-century American abortion debates. Privileged pro-lifers believe they are committed to parenting every child they sire, knowing they will have the power to change their minds should the unexpected pregnancy occur. Pro-choice Republican suburbanites vote for pro-life, antitax candidates, knowing they are not really placing their privately financed means of controlling their fertility in jeopardy. Affluent pro-choice activists adopt all-or-nothing strategies when litigating the constitutional status of abortion rights, knowing they will still have access to abortion almost on demand should *Roe* be overruled. The result has been an abortion controversy long on political posturing but short on serious analysis of the actual costs and benefits of different abortion policies.

Abortion issues deserve a more honest and intelligent debate. Pro-life positions may charm many Americans, and the number of abortions performed annually is indeed scandalous. Nevertheless, our society is pro-choice in practice. Statutory restrictions on reproductive liberty do little to lessen the demand for safe abortions and result in law enforcement practices that are a national disgrace. Pro-life laws that are honored only in the breach have no business being in the penal code of a nation constitutionally committed to equal justice and rule by law. If nothing else, American abortion policies teach the valuable lesson that the ignorance and hypocrisy of the majority pose as great a threat as the more-often attacked tyranny of the majority to a just democratic order.

Introduction
Sublime Theories, Ugly Facts

1. 410 U.S. 113 (1973).

2. Following conventional scholarly practice, I describe proponents and opponents of abortion rights as pro-choice and pro-life, respectively, even though, as Kristin Luker points out, "each side is emphatic that the label used by the other is a mockery of what it is really up to" (Luker 1984b, p. 2 n. *). See Cook, Jelen, and Wilcox 1992, p. xvi.

3. Piercy 1988, p. x.

4. See chap. II.

5. The leadership of the Democratic party is firmly pro-choice and is likely to remain so for at least a generation.

6. See Craig and O'Brien 1993, pp. 284–92.

7. See chap. II.

At 1991 prices, taking one of my daughters on an emergency two-day trip from Austin, Texas (where we were then living) to Hartford, Connecticut, for the purpose of obtaining a second trimester abortion would cost approximately $2,700 (two round-trip tickets on American Airlines at $902 each, accommodations for two nights for two persons at the Holiday Inn at $109 a night, a second trimester abortion for $495, and $200 in assorted expenses [food, transportation]). Needless to say, we would probably be able to obtain as safe an abortion for much less money (the airfare alone would be a thousand dollars less if we could schedule the trip two weeks in advance). My family would prefer spending the money on a European vacation, but the loss would not put a serious dent in our budget. I could more than recoup our losses by teaching one six-week course during the following summer.

8. Olsen 1989, p. 105; Braucher 1991, p. 609; Hirschman 1988, p. 181. See also Hirschman 1988, pp. 224–30; Estrich and Sullivan 1989, p. 130; Baer 1991, pp. 291–93; Robertson 1994, p. 25.

Responding to claims that I might feel more threatened by recent political and judicial developments if I were a woman is difficult because I am not a woman. On the other hand, I am Jewish but I do not worry about a serious resurgence of anti-Semitism in the United States even though much of the cultural right wing seems to be as hostile to liberal Jewish intellectuals as they are to abortion rights (see, e.g., A. Dworkin 1983, pp. 107–46). More generally, although I understand why female (and male) professors and activists might find any call for restrictive abortion policies distressing, I know of no serious scholarship that suggests that elite reproductive choices are likely to be significantly curtailed in the near future. Indeed, twenty pages after Frances Olsen asserts that women of all classes feel threatened by the holding of *Webster v. Reproductive Health Services*, 492 U.S. 490 (1989), she notes that justices "come from a socioeconomic class that has long been able to obtain abortions" (Olsen 1989, p. 123). Law professors at U.C.L.A. presumably belong to that same socioeconomic class.

9. See Graber 1993b; chap. V.

10. See Luker 1984b; F. Ginsburg 1989. See also chap. V.

11. Roberts 1992, p. 312. See *Congressional Record*, 95th Cong., 1st sess., 1977, 123, pt. 16:19700 (quoting Representative Henry Hyde, R-Ill.).

12. Funding programs marginally increase the federal deficit and enable poor women to procure abortions without sacrificing basic necessities. Nevertheless, the Hyde Amendment and related measures are rarely debated in those terms.

13. 505 U.S. ___, 120 L. Ed. 2d 674 (1992).

14. 492 U.S. 490 (1989).

15. The limited impact of Supreme Court decisions permitting states to regulate abortion is discussed later in this introduction and in chap. II.

16. Roberts 1992, p. 192; Culp 1994, p. 196.

17. When women are unable to obtain wanted abortions, the barrier is more likely to be practical—the lack of a nearby provider—than legal.

18. Hamilton, Madison, and Jay 1961, pp. 352–53.

19. My own philosophical instincts are weakly pro-life and I do not believe the Constitution protects abortion per se. See conclusion.

20. One study found that police officers failed to arrest criminal suspects in half the cases in which they had probable cause to believe a crime had been committed (Reiss 1971). See J. Goldstein 1960. The Constitution permits and in some cases may even require such discretion. See *Town of Newton v. Rumery*, 480 U.S. 386, 396 (1987); *Wayte v. United States*, 470 U.S. 598, 607–8 (1985); *Williams v. Illinois*, 399 U.S. 235, 243 (1970); *Williams v. New York*, 337 U.S. 241, 247 (1949); Note 1988, pp. 1620–21.

21. The relationship between equal choice and failed constitutional attacks on the death penalty is discussed at length in chap. III.

22. See chap. V.

23. See chap. II.

24. *Congressional Record*, 95th Cong., 1st sess., 1977, 123, pt. 16:19700.

25. Nor does any precise formula exist for determining how confident persons must be that abortion is a serious evil before they can reject equal choice arguments.

26. Professor Stephen Carter of Yale Law School bemoans that "as each new article or book comes out, one is left with the dreadful and yet unavoidable sense that everything has been said. Not only that, but most of it was said ten years ago. . . . As eyes glaze over, it often has seemed that during the past two decades that only the names of the authors who offer the arguments have changed" (Carter 1991a, p. 2747). See L. Epstein and Kobylka 1992, p. 272 (noting that the numerous briefs in *Webster* all essentially repeated the same arguments that had been made in the past).

27. Blake and Del Pinal 1981, p. 312. See Blake and Del Pinal 1981, p. 318 ("although out-and-out negation is rare, so is support for basic planks of the pro-choice platform"); Lamanna 1984, pp. 4–6, 9; Robertson 1994, pp. 241–42 n. 4; Craig and O'Brien 1993, pp. 245–51.

28. See Lamanna 1984, p. 23.
29. See Bobbitt 1982 (discussing various forms of constitutional argument).
30. R. Dworkin 1978, p. 149.
31. 481 U.S. 279 (1987).
32. See D. Harris 1994.

Chapter I
The Clash of Absolutes Revisited

1. See Craig and O'Brien 1993, pp. 35–36 ("the rhetoric of war is a prominent feature of abortion politics").
2. R. Dworkin 1993, p. 29.
3. Tribe 1990a. See Robertson 1994, p. 48.
4. Rosenblatt 1992, p. 50.
5. Rosenblatt 1992, p. 50.
6. See Rawls 1971.
7. For a general discussion of gross concepts in political argument, see I. Shapiro 1989.
8. See sources cited in nn. 81–84.
9. See Pound 1910.
10. Reagan 1991b, p. 6
11. Llewellyn 1960, p. 3.
12. Tribe does recognize that before *Roe*, "legal abortion remained available for a variety of conditions that were not explicitly included in the statute books" (1990a, p. 38). He does not, however, treat this insight as having any normative significance.
13. Olsen 1989, p. 107. Similar assertions can be found in virtually every legal commentary on abortions rights.
14. See sources cited in n. 19, below; see also introduction, n. 8.
15. Glendon 1987, pp. 21, 15.
16. Ely 1973, pp. 923, 936 n. 94. Glendon 1987, pp. 59–60, does note that "strict and lenient laws do not appear to be related in any simple way to abortion rates." Nevertheless, she implies that different abortion statutes in the United States may fairly reflect practice (pp. 47–49) and at no point attaches any constitutional significance to disparities between abortion law and abortion practice.
17. See chap. II.
18. See Luker 1984b, pp. 88, 94; Garrow 1994, pp. 411, 457; Sarvis and Rodman 1973, p. 51. See also chap. II.
19. Law 1984, p. 1017. See Rubenfeld 1989, p. 788 (restrictions on abortion "take diverse women with every variety of career, life-plan, and so on, and make mothers of them all"); Tribe 1990a, p. 104; Rhode 1989, p. 214; sources cited in introduction, n. 8.
20. See chap. II.
21. Burt 1992, p. 368.
22. See chap. II.
23. *Harris v. McRae*, 448 U.S. 297 (1980); *Maher v. Roe*, 432 U.S. 464 (1977).

24. West 1990, p. 51; MacKinnon 1991, p. 1320. See *Harris*, at 338 (Marshall, J., dissenting); Rhode 1989, pp. 213–14; Olsen 1989, pp. 105, 113, 116; Colker 1992, pp. 136–41; Milbauer 1983, p. 270 (quoting Rhonda Copelon); Robertson 1994, p. 47. See also Ely 1980, p. 246 n. 38; L. Epstein and Kobylka 1992, p. 136.

25. *Harris*, at 338 (Marshall, J., dissenting). For a discussion of the impact of funding cut-offs, see chap. II.

26. The impact of legal abortion is discussed at length in chap. II.

27. Dellinger and Sperling 1989, p. 108. See Olsen 1989, p. 123; Rhode 1989, p. 206; R. Dworkin 1989a, p. 49; R. Dworkin 1989b, p. 49; Karst 1977, p. 59; Estrich and Sullivan 1989, p. 154; R. Ginsburg 1985, p. 380 n. 36 (citing other sources). See also Glendon 1987 (discussed above at n. 16); Cohen 1989, p. 1248 n. 37.

28. See Glendon 1987, pp. 2, 45, 47; Perry 1988, p. 177; R. Epstein 1974, p. 168; Bryson et al. 1989, p. 21 n. 15. A number of commentators who support legal abortion, most notably Justice Ruth Bader Ginsburg, suggest that the Supreme Court curtailed public debate on abortion by handing down too specific a decision in *Roe*. See R. Ginsburg 1992, pp. 1198–99, 1205; Burt 1992, pp. 357–58; Rosenblatt 1992, p. 34.

29. See R. Dworkin 1989a, p. 50; Tribe 1990b, p. A13. See also Estrich and Sullivan 1989, pp. 150–55.

30. See Luker 1975, pp. 125–26, 137; F. Ginsburg 1989, pp. 43, 72; Craig and O'Brien 1993, p. 32; L. Epstein and Kobylka 1992, pp. 207, 292; E. Rubin 1987, pp. 186–88; Faux 1988, p. 179. See also Cohen 1989, p. 1236 ("we cannot stop legislating and adjudicating about [abortion], or talking and writing about it, or imagining and even imaging it"). For the rare law professor who recognizes how *Roe* promoted public and legislative dialogue, see Colker 1992, pp. 115–25.

Burt's claim that *Roe* "redirected the attention of abortion reform (pro-choice) advocates away from their partly successful campaign for legislative change" (1992, pp. 357–58) is similarly belied by the available empirical evidence. Studies of abortion politics consistently find that the leading proponents of legal abortion had eschewed grassroots mobilization in favor of litigation long before *Roe* was handed down. See, e.g., L. Epstein and Kobylka 1992, pp. 154–55, 160, 211, 351 n. 47; sources cited in chap. V, nn. 2–8.

31. Empirical facts, of course, are rarely independent of the theories they support; see Kuhn 1970. Some scholars even assert that normative theories inevitably predetermine the results of empirical investigation. Most academic lawyers, however, rarely bother conducting any empirical investigation before making their definite assertions about abortion politics.

32. Tinnelly 1959, p. 190.

33. Noonan 1970; S. Callahan 1984, p. 296; Meehan 1984, p. 146. See Hentoff 1992b. For general discussions of pro-life feminism and pro-life feminist readings, see Sweet 1985; S. Callahan and D. Callahan 1984; Mensch and Freeman 1991, p. 934; Tatalovich and Daynes 1981, p. 155.

34. See Noonan 1979; Herbert 1965, pp. 284–85, 292.

35. Perry 1988, p. 174. See Bork 1990, p. 111; R. Epstein 1974, pp. 169–70; Ely 1973, pp. 924–26.

36. R. Epstein 1974, p. 170. See Perry 1988, pp. 174–75; Ely 1973, pp. 929–30; J. Rosen 1993b, pp. 38–40.

37. Dellinger and Sperling 1989, p. 106.

38. Those who attack *Roe* also fail to explain why communities whose penal codes declare that human life begins at conception nevertheless permit residents to obtain in other localities what, by statutory definition, is the murder of a state citizen. See R. Dworkin 1989b, p. 50; Dellinger and Sperling 1989, p. 108.

39. These studies are discussed at length in chap. II.

40. Syska, Hilgers, and O'Hare 1981, especially pp. 164–69; Rosenberg 1992, pp. 353–54 (noting the problems with data on abortion fatalities); E. Gold, Erhardt, Jacobziner, and Nelson 1965 (data on race and abortion fatalities). The Syska, Hilgers, and O'Hare study is cited by Krason 1984, p. 303. Another study that opponents of *Roe* frequently cite determined the national abortion rate by surveying married white Protestants, the demographic group least likely to terminate an unwanted pregnancy. See Louisell and Noonan 1970, p. 242 (citing Taylor 1944, p. 18); Krason 1984, p. 303 (citing the same).

41. Some opponents of abortion point to a study done by researchers at the CDC that found that approximately 130,000 illegal abortions were performed in 1972. See, e.g., Reardon 1987, pp. 287–91 (citing Cates and Rochat 1976). These pro-life advocates "forget" to note that over 600,000 legal abortions were performed that year. Needless to say, 1972 figures provide a very poor basis for estimating the number of illegal abortions performed before 1967, when fewer than 8,000 legal abortions were performed annually. Indeed, given the transitional status of abortion in 1972, no data confined to that year can offer a reliable picture of abortion practices during the 1950s and 1960s.

42. See chap. II. In their eagerness to discredit pro-choice figures, some opponents of legal abortion criticize studies for flaws that indicate that the researchers underestimated the total number of illegal abortions. John Finnis and Stephen Krason lambast the Kinsey Institute's claim that 600,000 illegal abortions were performed annually during the 1950s because that study underrepresented persons of color and urban dwellers. Persons of color, urban dwellers, and unmarried women (also underrepresented), however, have much higher illegal abortion rates than the women Kinsey surveyed. Hence, if anything, Finnis and Krason demonstrate that no fewer than 600,000 abortions were taking place annually during the 1950s (Krason 1984, p. 302; Finnis 1970, p. 181). See also Louisell and Noonan 1970, p. 242.

43. 52 Fed. Reg. 33210 (1987); Rosoff 1988, p. 317.

44. McWilliams 1991, p. 11. The Family Protection Act of 1981 would have denied federal funds to any program that "provid[ed] any *contraceptive device* or abortion service . . . to an unmarried minor" without first notifying his or her parents (*Congressional Record*, 97th Cong., 1st sess., 1981, 127, pt. 10:12699; emphasis added). See Barber 1984, p. 67. The brief for the American Historical Association in *Webster* similarly notes that concern for the fetus has never been the primary force behind movements for restricting abortion (Spillenger, Larson, and Law 1989). See Gordon 1976, p. 415 (noting the "fus[ion of] abortion with contraception").

45. Rosoff 1988, p. 320.

46. Hesburgh 1980, p. viii.

47. Vinovskis 1980b, p. 246. In March 1995, congressional Republicans nominally committed to reducing abortion voted overwhelmingly to deny additional welfare benefits to unmarried mothers under eighteen and women who had babies while on government assistance, even though such policies clearly make abortion a more attractive choice for poor women. To their credit, the Roman Catholic Church, the National Right to Life Committee, and several prominent pro-life Republicans vigorously fought against that measure. See Pear 1995, p. A1.

48. Bork actually makes this argument when defending restrictions on birth control, but he explicitly asserts that the same logic applies to all constitutional arguments (1990, p. 257).

49. Bork 1990, p. 258.

50. For evidence that this latter fear inspired many restrictions on abortion, see Mohr 1978, pp. 166–67; Siegal 1992, pp. 297–99; Rosoff 1988, p. 313.

51. Ely 1973, pp. 923–24. See also R. Epstein 1974, p. 175 (the existence of abortion laws demonstrates that popular majorities support pro-life policies). Ely admits that "a law that has been neither legislatively considered *nor enforced* for decades" might present a more problematic case (1973, p. 935 n. 89; emphasis added). Nevertheless, as long as state statutes and judicial decisions have some effect on abortion practices, conventional philosophical and constitutional defenses of pro-life policies regard such measures as necessarily representing the will of present majorities.

52. Bork 1990, p. 116; see also p. 264 ("when a court strikes down a statute, it *always* denies the freedom of the people who voted for the representatives who enacted the law"; emphasis added). See Perry 1988, p. 175; Bickel 1975, pp. 28–29.

53. J. Rosen 1993b, p. 38.

54. R. Epstein 1974, p. 168 n. 34. See Bork 1990, p. 113 ("a statute may be enacted for one reason, retained for another, and be none the less constitutional for that").

55. Pro-life advocates, I should note, argue that restrictions on abortion were originally designed to protect fetal life.

56. Ely 1973, p. 935 n. 89.

57. *Roe v. Wade*, 410 U.S. 153 (1973); R. Dworkin 1989a, p. 51. See R. Dworkin 1992b; R. Dworkin 1989a, p. 50; Heymann and Barzelay 1973; Rubenfeld 1989; Dellinger and Sperling 1989, p. 93; Estrich and Sullivan 1989, p. 125; Robertson 1994.

58. Sands 1966, pp. 304–6; G. Williams 1966, pp. 197–201; Model Penal Code 1980 230.3, p. 428; R. Dworkin 1992b, p. 403.

59. *Roe*, at 158. See R. Dworkin 1992b, p. 398.

60. Thomson 1971.

61. West 1988, pp. 59–60, 66; Rhode 1989, p. 212. See Law 1984, p. 1017; R. Dworkin 1992b, p. 395.

62. Sunstein 1992, p. 31; Tribe 1990a, p. 131. See Dellinger and Sperling 1989, pp. 92–93 ("restrictive state abortion laws require women, and only women, to endure government-mandated physical intrusions significantly more substantial than those the Court has held to violate the constitutional principle of

bodily integrity"); Koppelman 1990; Regan 1979; Rhode 1989, p. 212; Calabresi 1991, pp. 91–96; Robertson 1994, pp. 66–67. See also J. Rosen 1993b, p. 40. But see Rhode 1989, p. 385 n. 27 (expressing some doubts about the Good Samaritan constitutional defense of abortion rights).

63. Garrow 1994, p. 705; Estrich and Sullivan 1989, p. 130.

64. The rhetoric of choice also suggests that a man has a right not to become an involuntary father whenever a woman he impregnates elects to carry the pregnancy to term. Thus, as presently conceptualized, liberal pro-choice arguments either entail that men have the right to force women to have unwanted abortions or that men have the right not to support their biological children. See Feaver, Kling, and Plotchan 1992–93, pp. 212–13.

65. Torres and Forrest 1988, p. 170. The extremely low incidence of abortion after rape casts doubt on Sunstein's suggestion that "the only realistic way to protect th[e] right [to abortion after rape] seems to be to create a general right to abortion" (Sunstein 1992, p. 40). A strict requirement that women prove they were raped in order to obtain a legal abortion might force a majority of the relatively few pregnant rape (or incest) victims to bear their assailant's child. At some point, however, a legal system must tolerate some grievous injustices or cease to function. No one would suggest we should abandon the criminal justice system because that is the only realistic way to prevent innocent persons from being sentenced to prison. Hence, if virtually all abortions are an unjustified taking of human life, the social benefits of statutory bans on abortion probably outweigh the hideous cost such policies impose on those few rape victims who fail to report the crime against them in the time necessary to secure a legal abortion.

66. See R. Dworkin 1993, pp. 169–71; R. Goldstein 1988, pp. 3, 47–48, 54–62.

67. Bork 1990, p. 111.

68. Robert Goldstein grossly miscites Kristin Luker's *Taking Chances* when he declares that "students of female sexual acculturation [maintain] that the misinformation that young women have acquired by education and experience . . . lead them to believe that impregnation is so unlikely that the nonuse of contraception cannot by itself be said to make impregnation an intended or reasonably foreseeable outcome of any one act of intercourse" (1988, p. 14). Luker's work, discussed at length later in this chapter, set out to "refut[e] the thesis that unwanted pregnancies result from a lack of contraceptive skills" (Luker 1975, p. 21). Thus, *Taking Chances* explores why many women with the knowledge necessary to avoid pregnancy nevertheless take contraceptive risks; see Luker 1975, pp. xv–xvii. The reasons Luker gives for this phenomenon do support legal abortion rights (see pp. 140–47), but no pro-choice commentator has integrated her actual findings into a constitutional defense of the result in *Roe*.

69. Koppelman 1990, p. 504.

70. American Psychiatric Association 1994.

71. Of the 130,000 women who responded to Ann Lander's question, 72 percent were willing to adjure forever "the act." Nearly half of those women were under 40. See Grossvogel 1987, p. 216.

72. D. Granberg 1981, pp. 161–62. For similar findings, see Fried 1988, p. 151; Luker 1984b.

73. Quoted in Arnold 1962, p. 101.

74. R. Dworkin 1989a, pp. 50–51. For similar claims, see Tribe 1990a, pp. 6–7, 16; Rhode 1989, p. 210.

75. R. Dworkin 1989a, p. 51. Dworkin also regards legislative efforts to restrict abortion as undemocratic, because such "moral issues are particularly likely to produce a paralysis of legislative inertia" and because "democracy . . . requires a system of individual rights guaranteeing the integrity of each person's basic interests and needs" (p. 51 with n. 18).

76. See L. Epstein and Kobylka 1992, p. 232; and see chap. V, which questions how influential pro-life voters have been. See also Tribe 1990a, pp. 149, 165.

77. See, e.g., Luker 1984b; Rodman, Sarvis, and Bonar 1987.

78. See Page and Shapiro 1992; Popkin 1991. For a sampling of the early literature, see Campbell, Converse, Miller, and Stokes 1960; Converse 1964.

79. See, e.g., Tufte 1975; Kramer 1971.

80. Academic disputes rage over who is a feminist. See Bartlett 1990, pp. 833–36; MacKinnon 1987, pp. 198–205. This book treats as feminists persons who label themselves as feminists or who make claims similar to those made by persons who so label themselves. Not all self-described feminists, however, are pro-choice. A small pro-life feminist group has also been active in the abortion controversy. See Sweet 1985; see also sources cited in n. 33.

81. Rhode 1990, p. 621 (quoting, in part, Bartlett 1990, p. 831); Binion 1993, p. 143. For general overviews of feminist critical theory, see Rhode 1990; A. Harris 1990.

82. MacKinnon 1991, p. 1324. But see Bartlett 1990 (discussing various feminist legal methods and the extent to which they differ from masculine reasoning).

83. Law 1984, p. 55; MacKinnon 1989, pp. 249, xii. See Rhode 1989, pp. 214 ("we need less preoccupation with abstract rights and more concern with the context in which they are exercised"), 315–17; Binion 1993, p. 143. See also Braucher 1991, p. 607 (asserting that Laurence Tribe fails "to take seriously women's situations, subjective experiences, aspirations and values").

84. West 1990, p. 84.

85. MacKinnon 1987, p. 94.

86. MacKinnon 1989, p. 193; MacKinnon 1984, pp. 46–48.

87. MacKinnon 1989, pp. 46–48.

88. MacKinnon 1991, p. 1312. See Olsen 1989, p. 124 (the "assumption" that women "exercise a free autonomous choice regarding sexual intercourse" "overlooks the level of force and coercion that governs that life of many women"); Koppelman 1990, pp. 503–4.

89. MacKinnon 1991, p. 1312. Indeed, Ruth Colker suggests that physical coercion is responsible for a significant number of unwanted pregnancies (1992, pp. 42–46, 68–69). But see Torres and Forrest 1988, p. 170 (finding that coercion is responsible for only 1 percent of all abortions).

90. See, e.g., Luker 1975, especially p. 23.

91. MacKinnon 1984, p. 47. See Koppelman 1990, p. 505.

92. MacKinnon 1989, p. 188.

93. MacKinnon 1984, p. 47.

94. MacKinnon 1984, pp. 50–51. For similar arguments, see Olsen 1989, pp. 112, 124–25; Koppelman 1990, pp. 503–5.

95. See especially MacKinnon 1979.

96. MacKinnon 1989, p. 299 n. 3. For Luker's credentials as a feminist, see MacKinnon 1989, p. xv.

97. See Luker 1975, p. xvii.

98. Luker 1975, p. 57.

99. Henshaw and Silverman 1988, p. 167.

100. Luker 1975, pp. 63, 68–69.

101. Luker 1975, pp. 49–51.

102. Luker 1975, pp. 59–60, 49–50. See also Rodman, Sarvis, and Bonar 1987, pp. 77–78 (citing numerous studies that reach similar conclusions).

103. MacKinnon 1989, pp. 184–85.

104. Luker 1975, pp. 56–59. A few women indicated that their lovers had philosophical opposition to birth control (p. 57).

Taking Chances also challenges MacKinnon's assertion that "a good user of contraception can be presumed sexually available and, among other consequences, raped with relative impunity" (MacKinnon 1989, p. 185). Luker found that many women avoid ongoing use of contraception not because they fear unwanted sex, but because these women believe that were they to give indications that they are "frankly expecting sex," they would "not be courted on the same terms as a woman whose sexual availability is more ambiguous" (1975, pp. 51, 49).

105. See generally MacKinnon 1989, pp. 83–105.

106. As this suggests, women (and men) may want sex for reasons other than arousal.

107. Luker 1975, p. 32. See Luker 1975, pp. 16, 138–39; Sarvis, Rodman, and Bonar 1987, p. 78.

108. Luker 1975, pp. 66–76.

109. See Luker 1975, p. 147.

110. MacKinnon 1984, p. 47.

111. Luker 1975, p. 29; Luker 1984a, p. 26. See also Luker 1975, pp. 140–41.

112. See nn. 43–45, above.

113. See nn. 97, 102, above.

114. See Alan Guttmacher Institution 1994, pp. 22–23.

115. Olsen 1989, p. 120.

116. Law 1984, pp. 1006, 1017; see also pp. 1008–9, 1014.

117. Law 1984, pp. 978, 1016. See R. Ginsburg 1985, p. 382; Colker 1992, p. 87. See generally Rhode 1989; Karst 1977; Taub and Schneider 1990; Estrich and Sullivan 1989; Braucher 1991; West 1990.

118. Estrich and Sullivan 1989, p. 151. See Estrich and Sullivan 1989, pp. 137, 152; Colker 1992, pp. xvii, 124.

119. MacKinnon 1991, pp. 1309, 1314. See Colker 1992, p. 161.

120. MacKinnon 1991, p. 1324; Olsen 1989, p. 1324. See MacKinnon 1991, pp. 1327–28. See also Karst 1977, p. 54 n. 303.

121. Feminists correctly point out that late-twentieth-century American poli-

170 NOTES TO CHAPTER I

tics is still a predominately male preserve. No women has ever been president, vice president, secretary of the state, secretary of the treasury, secretary of defense, Speaker of the House, Senate Majority Leader, or chief justice. In 1991, only 1 of 9 Supreme Court justices, 2 of 100 senators, and 29 of 435 representatives were women. Women are only slightly better represented in state executive mansions (3 of 50), state legislatures (1,351 of 7,461) and state courts of last resort (35 of approximately 350). See Stanley and Niemi 1992, pp. 201, 396–97. With very few exceptions, men control such politically powerful institutions as business, law, and the academy.

122. See Blake and Del Pinal 1980, pp. 33, 42–45; Pomeroy and Landman 1973, p. 485; Blake 1971, p. 544; Blake 1973, p. 465; Blake 1977, pp. 53, 58; Jones and Westoff 1973, p. 475; Rodman, Sarvis, and Bonar 1987, pp. 140–43; Luker 1984b, p. 238; D. Granberg and B. Granberg 1980, p. 254; Rossi 1967, pp. 37–39; D. Granberg 1978, p. 418; Franklin and Kosaki 1989, pp. 758–59; Uslaner and Weber 1980, p. 213; D. Callahan 1986, p. 347; Noonan 1979, pp. 33–46, 49–51, 190; N. Lee 1969, p. 31; Manier 1977, p. 15; Baker, Epstein, and Forth 1981, p. 94; Tedrow and Mahoney 1979, pp. 184–85; Rossi and Sitaraman 1988, p. 276.

123. Luker 1984b, p. 194; D. Granberg 1981, p. 159. See F. Ginsburg 1989, pp. 6, 134–35; Craig and O'Brien 1993, p. 46.

124. See n. 122. But see Legge 1983, pp. 486, 489 (claiming that women are slightly more likely to support abortion when other variables are controlled for).

125. D. Callahan 1986, p. 347.

126. See chap. V.

127. Hansen 1993, p. 242 ("the proportion of women in state legislatures . . . emerges as a consistent predictor of continuation of abortion access guaranteed by *Roe*"). See Welch 1985; Diamond 1977, p. 50; Vinovskis 1980b, pp. 237–38; Richard 1991, p. 14. Democratic women legislators, in particular, play a vital role in committees that block pro-life initiatives. See Berkman and O'Connor 1993.

128. Surveys of medical students and doctors, for example, find that female physicians are more likely than male physicians to support legal abortion. Women in such lower-status occupations as nursing, in contrast, are far more sympathetic to pro-life positions. See Jaffe, Lindheim, and Lee 1981, p. 64; Bonar, Watson, and Koester 1983, p. 44; Weisman, Nathanson, Teitelbaum, Chase, and King 1986, p. 68; Zimmerman 1977, pp. 19–20. See also Rodman, Sarvis, and Bonar 1987, pp. 141–42; Hansen 1980, p. 392 (noting that "the most vocal groups supporting liberalized abortion laws have been middle- and upper-class white women").

129. Hill 1981, p. 159; Diamond 1977, pp. 5–7. Homemakers are more likely to be elected to nonprofessional, less competitive state legislatures. See Diamond 1977, pp. 51–60.

130. See Hill 1981, pp. 161, 164–65; Diamond 1977, pp. 3, 23–25, 50–51.

131. Welch 1985, p. 131; Vinovskis 1980b, pp. 237–38; Richard 1991, p. 24. The 1994 congressional election did, however, significantly increase the number of pro-life women in the House of Representatives. See Rosin 1995.

132. See Luker 1984b; F. Ginsburg 1989. See also Dodson and Burnbauer 1990, pp. 19, 73–74.

133. See Thomas 1991, p. 974 (women "are more likely than men to intro-
duce and successfully steer legislation through the political process that address
issues of women, children, and the family"); Thomas and Welch 1991; Diamond
1977, p. 45.

134. Rhode 1989, p. 622.

135. Olsen 1989, p. 120; Binion 1993, p. 143.

136. Olsen 1989, p. 112 n. 28. See MacKinnon 1991, p. 1300 n. 93;
A. Dworkin 1983, pp. 102–3.

137. See F. Ginsburg 1989, pp. 18, 109–10, 143, 172, 185, 196.

138. MacKinnon 1991, p. 1326.

139. See Cook, Jelen, and Wilcox 1992, p. 191.

140. Cook, Jelen, and Wilcox 1992, p. 171. See Barnes 1992; Casey 1992.

141. Cook, Jelen, and Wilcox 1992, pp. 170–71. See Stone 1992; Toner
1990. See also Craig and O'Brien 1993, p. 117 ("throughout the 1970s and
1980s, the battles in the Senate were fought with Republicans as the admirals on
both sides").

142. See, e.g., *Adarand Constructors, Inc., v. Pena*, ___ U.S. ___, 132 L. Ed.
2d 158 (1995) (overruling *Metro Broadcasting, Inc., v. FCC*, 497 U.S. 547
[1990]); *Coleman v. Thompson*, 501 U.S. 722 (1991) (overruling *Fay v. Noia*,
372 U.S. 391 [1963]); *Payne v. Tennessee*, 501 U.S. 808 (1991) (overruling *Booth
v. Maryland*, 482 U.S. 496 [1987] and *South Carolina v. Gathers*, 490 U.S. 805
[1989]); *Quill Corp. v. North Dakota*, 504 U.S. 298 (1992) (overruling *National
Bellas Hess, Inc. v. Department of Revenue*, 386 U.S. 753 [1967]); *Garcia v. San
Antonio Metropolitan Transit Authority*, 469 U.S. 528, 589 (1985) (O'Connor
J., dissenting) (calling for the overruling of the majority opinion). See generally
Maltz 1992, pp. 12–17; Gerhardt 1991, pp. 156–59. Indeed, Justices Souter,
Kennedy, and O'Connor had no difficulty abandoning the trimester system that
Roe originally established, overruling sub silento earlier decisions declaring un-
constitutional various statutes burdening the exercise of abortion rights. Compare
Planned Parenthood v. Casey, 505 U.S. ___, 120 L. Ed. 2d 674 (1992), to *Thorn-
burgh v. American College of Obstetricians and Gynecologists*, 476 U.S. 747
(1986), and *City of Akron v. Akron Center for Reproductive Health, Inc.*, 462 U.S.
416 (1983). See also J. Rosen 1993a, p. 27; Maltz 1992, p. 19.

Chapter II
Abortion Law in Action

1. Mohr 1984, p. 121. See nn. 38–90 and the relevant text.

2. See Louisell and Noonan 1970; Means 1968; Mohr 1978; Krason and Hollberg 1986; Buell 1991, pp. 1783–89; Quay 1960–61; Spillenger, Larson, and
Law 1989; Finnis 1994, pp. 10–19.

3. Although chap. II primarily discusses how statutory bans on abortion were
administered during the 1940s, 1950s, and 1960s, commentators writing in the
first third of the twentieth century also observed that "women of the upper economic classes" had privileged access to safe abortions (Note 1935, p. 94).

4. Young women who did not inform their affluent parents that they were
pregnant also had difficulty obtaining safe gray-market abortions.

5. The standard terminological distinction between "therapeutic" and "criminal" abortions is problematic. "The distinction between 'therapeutic' and 'illegal' abortion," the criminologist Edwin Schur points out, "represents merely a financial artifact: in many circumstances the difference between one and the other is $300 and knowing the 'right person'" (1965, pp. 29–30). See Buell 1991, p. 1798; Packer and Gampell 1959, p. 417. "Therapeutic abortions" not clearly necessary to save the life of the pregnant women (however *life* is defined) were, in some sense, "criminal abortions." See Rodman, Sarvis, and Bonar 1987, p. 89; Sarvis and Rodman 1973, p. 65; Niswander and Porto 1986, pp. 250–51. The label "criminal" hardly seems appropriate to describe an abortion the authorities have no intention to prosecute.

6. "Both Sides See Defeat in Decision" 1992, p. A1 (quoting Representative Patricia Schroeder, D-Colo.). See Benshoof 1993.

7. 492 U.S. 490 (1989).

8. 505 U.S. ___, 120 L. Ed. 2d 674 (1992).

9. Chap. III discusses whether these enforcement policies intentionally discriminated against poor persons and persons of color.

10. See Reagan 1991b, p. 116; Taussig 1936, p. 24. Contemporary records of legal abortions are not much better; see Rosenberg 1991, p. 178.

11. Aristotle 1980, p. 2; Braudel 1979, p. 39.

12. Rodman, Sarvis, and Bonar 1987, p. 89. See Sarvis and Rodman 1973, pp. 29–30.

13. Kahn, Bourne, Asher, and Tyler 1971, p. 430. For observations that legal texts do not adequately describe access to abortion in other countries, see Henshaw 1990, p. 78; Jones et al. 1988, p. 58; Sarvis and Rodman 1973, p. 30; Glendon 1987, pp. 13–15; Rosenblatt 1992, pp. 73–74.

14. Kahn, Bourne, Asher, and Tyler 1971, p. 425; Sarvis and Rodman 1973, p. 50. Indeed, the California and Maryland statutes nominally permitted abortion in fewer circumstances than the measures passed by the other states; see Kahn, Bourne, Asher, and Tyler 1971, p. 424.

15. See Russell and Jackson 1969, p. 760; A. Guttmacher 1986, p. 234 (Colorado); Garrow 1994, p. 341; A. Guttmacher 1967b, p. 15; Sarvis and Rodman 1973, pp. 50–52; Irwin 1970, p. 22 (more than 90 percent of all abortions in Maryland were performed in Baltimore).

16. Packer and Gampell 1959, p. 417.

17. Francome 1986, p. 47. See Steiner 1983a, pp. 2–3 (noting that for a "century," abortion "was both illegal in all of the states and yet widely performed"); Reagan 1991b, p. 32 (describing "the prevalent use of abortion by women as a means of controlling their reproduction, despite the prohibition against it"); Note 1935, p. 91 ("in marked contrast with this paucity of convictions is the prevalence of the practice").

18. Reagan 1991b, p. 35.

19. In the years immediately before legalization, the most statistically sophisticated attempt to determine the number of illegal abortions in the United States estimated that approximately 829,000 procedures were being performed annually (Abernathy, Greenberg, and Horvitz 1970, p. 26). Participants at a major Planned Parenthood conference in 1958 estimated that the number of unsanctioned abor-

tions was between 200,000 and 1,200,000 (Calderone 1958, p. 180). Subsequent scholarship suggested that the actual number was probably closer to the higher range of that approximation. The 1,000,000 figure has been obtained by scholars using mortality rates, birth rates, and statistical samples of women who were asked whether they had ever had an abortion. Christopher Tietze's finding that seven out of ten legal abortions in New York City replaced illegal abortions was replicated in Maryland and Oregon. See n. 200. Although no one claims that the 1,000,000 figure is cast in stone, that estimate best fits the available data. See Tietze and Martin 1957, p. 175 (one-fifth to one-quarter of all pregnancies are aborted); Gebhard, Pomeroy, Martin, and Christenson 1958, pp. 57, 93–94, 147 (same estimate); Harper and Skolnick 1962, p. 182 (20 to 25 percent); Kopp 1934, pp. 110, 121; Moore 1963, p. 251 (citing studies); Tietze 1981, p. 21; Hall 1967a, p. 1934; Leavy and Kummer 1962, p. 124; Herbert 1965, p. 285; Bates and Zawadski 1964, pp. 3–4; Lader 1966, p. 2; Lader 1973, p. 22; Zimmerman 1977, pp. 9, 17; Irwin 1970, p. 22; Starr 1965, p. 150; Ridgeway 1963, pp. 14, 16. See especially Rosenberg 1991, pp. 353–55 (pointing to a variety of reasons why 1,000,000 is probably the most accurate estimate); Note 1957, p. 193 ("the number of these illegal operations has assumed monstrous proportions"); A. Guttmacher 1973, p. 536 (in the years before *Roe*, "over half of . . . spontaneous abortions were . . . illegally induced abortions"). See also Calderone 1958, p. 171 (statement of G. Lotrell Timanus). For similar estimates concerning abortion rates in the late nineteenth century, see Mohr 1978, pp. 76–81.

Pro-life attempts to refute these claims are discussed in chap. I.

20. See Note 1935, p. 92; Gordon 1976, p. 53; Francome 1986, pp. 40–41; Petchesky 1990, p. 53.

21. Gebhard, Pomeroy, Martin, and Christenson 1958, p. 119 (85 percent).

22. Gebhard, Pomeroy, Martin, and Christenson 1958, pp. 54, 57, 196; Tietze and Martin 1957, pp. 174–75.

23. See Fisher 1951, p. 247; White House Conference on Child Health and Protection 1933, p. 463 (4,000–15,000 deaths); Voyles 1967, p. 496; Note 1935, p. 93; Moore 1963, p. 252; Mills 1958, p. 182; Herbert 1965, p. 285.

24. Miller 1993, p. 13. Authorities generally agree that deaths from illegal abortions were underreported. Dr. Robert Kimbrough of the American College of Obstetrics and Gynecology maintained that "the vast majority of abortion deaths are written off as something else" (Starr 1965, p. 150). See also Rosenberg 1991, pp. 353–54; Miller 1993, p. 147.

25. Gebhard, Pomeroy, Martin, and Christenson 1958, p. 204 n. 38; Ziff 1969, p. 6; G. Williams 1957, p. 213; Miller 1993, p. 327. The death rate for very poor women and women of color, however, increased in this period, at least in New York City. See E. Gold, Erhardt, Jacobziner, and Nelson 1971, p. 965; Reagan 1991b, pp. 323, 332–33.

26. Ziff 1969, p. 6; Voyles 1967, p. 496.

27. Mills 1958, p. 182 n. 9.

28. Voyles 1967, p. 496; G. Williams 1966, p. 194; Condit 1990, pp. 37 n. 4, 189; Starr 1965, p. 150.

29. Reagan 1991b, pp. 214, 219; Miller 1993, p. 74. See Miller 1993, pp. 119, 156–57, 221, 285.

30. Reagan 1991b, pp. 214, 219, 334–35; Harper and Skolnick 1962, p. 182; Mills 1958, p. 182. See also Swartz 1973, p. 95 (before legalization, there was one admission for septic abortion for every three births at Harlem Hospital in New York City).

31. Compare Burns et al. 1989, p. 12, with Syska, Hilgers, and O'Hare 1981.

32. Compare Burns et al. 1989, p. 13 (5,000 deaths annually "may be a minimum estimate"), with Burtchaell 1982 (133 deaths annually).

33. R. Bell 1971, pp. 125, 142; Schur 1965, p. 25. See also Rodman, Sarvis, and Bonar 1987, p. 190; Lucas 1968, p. 751; Voyles 1967, p. 496.

34. Bates 1954, p. 161.

35. G. Williams 1957, p. 214; Harper and Skolnick 1962, p. 181; Moore 1963, p. 251. See White House Conference on Child Health and Protection 1933, p. 463.

36. Note 1935, pp. 92–93. See G. Williams 1957, p. 213 (prohibitions do little more than "prevent the operation from being performed under proper conditions and by proper persons"); Ziff 1969, p. 7 ("almost all abortions performed by persons other than qualified physicians cause medical complications which require treatment").

37. White House Conference on Child Health and Protection 1933, p. 470; Moore 1963, p. 251. See G. Williams 1957, p. 233 ("the widespread demand for abortion . . . has reduced the law to impotence"); Calderone 1958, p. 181 ("present laws . . . have not served to control the practice of illegal abortion"); Model Penal Code 1980 230.3, p. 427; Note 1935, pp. 90–91; Ziff 1969, p. 8; Sands 1966, p. 306; Adelstein 1960, p. 84; Note 1957, p. 196.

38. See Steiner 1983a, p. 3 ("whether a sustained effort to destroy the abortion underground could have succeeded is an imponderable").

39. Mohr 1978, pp. 239, 244–45. See Francome 1986, p. 36 (noting that bans on abortion were rarely enforced even immediately after they were passed in the late nineteenth century); Rosenblatt 1992, pp. 85, 88; Grossberg 1985, pp. 179–88; D'Emilio and Freedman 1988, p. 66.

40. See Mohr 1984, pp. 119–20; Reagan 1991b, p. 151.

41. Rosenblatt 1992, p. 124. See Reagan 1991b, pp. 63–64.

42. Mohr 1984, p. 120; see also pp. 119–20.

43. Taussig 1936, p. 422. See Pollak 1950, p. 44 ("if there is any one offense which occurs in tremendous volume but is practically unprosecuted, it is criminal abortion"); G. Williams 1957, p. 215 ("the legal prohibition has broken down"); Fisher 1967, p. 6 ("it is doubtful if any other felonious act is as free from punishment as criminal abortion"); Leavy and Kummer 1962, p. 422; Mohr 1984, pp. 120–21; Buell 1991, p. 1798; Voyles 1967, p. 510.

44. Buell 1991. See Note 1935, p. 91; Schur 1965, p. 36; Reagan 1991a, pp. 1243–44. Professor Leslie Reagan notes that states "did punish women through persistent questioning by doctors and police and through public exposure of their abortion" (1991a, p. 1263).

45. *State v. Murphy*, 27 N.J. L. 112, 114–15 (1858). See Buell 1991, pp. 1790–91 (citing other cases); Model Penal Code 1980 230.3, pp. 437–38.

46. Leavy and Kummer 1962, p. 126. See Gebhard, Pomeroy, Martin, and Christenson 1958, p. 192; Rosenblatt 1992, p. 88; A. Guttmacher 1959, p. 179.

47. Buell 1991, pp. 1789–90. See Moore 1963, p. 252; Note 1957, p. 199; Miller 1993, p. 264.

48. Schur 1965, p. 34. See G. Williams 1957, p. 207 ("remarkable lack of prosecution"); Miller 1993, pp. 144, 189–90, 257; Moore 1963, p. 253; Note 1957, p. 200; Adelstein 1960, pp. 77, 85–86; Ziff 1969, p. 8. But see Bates and Zawadski 1964, p. 94.

Roe v. Wade may have been one consequence of the low priority prosecutors placed on fighting abortion. Absorbed with other matters, Texas state attorneys were consistently unprepared throughout the *Roe* litigation. Texas state attorneys "practically gave away [the] case" during oral argument before the Supreme Court by unnecessarily conceding that women would have a right to abortion if the fetus was not a constitutional person. L. Epstein and Kobylka 1992, p. 192. See L. Epstein and Kobylka 1992, pp. 173, 180, 182, 189; Garrow 1994, pp. 436, 569–70. See also Ely 1973, p. 926 (noting that "the argument that fetuses lack constitutional rights is simply irrelevant"). No other state expressed any interest in defending the law at stake in *Roe* from constitutional attack. See L. Epstein and Kobylka 1992, p. 178. Both Henry Wade and Arthur Bolton (of *Doe v. Bolton*, 410 U.S. 179 [1973], the companion case to *Roe*) later indicated that they were rather pleased with the Court's decision to protect abortion rights. See Garrow 1994, p. 602.

49. Mohr 1984, p. 120; Miller 1993, p. 132. See Gebhard, Pomeroy, Martin, and Christenson 1958, p. 192 ("defense lawyers know that their best way to win an abortion case is to secure a jury rather than a court trial"); Note 1935 pp. 90–91 (citing statistics); Note 1957, p. 193 (same); Adelstein 1960, p. 85 (same); Ziff 1969, p. 8 (same); Buell 1991, pp. 1790, 1795, 1828; Voyles 1967, p. 500; Harper and Skolnick 1962, p. 184; Moore 1963, p. 252; Calderone 1958, pp. 36–40; H. Rosen 1967c, p. 92; E. Rubin 1987, pp. 18, 36; Faux 1988, p. 88; Luker 1984b, p. 53; Tribe 1990a, p. 35; Kummer and Leavy 1966, p. 97; Davis 1985, p. 103; Schur 1965, p. 38; R. Bell 1971, p. 126; Gordon 1976, p. 57; Ridgeway 1963, p. 14; Burtchaell 1982, p. 244; L. Lee 1973, p. 351; Reagan 1991a, pp. 1247–48; Reagan 1991b, p. 11; Miller 1993, pp. 261–62; Mohr 1984, pp. 120–21; D'Emilio and Freedman 1988, pp. 253–54. See also Mohr 1978, pp. 230, 237.

50. D'Emilio and Freedman 1988, pp. 253–54; Greenhouse 1993, p. 30.

51. See Leavy and Kummer 1962, p. 130; Calderone 1958, p. 35 (statement of Edwin Schur); Rodman, Sarvis, and Bonar 1987, p. 172; Sarvis and Rodman 1973, pp. 36, 62; Schur 1965, pp. 55–56; R. Bell 1971, p. 140.

52. *People v. Ballard*, 167 Cal. App. 2d 803, 815, 817 (1959). But see Model Penal Code 1980 230.3, p. 435 (noting that this was the minority rule).

53. See Grossberg 1985, pp. 179–88; Miller 1993, p. 103; Reagan 1991b, pp. 12–13, 283. Many abortionists had valid entrapment claims. Still, judges seemed more sensitive to the constitutional rights of competent abortionists than to the rights of other persons accused of penal violations.

54. Mohr 1984, p. 121.

55. The public uproar over Sherri Finkbine's attempt to procure an abortion after discovering she had taken thalidomide, a drug that often caused horrible birth defects, took place only because Finkbine's scheduled abortion was canceled

when she publicized her reasons for seeking to terminate her pregnancy. See Finkbine 1967.

56. Reagan 1991b, pp. 136–55 (discussing midwives); Bates and Zawadski 1964, pp. 48, 35. See Garrow 1994, p. 299 (illegal abortions were "easy to find in Dallas"); Starr 1965, p. 150; Ziff 1969, pp. 6–7; Messer and May 1988, pp. 139–40, 165 ("it's easy to find the underground when you live in the ghetto").

57. Miller 1993, pp. 10, 93, 114–15, 217–18, 252, 275; Messer and May 1988, pp. 6, 188.

58. See Mohr 1984, pp. 120–21; Miller 1993, pp. 12, 112, 157–58, 264, 286.

59. Reagan 1991a, pp. 1242, 1256. See also Note 1957, p. 199.

60. Bates and Zawadski 1964, pp. 10–11, 64. See Calderone 1958, pp. 36, 39; Davis 1985, p. 57; Lader 1966, p. 70; N. Lee 1969, p. 6; Sarvis and Rodman 1973, p. 65.

61. Bates and Zawadski 1964, pp. 78–82. See Miller 1993, pp. 145–46.

62. Gebhard, Pomeroy, Martin, and Christenson 1958, p. 192; Miller 1993, p. 263; Moore 1963, p. 253. See Bates and Zawadski 1964, p. 10 ("there is no aggressive campaign to eliminate abortion").

63. For studies of police corruption and abortion, see Bates and Zawadski 1964, pp. 66–70; Bates 1954, pp. 164–66; Ziff 1969, p. 6; Schur 1965, pp. 34–35; Lader 1966, pp. 71–74; Reagan 1991b, pp. 249–50.

64. Davis 1985, p. 57. See Davis 1985, p. 51; Bates and Zawadski 1964, pp. 5–6, 134; Schur 1965, p. 61; Sarvis and Rodman 1973, p. 65; E. Rubin 1987, p. 18; D'Emilio and Freedman 1988, pp. 253–54.

65. Bart 1987, p. 346; Petchesky 1990, p. 129. See Gebhard, Pomeroy, Martin, and Christenson 1958, p. 192; Garrow 1994, pp. 486–87.

66. Bart 1987, p. 346.

67. Davis 1985, pp. 89–90; Miller 1993, p. 262. See Bart 1987, p. 342; Joffe 1991, p. 60; Lader 1966, p. 28.

68. Davis 1985, pp. 49–50, 90.

69. Davis 1985, p. 142; also p. 61.

70. Lader 1973, p. 48. For a similar incident in Baltimore, see Lader 1966, p. 48. A private physician-abortionist dissuaded a would-be blackmailer by flatly declaring, "the police know I'm doing abortions, sometimes they refer people to me" (Joffe 1991, p. 60).

71. See Luker 1984b, pp. 32–35; Mohr 1978, pp. 147–70.

72. Luker 1984b, pp. 85, 36. See Leavy and Kummer 1964, p. 52 ("the community at large has no desire to hold criminally responsible the licensed physician who in good faith exercises sound medical judgment consistent with standards and practices generally accepted by his profession"); Starr 1965, pp. 153–54; Moore 1963, p. 253.

73. Luker 1984b, p. 85.

74. Garrow 1994, p. 306.

75. Joffe 1991, p. 47.

76. Reagan 1991b, pp. 79, 84, 101–2.

77. Messer and May 1988, pp. 179–80. See B. Nathanson 1979, pp. 21–22; Joffe 1991, p. 54. See also Reagan 1991b, p. 107.

78. Joffe 1991, p. 54.

79. A. Guttmacher 1959, p. 208.

80. Even physicians attempting to bring test cases challenging abortion laws had difficulty getting arrested. See Lader 1973, pp. 53, 180–81, 191–92; Fujita and Wagner 1973, p. 241; L. Epstein and Kobylka 1992, p. 161; Garrow 1994, pp. 315, 384. One physician-abortionist waived a jury trial in order to obtain the conviction necessary for challenging local abortion laws in federal court. See Garrow 1994, p. 467.

81. Bates 1954, p. 161; Starr 1965, p. 153; Tatalovich and Daynes 1981, p. 43; Reagan 1991b, p. 235; Joffe 1991, p. 60; Garrow 1994, pp. 275, 361–64, 383; A. Guttmacher 1959, pp. 208–13; Lader 1966, pp. 45–50.

82. Gebhard, Pomeroy, Martin, and Christenson 1958, p. 199. See Greenhouse 1993, p. 30 (claiming that Dr. Milan Vuitch "performed thousands of abortions a year" in Washington, D.C.); Reagan 1991b, p. 235 (Dr. Edgar Keemer "performed over 30,000 abortions").

83. Miller 1993, pp. 123–25, 135.

84. Miller 1993, p. 127. But see Garrow 1994, pp. 362–63 (suggesting that Spencer may have performed only 30,000 to 40,000 abortions).

85. A. Guttmacher 1959, p. 181; Calderone 1958, pp. 35–36. See Reagan 1991b, p. 291; A. Guttmacher 1967a, p. 11 ("the District Attorney allows ethical hospitals to police themselves with respect to abortion"); Calderone 1958, pp. 34 (statement of Edwin Schur), 40, 164 (statement of Sophia Kleegman); Schur 1965, p. 36; Rodman, Sarvis, and Bonar 1987, pp. 190–91; Packer and Gampell 1959, p. 449; Lucas 1968, p. 749; Davis 1985, pp. 69, 72; George 1967, p. 25; Pilpel 1967, p. 104; Leavy and Kummer 1962, p. 128; Leavy and Kummer 1964, p. 52.

86. George 1967, p. 25.

87. Hall 1967a, p. 1933.

88. Kummer 1967, p. 121; A. Guttmacher 1960. See Niswander, Klein, and Randall 1966, p. 1143; H. Rosen 1967c, p. 87; Hall 1967a, p. 1933; Hall 1967b, pp. 224–25; Schur 1965, pp. 14–18; Lucas 1968, pp. 748–49; Davis 1985, pp. 4–5; Kummer and Leavy 1966, p. 97; Packer and Gampell 1959, pp. 430, 447; Rodman, Sarvis, and Bonar 1987, p. 190; Sarvis and Rodman 1973, p. 65; Pilpel 1967, p. 104; Leavy and Kummer 1962, p. 126; Leavy and Kummer 1964, p. 52; Adelstein 1960, pp. 79, 86; Trout 1964, p. 173; Ziff 1969, p. 9; Model Penal Code 1980 230.3, pp. 426–27; Quay 1960–61, pp. 178–79; Garrow 1994, pp. 278–80.

89. Niswander 1967, p. 53 (noting that hospitals routinely performed "illegal" abortions when the women had rubella); Imber 1986, p. 22; Schur 1965, p. 15; Cushner et al. 1973, p. 136; Sands 1966, pp. 286, 292.

90. A. Guttmacher 1960, pp. 51–53. See Starr 1965, p. 155.

91. See Lucas 1968, pp. 767–69; Dubin 1961, pp. 147–48; Voyles 1967, p. 501. See also Rosenberg 1991, p. 181 (citing judicial decisions striking down abortion restrictions on vagueness grounds).

92. See sources cited in nn. 87–90.

93. Personal attitudes encompass not only beliefs about the morality of abortion but more general willingness to perform the procedure. Many pro-

choice physicians would rather not perform many abortions. See Burtchaell 1982, pp. 49, 218.

94. See Hall 1967a, p. 1935 (documenting disparities between doctors working with the same kinds of patients in the same hospital, but on different wards); Rodman, Sarvis, and Bonar 1987, p. 46; Sarvis and Rodman 1973, p. 96.

95. A. Guttmacher 1986, pp. 231–32. See Adelstein 1960, p. 75; G. Williams 1966, p. 189.

96. Hall 1965, pp. 524–25; Packer and Gampell 1959, p. 427 n. 24. See Niswander 1967, p. 54. See generally Rodman, Sarvis, and Bonar 1987, pp. 166–67; Luker 1984b, pp. 45–46; Mandy 1967, pp. 285–86; Davis 1985, p. 61; Gebhard, Pomeroy, Martin, and Christenson 1958, p. 196; Quay 1960–61, p. 183.

97. H. Rosen 1967c, p. 95.

98. Rodman, Sarvis, and Bonar 1987, p. 74. See Sarvis and Rodman 1973, pp. 82, 96.

99. R. Schwartz 1986, p. 327. See Garrow 1994, p. 379.

100. Packer and Gampell 1959, p. 447.

101. Packer and Gampell 1959, pp. 431–33, 443–44.

102. Packer and Gampell 1959, p. 446. The Packer and Gampell study was later replicated in Chicago with similar results (Broeman and Meier 1971). See Reagan 1991b, pp. 349–50.

103. Charles and Alexander 1971, pp. 150–51. See Joffe 1991, p. 55; Reagan 1991b, pp. 217, 333–37, 389; Voyles 1967, p. 501; Rodman, Sarvis, and Bonar 1987, pp. 17, 149–50; Lucas 1968, p. 771; Sarvis and Rodman 1973, p. 56; Cates 1982, p. 1588; Tietze 1981, p. 39; N. Lee 1969, pp. 163–64; Niswander and Porto 1986, p. 250.

104. A. Guttmacher 1959, p. 178.

105. Luker 1984b, p. 36. See A. Guttmacher 1967a, pp. 8–9; Mannes 1967, p. 55; Newman 1967, p. 64; F. Ginsburg 1989, p. 33; Davis 1985, p. 6; Schur 1965, p. 21; Calderone 1958, pp. 162, 183. Having a physician in the family or in one's circle of close friends was particularly useful. See N. Lee 1969, p. 164. For claims of similar discrimination in the late nineteenth century, see Mohr 1978, pp. 94–98.

106. Reagan 1991b, pp. 268, 312 (noting that abortions became more difficult to obtain for many women in the 1940s and 1950s); Miller 1993, p. 263.

107. Joffe 1991, p. 53. See Joffe 1991, pp. 50–54; Messer and May 1988, p. 180.

108. A. Guttmacher 1967a, p. 11; Sarvis and Rodman 1973, pp. 172–73. See Charles and Alexander 1971, p. 165; Mandy 1967, p. 288; Kleegman 1967, p. 256; Miller 1993, p. 113.

109. See nn. 115–17.

110. Mandy 1967, p. 288. See Charles and Alexander 1971, pp. 151–52; Irwin 1970, p. 23; Davis 1985, p. 5 ("a two-tiered system").

111. See Rodman, Sarvis, and Bonar 1987, p. 154; Irwin 1970, p.22–23; Calderone 1958, p. 77 (statement of Carl Erhardt); L. Lee 1973, p. 346.

112. Hall 1965, p. 519; Hall 1967a, p. 1934.

113. Hall 1965, pp. 519, 524–25.

114. Hall 1965, pp. 524–25.

115. E. Gold, Erhardt, Jacobziner, and Nelson 1965, pp. 970–71. See Hall 1965, p. 519 (noting that at Sloane Hospital, private patients were eleven times more likely than ward patients to have abortions for psychiatric indications); Niswander, Klein, and Randall 1966; Hall 1967a, p. 1935; Calderone 1958, p. 80 (statement of Carl Erhardt); Charles and Alexander 1971, pp. 153–54; R. Bell 1971, p. 135.

116. Hall 1965, p. 522.

117. Hall 1965, p. 523.

118. A. Guttmacher 1967a, p. 11.

119. E. Gold, Erhardt, Jacobziner, and Nelson 1971, p. 970. See Niswander, Klein, and Randall 1966, p. 1143 ("no reliable evidence that [affluent] women . . . are more likely to be seriously ill or mentally disturbed").

120. E. Gold, Erhardt, Jacobziner, and Nelson 1971. See Rodman, Sarvis, and Bonar 1987, p. 154; Niswander 1967, p. 39 ("the indigent patient may still have a more difficult time than the wealthy in obtaining legal sanction for even a medically indicated abortion").

Physicians were also more willing to provide comprehensive contraceptive services to their private patients. See Kleegman 1967, pp. 256–58; Rodman, Sarvis, and Bonar 1987, p. 17; Calderone 1958, pp. 162, 183; Newman 1967, p. 67.

121. Rodman, Sarvis, and Bonar 1987, p. 150. See Sarvis and Rodman 1973, p. 172.

122. Rochat, Tyler, and Schoenbucher 1971, p. 548. See Rodman, Sarvis, and Bonar 1987, pp. 149–50. See H. Rosen 1967c, p. 73 (racially discriminatory distribution of abortions in Baltimore).

123. Niswander 1967, p. 40 (discussing Niswander, Klein, and Randall 1966).

124. E. Gold, Erhardt, Jacobziner, and Nelson 1965, pp. 964–66. See Pilpel 1967, p. 101. For an earlier study, see Calderone 1958, p. 73 (statement of Carl Erhardt). See also Legge 1985, p. 117; Tietze 1968, p. 786; Tietze 1981, p. 39.

125. Bates and Zawadski 1964, pp. 79–80; Burtchaell 1982, p. 49. Several persons who wish to remain anonymous have informed me that large hospitals in New York City, Boston, and St. Louis also practiced this subterfuge.

126. Rodman, Sarvis, and Bonar 1987, p. 151. See Sarvis and Rodman 1973, pp. 188–93; Miller 1993, p. 64.

127. H. Rosen 1967b, pp. 53–54. See Myers 1967, pp. 87, 93–94; M. Guttmacher 1967, p. 182; D. Wilson 1967, p. 194; Lidz 1967, pp. 281–82; Mandy 1967, pp. 281–82; Davis 1985, pp. 54, 69; Schur 1965, p. 22; Simon, Senturia, and Rothman 1967, pp. 59–60; Calderone 1958, pp. 88–89. See also Mensch and Freeman 1991, pp. 1124–25.

128. Eliot, Hall, Willson, and Houser 1970. See Rodman, Sarvis, and Bonar 1987, p. 151.

129. H. Rosen 1967a, pp. 239–40.

130. Hall 1965, pp. 519, 526; Russell 1953, p. 111. See Reagan 1991b, pp. 305–6 (60 percent sterilization rate in Chicago municipal hospital), 334; Rodman, Sarvis, and Bonar 1987, p. 151.

131. See generally Reagan 1991b, p. 323.

132. For a description of how review boards functioned, see Hammond 1964; Reagan 1991b, pp. 286–97.

133. H. Rosen 1967c, pp. 89–90.

134. Luker 1984b, p. 57. See F. Ginsburg 1989, p. 266 n. 21; Charles and Alexander 1971, pp. 165–66; Petchesky 1990, pp. 126–27; Lader 1966, pp. 8, 29–30.

135. Pilpel 1967, p. 101. See Davis 1985, pp. 77, 79.

136. Model Penal Code 1980 230.3, p. 422. See Model Penal Code 1980 230.3, p. 442; Buell 1991, pp. 1796–97; Ziff 1969, pp. 4–5; Tribe 1990a, p. 36.

137. Packer 1968, p. 344; Jaffe, Lindheim, and Lee 1981, p. 25. See Lader 1973, p. 86; Irwin 1970, p. 23.

138. Kahn, Bourne, Asher, and Tyler 1971, pp. 425–26; A. Guttmacher 1986, p. 233. See Irwin 1970, p. 22.

139. B. Nathanson 1979, pp. 40–41. See Joffe 1991, p. 54; Messer and May 1988, pp. 143, 176.

140. A. Guttmacher 1986, p. 234.

141. Packer 1968, p. 344. See R. Bell 1971, p. 127; Irwin 1970, pp. 22–23; G. Williams 1966, p. 189.

142. Quay 1960–61, p. 184. See Quay 1960–61, pp. 183–220, 229–33 (detailing increased medical capacities to bring to term pregnant women with a variety of ailments). See also Niswander and Porto 1986, pp. 251–54; Niswander, Klein, and Randall 1966, p. 1141; Russell 1953, p. 108; Adelstein 1960, pp. 80–81; Mills 1958, pp. 194–95 n. 80; Herbert 1965, pp. 288–89; Dubin 1961, p. 149; Reagan 1991b, pp. 272, 335–36.

143. Herbert 1965, p. 289 n. 44. See Reagan 1991b, p. 349.

144. A. Guttmacher 1967b.

145. A. Guttmacher 1986, p. 233; Calderone 1958, pp. 83–84 (statement of Christopher Tietze); Niswander, Klein, and Randall 1966, p. 1141. See Sarvis and Rodman 1973, p. 30 n. *; R. Bell 1971, p. 135; Sands 1966, p. 297; A. Guttmacher 1959, p. 185.

146. See Reagan 1991b, p. 305.

147. Calderone 1958, p. 101 (statement of Charles McLane).

148. Lader 1973, pp. 13, 22 (noting that "New York's Metropolitan Hospital . . . performed only one [abortion] in 13,000 live births between 1959 and 1961"); Russell 1953, p. 111. For other studies decrying the low rate of abortion at municipal hospitals, see Niswander 1967, p. 54; A. Guttmacher 1967a, p. 9 (doctors on the private services of voluntary hospitals perform twenty times as many abortions as doctors at municipal hospitals); Kleegman 1967, p. 256. See generally G. Williams 1957, p. 167; Ridgeway 1963, p. 14; Starr 1965, p. 156.

149. Niswander 1967, p. 53. See Niswander, Klein, and Randall 1966 (presenting the actual data).

150. E. Gold, Erhardt, Jacobziner, and Nelson 1965, p. 966. See Rodman, Sarvis, and Bonar 1987, p. 150; Sarvis and Rodman 1973, p. 162.

151. Jaffe, Lindheim, and Lee 1981, p. 24; Sarvis and Rodman 1973, pp. 170–71.

152. Rochat, Tyler, and Schoenbucher 1971, pp. 543–44.

153. Packer 1968, p. 343.

154. See Luker 1984b, pp. 74–75.

155. See Miller 1993, p. 10.

156. Compare Miller 1993, p. 101, with pp. 59, 63 (sex plus $1,000); Reagan 1991b, pp. 329–30.

157. Bates 1954, pp. 158–60. See Gebhard, Pomeroy, Martin, and Christenson 1958, p. 199.

158. N. Lee 1969, pp. 13–14. See N. Lee 1969, pp. 77, 154, 166; Rodman, Sarvis, and Bonar 1987, p. 191.

159. Steiner 1983a, p. 3; Hardin 1967, p. 84. See Lidz 1967, p. 277; Starr 1965, p. 153.

160. Sarvis and Rodman 1973, p. 170. See N. Lee 1969, pp. 166–68.

161. Newman 1967, p. 67; Miller 1993, p. 76. See Miller 1993, p. 209; Messer and May 1988, p. 5.

162. See Charles and Alexander 1971, p. 155; Lader 1966, pp. 64–66; Schur 1965, pp. 32, 46; Niswander 1967, p. 39; Reagan 1991b, p. 333; Miller 1993, pp. 119, 221, 285.

163. Burns et al. 1989, p. 17.

164. Messer and May 1988, pp. 11–12. For similar experiences, see Burns et al. 1989; Messer and May 1988; Miller 1993.

165. Miller 1993, p. 108.

166. Luker 1984b, pp. 74–75.

167. Calderone 1958, p. 170 (statement of G. Lotrell Timanus); Joffe 1991, p. 50 n. 8; Miller 1993, pp. 99, 104, 157; Bates 1954, pp. 166–67. See Schur 1965, p. 32; Kummer and Leavy 1966, p. 97; H. Rosen 1967c, p. 92; A. Guttmacher 1959, pp. 209–10; A. Guttmacher 1986, p. 231; Garrow 1994, pp. 270–71; Gebhard, Pomeroy, Martin, and Christenson 1958, pp. 198–99; Moore 1963, p. 253; Miller 1993, pp. 32, 97, 101, 110–11; Messer and May 1988, pp. 140, 148; Bart 1987, p. 342; Reagan 1991b, pp. 9–10, 75–84, 104, 136–37, 238–41; Joffe 1991, p. 50. Doctors were often paid for making referrals to illegal abortionists; see Reagan 1991b, p. 104.

168. Jaffe, Lindheim, and Lee 1981, p. 22.

169. Lader 1973, p. 23.

170. Luker 1984b, pp. 74–75. Rodman, Sarvis, and Bonar 1987, p. 150; Niswander 1967, p. 39; E. Gold, Erhardt, Jacobziner, and Nelson 1971, pp. 964–66 (discussed above).

171. Rochat, Tyler, and Schoenbucher 1971, pp. 543–44 (88 percent of the women who died from criminal abortions in this time period were black).

172. See Liu 1977, p. 146; Joffe 1991, p. 50; B. Nathanson 1979, p. 26; Miller 1993, p. 33, 172; Messer and May 1988, pp. 9, 72–73, 113–14; Pilpel 1967, p. 101; George 1967, p. 23; Condit 1990, pp. 41–42 n. 46 (citing sources). For a good anecdotal account of the options available for those who elected to have legal abortions overseas, see Finkbine 1967.

173. Davis 1985, p. 119. Jack Starr of *Look* claimed that ten thousand women annually went to Puerto Rico where "abortion [was] illegal, but easy to get" (1965, p. 154). See G. Williams 1966, p. 188; B. Nathanson 1979, p. 23 (a doctor describes how he routinely referred patients to a relatively trusted abortionist in San Juan).

174. Compare Messer and May 1988, pp. 72–73, 113–14, with Miller 1993, p. 33.

175. See Lader 1973, p. 179.

176. A local travel agency was indicted for advertising trips to London for abortion-seeking women (see Tribe 1990a, p. 127; "Ads for London Abortions Stir Legal Questions" 1970, p. 20; "Lawyer Pleads Not Guilty in Abortion Package Deal" 1970, p. 40), but that prosecution was apparently dropped for unknown reasons.

177. See Davis 1985, p. 61.

178. J. Kahn, Bourne, Asher, and Tyler 1971, p. 428. See Sarvis and Rodman 1973, p. 52.

179. Pakter, O'Hare, Nelson, and Svigir 1973, p. 524.

180. Davis 1985, p. 199; Bart 1987, p. 33; Pakter, O'Hare, Nelson, and Svigir 1973, p. 529. See Reagan 1991b, pp. 346–48.

181. Sarvis and Rodman 1973, p. 167. See Davis 1985, p. 99; Jaffe, Lindheim, and Lee 1981, p. 21; David 1980, p. 87.

182. George 1967, p. 25. See Mohr 1978, p. 255; Condit 1990, p. 34; L. Lee 1973, p. 346.

183. Mid-twentieth-century proponents of abortion reform and repeal emphasized other details of the system of abortion regulation then in place. Many early participants in the abortion reform movement wanted to make the law on the books conform to the law in action. Doctors, in particular, needed more assurance that public authorities would not interfere with their abortion decisions. See Luker 1984b, pp. 78, 82; Rodman, Sarvis, and Bonar pp. 89–90; E. Rubin 1987, pp. 28–29; Irwin 1970, p. 80; Condit 1990, pp. 22–23, 189; Sands 1966, p. 286; Voyles 1967, p. 511. Most advocates of abortion reform were concerned with eradicating the evils associated with black-market abortions. "Many physicians throughout the world," Rodman, Sarvis, and Bonar (1987) note, "urged that abortions be legalized because it was clear that desperate women will have an abortion even though it was illegal and dangerous" (p. 30). See G. Williams 1966, p. 191 ("the most that a penal law can do is ensure that the operations are performed by the only people who are competent to do it, medical practitioners"); Rodman, Sarvis, and Bonar 1987, pp. 1, 62; Condit 1990, pp. 24–28, 189; A. Guttmacher 1960, p. 54; Tribe 1990a, pp. 43–44, 47–48; E. Rubin 1987, pp. 28–29. Mainstream abortion reformers also spoke of the "dubious value of keeping unenforced laws on books" (Dubin 1961, p. 146). See Ziff 1969, p. 8; Sands 1966, pp. 306–07 n. 139; Model Penal Code 1980 230.3, p. 428; Moore 1963, p. 253.

184. Calderone 1958, p. 183; Pilpel 1967, p. 101. See Calderone 1958, p. 162.

185. Mohr 1978, p. 255; A. Guttmacher 1967a, p. 12. See Tatalovich and Daynes 1981, p. 90; Reagan 1991b, pp. 391–92; B. Nathanson 1979, p. 31; Roemer 1973, p. 291; Pilpel 1967, p. 107; E. Gold, Erhardt, Jacobziner, and Nelson 1965, p. 971; Hall 1967a, p. 1936; E. Rubin 1987, p. 94; Jaffe, Lindheim, and Lee 1981, pp. 1, 11–12; Tietze 1981, p. 7; Hardin 1967, p. 84; David 1980, p. 67; Condit 1990, pp. 63–65; A. Guttmacher 1960, p. 52; L. Epstein and Kobylka 1992, p. 147; Garrow 1994, p. 370.

186. Calderone 1958, p. 112 (quoting Sophia Kleegman).

187. Charles and Alexander 1971, p. 168. See Lucas 1968, pp. 763, 771–73. See also L. Epstein and Kobylka 1992, p. 160 (noting that the *1976 Policy Guide of the American Civil Liberties Union* stated that abortion law in action unconstitutionally discriminated against poor women; see American Civil Liberties Union 1976, p. 231).

188. L. Epstein and Kobylka 1992, pp. 174–76, 179.

189. Davis 1985, p. 9.

190. Powe 1994, p. 208. See Jeffries 1994, p. 347.

191. 305 F. Supp. 1032, 1035 (D. D.C. 1969).

192. *People v. Belous*, 458 P.2d 194 (Cal. 1969); *People v. Barksdale*, 503 P.2d 257 (Cal. 1972); *Doe v. Bolton*, 319 F. Supp. 1048 (N.D. Georgia 1970); *Roe v. Wade*, 314 F. Supp. 1217 (N.D. Tex. 1970); *Walsingham v. State*, 250 So.2d 857 (Fla. 1971); *Abele v. Markle*, 342 F. Supp. 800 (D. Conn. 1972); *Abele v. Markle*, 351 F. Supp. 224 (D. Conn. 1972); *Beecham v. Leahy*, 287 A.2d 836 (Ver. 1972); *YWCA v. Kugler*, 342 F. Supp. 1048 (D. N.J. 1972); *Doe v. Scott*, 321 F. Supp. 1385 (N.D. Ill. 1971); *Babbitz v. McCann*, 306 F. Supp. 400 (E.D. Wisc. 1970); *Poe v. Menghini*, 339 F. Supp. 986 (D. Kan. 1972); *United States v. Vuitch*, 305 F. Supp. 1032 (D. D.C. 1969). See Garrow 1994, pp. 377, 382–83, 415–17, 480–81, 496, 538–41, 544, 561, 565–66, 579; Roemer 1973, pp. 288–90. In 1969, Oregon passed a very permissive abortion law which, in practice, amounted to legalized abortion on demand (Roemer 1973, p. 286; Quick 1978).

193. *Roe v. Wade*, 410 U.S. 164 (1973).

194. *Planned Parenthood v. Casey*; *Rust v. Sullivan*, 500 U.S. 173 (1991); *Ohio v. Akron Center for Reproductive Health*, 497 U.S. 502 (1990); *Webster v. Reproductive Health Services*; *Harris v. McRae*, 448 U.S. 297 (1980); *Maher v. Roe*, 432 U.S. 464 (1977).

195. *Roe v. Wade* has become the symbol of legalized abortion. That case, however, was only one cause of the increase in legal abortions that has taken place over the past thirty years. See Rosenberg 1991, pp. 178–80.

196. Bracken, Freeman, and Hellenbrand 1982, p. 34. See Niswander and Porto 1986, p. 260.

197. See Condit 1990, pp. 191–92.

198. Tietze 1973, p. 41. See Jaffe, Lindheim, and Lee 1981, p. 21; Tietze and Bongaarts 1976, pp. 707–8; Quick 1978, p. 1007; Cates 1986, p. 308; Fujita and Wagner 1973, p. 256.

199. See Adamek 1980, p. 21.

200. Tietze and Bongaarts 1976, p. 706; Quick 1978, p. 1007. See Cates 1982, p. 1586; Oppel and Sanford 1973, pp. 405–8. For a discussion of pro-life critiques of these figures, see chap. I.

201. Hansen 1980, p. 377.

202. Lamanna 1980, p. 140. See Tietze 1981, p. 103; Zimmerman 1977, p. 9. Abortion has clearly not proven an alternative to contraception. Women who have abortions tend to improve their contraceptive skills. See E. Freeman 1978, pp. 153–54; Lamanna 1980, p. 142 (citing studies); Tietze 1973, pp. 40–41; Swartz 1973, p. 114; Petchesky 1990, p. 190.

203. Sarvis and Rodman 1973, p. 173.

204. See Rosenberg 1991, p. 198. Abortions are also moneymakers in hospitals; see p. 198.

205. Cates 1982, p. 1588.

206. Jaffe, Lindheim, and Lee 1981, p. 25. See Sheeran 1987, pp. 30, 45; Sarvis and Rodman 1973, p. 55. The average fee in 1985 was estimated to be $213 (Henshaw, Forest, and Van Vort 1987, p. 69).

207. See generally Cates 1981, p. 1111 (noting the role of "reduced provider fees . . . and philanthropic contributions" when Medicaid payments were halted).

208. Pakter, O'Hare, Nelson, and Svigir 1973. See Legge 1985, p. 97; Jaffe, Lindheim, and Lee 1981, p. 11.

209. Petchesky 1990, pp. 156–57. See Niswander and Porto 1986, p. 250.

210. Cates 1977, p. 280; Rodman, Sarvis, and Bonar 1987, p. 153. See Cates 1977, pp. 267–68; Hansen 1980, p. 392; Mensch and Freeman 1991, p. 1107 n. 692; Tietze 1986, p. 296; L. Lee 1973, p. 346; Petchesky 1990, p. xvi; Steinhoff 1973, p. 208.

211. Women of color continue to suffer much higher mortality and morbidity rates from illegal and legal abortions. See Binkin, Gold, and Cates 1982, p. 164 (from 1972 to 1979, the death rate among Hispanics was ten times that of whites, and the death rate of blacks was fourteen times that of whites); Cates 1977, p. 277 (noting that even when other factors are controlled, blacks are twice as likely as whites to die from a legal abortion); Rodman, Sarvis, and Bonar 1987, pp. 66–67.

212. Tietze 1984, p. 26. See Cates 1982, pp. 1586–87; Jaffe, Lindheim, and Lee 1981, p. 23; Rodman, Sarvis, and Bonar 1987, p. 46; L. Lee 1973, pp. 340–41; Niswander and Porto 1986, p. 248; Cates 1986, pp. 307–8; Petchesky 1990, p. 157; Roemer 1973, p. 296. See also Condit 1990, p. 197 n. 16. These estimates may be too low for reasons discussed in n. 24, above.

Although no one would claim that abortion saves fetal lives, research suggests that legalization has reduced infant mortality. See, e.g., Quick 1978; A. Guttmacher 1986, p. 536; L. Lee 1973, pp. 340–41.

213. Sewart, Ballard, and Ulene 1973, p. 336. For earlier California studies showing that these medical effects only took place in communities that liberalized abortion practices, see P. Goldstein and Stewart 1972; Stewart and Goldstein 1971. For similar findings in other states, see Harting and Hunter 1971, p. 2101–2 (New York); Kahan, Baker, and Freeman 1975 (Georgia).

214. Neubardt and Schulman 1977, pp. viii-ix. See Miller 1993, p. 8 ("after January 1973, the septic abortion wards . . . simply disappeared"); Rodman, Sarvis, and Bonar 1987, pp. 62–63.

215. See Cates 1982, pp. 1587–88; Cates 1986, pp. 307, 311–15; Tietze 1986, pp. 297, 302–3; Cates, Schulz, Grimes, and Tyler 1977; Harting and Hunter 1971, p. 2104; Hansen 1980, p. 379; Davis 1985, pp. 226–27, 230; Sheeran 1987, p. 45; Niswander and Porto 1986, p. 259.

216. Sheeran 1987, p. 22. See Cates 1986, p. 308; Tietze 1986, p. 301.

217. See Tribe 1990a, pp. 205–6; MacKinnon 1991, p. 1320; West 1990, p. 51; Rhode 1989, pp. 213–14; Olsen 1989, p. 105, 113, 116; Roberts 1992.

218. 432 U.S. 464 (1977).

219. 448 U.S. 297 (1980).

220. Cates 1981, p. 1112. See Cates 1986, pp. 315–16; Legge 1985, p. 7;

R. Gold and Macias 1986, p. 263; Trussell, Menken, Lindheim, and Vaughan 1980, p. 130; Rodman, Sarvis, and Bonar 1987, pp. 155–56; Rosenberg 1991, p. 187. See also E. Rubin 1987, p. 176.

221. Wolpert and Rosenberg 1990, p. 15. See also Hansen 1993, pp. 240–42.

222. Legge 1985, p. 7. See also Francome 1986, p. 192 ("an unwanted pregnancy is such a traumatic experience that women will go great distances, take enormous risks and use up large parts of their savings to get abortions").

223. See Henshaw and Wallisch 1984; Trussell, Menken, Lindheim, and Vaughan 1980, p. 130. See also E. Rubin 1987, p. 176; Petchesky 1990, p. 160.

224. See Cates 1981 (discussed above).

225. Cates 1986, p. 316.

226. Legge 1985, p. 124.

227. See Althaus and Henshaw 1994, p. 228 (only seven of fifteen states are enforcing legally mandated waiting periods); Craig and O'Brien 1993, pp. 85, 88, 91; Lewin 1992.

228. Yates and Pliner 1988, p. 647.

229. "Pennsylvania Abortion Foes Say Law Is Being Underminded," 1994, p. A14; Abortion Political Network 1994.

230. Applebome 1992, p. A14 (waiting periods in Mississippi); Althaus and Henshaw 1994 (waiting periods in Pennsylvania and Mississippi); Cartoof and Klerman 1986 (parental consent in Massachusetts). See also Henshaw 1995 (parental consent laws in Mississippi are merely increasing the number of out-of-state abortions procured by Mississippi minors).

231. Wolpert and Rosenberg 1990, p. 15. Wolpert and Rosenberg did not explore whether such laws increased abortions in neighboring states.

232. Althaus and Henshaw 1994, p. 231.

233. Althaus and Henshaw 1994, pp. 231–33. But see Blum, Resnick, and Stark 1990, p. 160 (suggesting that affluent teenagers are more likely to use judicial bypass mechanisms in states that require parental consent before abortion).

234. R. Gold 1990, pp. 44–46; Yates and Pliner 1988, pp. 648–49; Althaus and Henshaw 1994. See also Henshaw 1995, p. 121.

235. R. Gold 1990, p. 45. See Lupfer and Silber 1981; Althaus and Henshaw 1994.

236. Blum, Resnick, and Stark 1987, p. 620; Blum, Resnick, and Stark 1990, p. 160.

237. C. Nathanson and Becker 1981, p. 218.

238. Rodman, Sarvis, and Bonar 1987, p. 83. See E. Rubin 1987, pp. 168–69; Henshaw and Van Vort 1990, p. 107; Davis 1985, p. 9; Jaffe, Lindheim, and Lee 1981, pp. 191–92; Petchesky 1990, p. 157.

239. Alan Guttmacher Institute 1979, p. 13; Jaffe, Lindheim, and Lee, p. 205; R. Gold 1980, p. 205; Forrest, Tietze, and Sullivan 1978, p. 279.

240. Rosenberg 1991, p. 195. See L. Epstein and Kobylka 1992, p. 205.

241. Henshaw and Van Vort 1994, p. 104; Henshaw and Van Vort 1990, p. 107; Rosenberg 1991, pp. 190, 194. See Rosenthal 1995, p. A1 ("over the past 10 years, almost all of New York City's full-service hospitals have backed out of the abortion business"); Henshaw 1986, p. 253; Garrow 1994, pp. 608, 618, 683; Jaffe, Lindheim, and Lee 1981, pp. 15, 22–23; Tietze 1981, p. 9; E. Rubin 1987,

186 NOTES TO CHAPTER II

p. 109; F. Ginsburg 1989, p. 55; Tietze 1986, pp. 292–93; Petchesky 1990, p. 157; Zimmerman 1977, p. 13; Tatalovich and Daynes 1981, p. 206; Rosenblatt 1992, p. 17; Craig and O'Brien 1993, pp. 77–78. See also Lindheim and Cotterill 1978, p. 11 (noting that many teaching hospitals do not require that obstetric residents learn to perform abortions); Rosenberg 1991, p. 194.

242. Imber 1986, p. 115. See Imber 1986, pp. 23, 73, 76, 114, 122–23; Seims 1980, p. 88; C. Nathanson and Becker 1977, pp. 162–63; Petchesky 1990, pp. 158–59; Orr and Forrest 1985.

243. Henshaw and Van Vort 1994, p. 106; Henshaw and Van Vort 1990, p. 107. See Henshaw, Forrest, and Van Vort 1987, p. 67; Rosenberg 1991, pp. 195–98; F. Ginsburg 1989, pp. 55–56; Wolpert and Rosenberg 1990, pp. 5–6; Cates 1982, pp. 1587–88; Jaffe, Lindheim, and Lee 1981, pp. 32, 191–92; Cates 1986, pp. 314–15; Petchesky 1990, p. 157.

244. Jaffe, Lindheim, and Lee 1981, pp. 191–92.

245. Henshaw and Van Vort 1994, p. 103; Henshaw and Van Vort 1990, p. 107. See Henshaw, Forrest, and Van Vort 1987, pp. 64–65; Jaffe, Lindheim, and Lee 1981, pp. 34, 191–92; F. Ginsburg 1989, p. 56. See also Tietze 1986, pp. 292–93.

246. Craig and O'Brien 1993, p. 78 (discussing Rosenberg 1991, p. 192). See Henshaw and Van Vort 1994, p. 102.

247. Henshaw and Van Vort 1994.

248. See Henshaw 1991, pp. 250–51; National Abortion Federation 1993; National Abortion Federation 1994; Donovan 1985; Forrest and Henshaw 1987; Kifner 1994; Rimer 1993; Lapidus and Albisa 1994; Cowles and Finley 1994. But see Forrest and Henshaw 1987, p. 13 ("harassment of abortion providers has not succeeded in reducing the number of abortions performed by the facilities [surveyed]").

249. Boodman 1993; Rimer 1993. For a good summary of the variety of pressures on abortion clinics, in particular "financial pressures—from competition, from managed health-care plans, [and] from a dropping abortion rate"—see Vrazo 1995, p. B4.

250. F. Ginsburg 1989, p. 57. See Hansen 1980, pp. 383, 386, 390–91; Hansen 1993, p. 241.

251. Shelton, Brann, and Schulz 1976, p. 262; Jaffe, Lindheim, and Lee 1981, p. 34. See Henshaw and Van Vort 1990, p. 105; Wolpert and Rosenberg 1990, p. 15 ("the higher the proportion of residents living in metropolitan areas, the higher the abortion rate"); Henshaw and Silverman 1988, p. 156; Zimmerman 1977, p. 13.

252. Henshaw and Van Vort 1990, p. 104. In the same year, 163 out of every 1,000 women in Washington, D.C., terminated a pregnancy (p. 104).

253. See nn. 131–233 and the relevant text.

254. Wolpert and Rosenberg 1990, p. 15. For similar findings, see Hansen 1980, pp. 383, 386.

255. See A. Rubin 1992.

256. Some commentators speculate that pro-choice policies enable men to coerce women into unwanted abortions. Reardon 1987; Mensch and Freeman 1991, p. 1124. Anecdotes do exist of men pressuring women to have abortions

against their will (see, e.g., Reardon 1987, pp. 30–31). Nevertheless, men also pressured women into having unwanted abortions when abortion was illegal (see Reagan 1991b, pp. 60–61). No evidence exists that coerced abortion is a major social problem or that coerced abortions have increased since legalization. Studies suggest that very few women later regret their abortions and that most women who have abortions become more sympathetic to pro-choice positions. See E. Freeman 1977, p. 506; D. Granberg 1981, p. 161; N. Lee 1969, pp. 38–39.

257. See Weigel and Kristol 1994, p. A21 ("the goal of pro-life Republican action should be unequivocal: 'an America in which every unborn child is protected in law and welcomed in life' "); Barnes 1994; A. Rubin 1995.

258. See Robertson 1994; Lader 1991.

259. Manier, Liu, and Solomon 1977, p. 197.

260. Although at present RU-486 would require consistent medical supervision; see Wickenden 1990, p. 27.

261. See generally D. Callahan 1984, pp. 313–14.

262. See Dellinger 1992; Tribe 1990a, pp. 197–228.

263. Laws limiting the number of abortion providers might have a more substantial and discriminatory effect on access to abortion services. Predictions about the impact of abortion laws in action that are based on abortion laws on the books, however, have seldom been accurate. Hospitals in states that ban specialized abortion clinics might perform more abortions; some specialized abortion clinics might be redefined as private hospitals. Thus, until some state actually requires that abortions be performed in hospitals, commentators are best advised to reserve judgment on the practical consequences of such measures.

264. See especially Glendon 1987, p. 49. See also Boling 1991, p. 11; Macedo 1991, p. 72; P. Freund 1983, p. 1480.

265. Calabresi and Bobbitt 1978, p. 207 n. 7. See Lamanna 1984, p. 12; Trout 1964, p. 188.

266. Niswander and Porto 1986, p. 251. See generally Niswander and Porto 1986, pp. 251–54.

267. Luker 1984a, p. 26. See Miller 1993, p. 2 ("the real public policy question is not *whether* we will have abortions but *what kind* of abortions we will have" [emphasis in original]).

Chapter III
Equal Choice

1. Thucydides 1954, p. 145. See Sealey 1987, pp. 99–102, 146; Dahl 1989, p. 14; Landes 1993, p. 68.

2. Kens 1990, p. 105. See nn. 18–25 and the relevant text.

3. Constitutional commentators engage in vehement historical debates over which persons were responsible for framing and ratifying the Constitution and various constitutional amendments, and in equally vehement theoretical debates over whether the intentions of framers or those of ratifiers are more authoritative (see, e.g., Brest 1980). Such problems need not concern proponents of equal choice. However the persons responsible for the constitutional provisions dis-

cussed in this chapter are designated, they clearly intended that the Fourteenth Amendment protect the right to formal legal equality defended here.

4. Hughes 1908, p. 139.

5. See chap. V.

6. 481 U.S. 279 (1987).

7. See chap. II.

8. That ban applies to both federal and state officials. See *Bolling v. Sharpe*, 347 U.S. 497 (1954); Graber 1993a.

9. *Slaughter-House Cases*, 83 U.S. 36, 71 (1873).

10. See *Regents of the University of California v. Bakke*, 438 U.S. 265 (1978) (white persons); *Craig v. Boren*, 429 U.S. 190 (1976) (women); *Sugarman v. Dougall*, 413 U.S. 634 (1973) (aliens); *Bowers v. Hardwick*, 478 U.S. 186 (1986) (homosexuals); *Cleburne v. Cleburne Living Center*, 473 U.S. 432 (1985) (the mentally retarded); *Mathews v. Lucas*, 427 U.S. 495 (1976) (the illegitimate); *Massachusetts Board of Retirement v. Murgia*, 427 U.S. 307 (1976) (the aged).

11. See Hyman and Wiecek 1982, pp. 317, 393; Kaczorowski 1986, p. 883; Nieman 1991, p. 61. Reconstruction Republicans also sought to ensure racial equality in commercial relationships. All persons of color, they agreed, must enjoy "the right to make contracts for their labor, the power to enforce the payment of their wages, and the means of holding and enjoying the proceeds of their toil" (Foner 1988, pp. 28–29). See Hyman and Wiecek 1982, p. 321; Nieman 1991, pp. 60–62; McCurdy 1984, pp. 26–27; Gillman 1993, pp. 44–45; Fredrickson 1971, pp. 152–81.

The strong racial prejudices that lingered even among many Northern abolitionists did prevent Reconstruction Republicans from clearly demanding policies that would ensure the future equality of persons of color in all spheres of political and social life. Historians and constitutional commentators debate the extent to which the framers of the Fourteenth Amendment intended to provide for racial equality and the extent to which the Fourteenth Amendment should be interpreted as protecting the rights of persons of color. For a sampling of this debate, see Nelson 1988; Curtis 1986; Berger 1977; Graham 1968; Maltz 1990a; Kousser 1988; Hyman and Wiecek 1982; Kaczorowski 1986; Foner 1988; TenBroek 1951; Bickel 1955.

12. Hyman and Wiecek 1982, p. 399.

13. T. Wilson 1965, p. 70. See Hyman and Wiecek 1982, p. 425.

14. 14 *U.S. Statutes at Large* 27 (1866).

15. See especially Berger 1977. See also Lofgren 1987, pp. 63, 65; Nelson 1988, p. 115.

16. Law enforcement officials in many communities also violated the Fourteenth Amendment by selectively prosecuting only those incompetent abortionists who maimed white women, leaving rank amateurs free to butcher women of color. See Kennedy 1988 (noting that the Fourteenth Amendment requires that persons of color receive the same police and prosecutorial services as white persons); Carter 1988, pp. 442–45; Reagan 1991a, pp. 1246–47.

17. See n. 10, above.

18. See Kens 1990, p. 105; Benedict 1985, pp. 304–26.

19. Pole 1978, p. 29 (quoting the Reverend Francis Allen, a leader of Philadelphia Presbyterians).

20. See Pole 1978, p. 49; Benedict 1985, pp. 321–22. The extent to which "men [and women] are by nature free and equal," however, remains controversial to this day. See Mansbridge 1986.

21. Goodman 1975, p. 69. See Wood 1992, p. 232 ("equality was in fact the most radical and most ideologically powerful force let loose by the Revolution").

22. *Dartmouth College v. Woodward*, 17 U.S. 518, 581 (1819). See *Clapp & Albright v. Administrator of Reynolds*, 2 Texas Reports 250, 252 (1851). See also Maltz 1990b, p. 252 n. 5. For a discussion of the relationship between the equality component of due process and the equal protection clause, see Mott 1926, pp. 275–99.

23. *Vanzant v. Waddell*, 2 Yerg. 260, 271 (Tenn., 1829) (Catron, J., concurring). See *State Bank v. Cooper*, 2 Yerg. 599 (Tenn., 1831). For a general discussion of class legislation before the Civil War, see Mott 1926, pp. 259–66. See also Mendelson 1985, pp. 195–96, 199–201; Gillman 1993, pp. 50–55, 59–60.

24. A. Jackson 1963, p. 274. See Pole 1978, pp. 144–46; Gillman 1993, pp. 35–37.

25. Leggett 1954, pp. 77–78. See *Democratic Review* 1954, p. 28; Pole 1978, p. 139 (quoting Robert Rantoul Jr., a leading Jacksonian jurist). See generally Benedict 1985, pp. 318–20; Hyman and Wiecek 1982, p. 29; Gillman 1993, pp. 38, 42–44.

26. TenBroek 1951, pp. 175–76; Foner 1988, p. 254. See also TenBroek 1951, pp. 213–14 (quoting Senator Jacob Howard); Curtis 1986, p. 61 (quoting Bingham), 62 (quoting Ignatius Donnelly); Kousser 1988, p. 956 (quoting the *Liberator*), 979 (quoting Charles Summer); Fredrickson 1971, pp. 178–79 (quoting Godkin). See generally Nelson 1988, pp. 71–80; Gillman 1993, p. 62.

27. *Congressional Globe*, 39th Cong., 1st sess., 1866, p. 2766.

28. *Edwards v. California*, 314 U.S. 160, 184–85 (1941) (Jackson, J., concurring). See *Edwards*, at 181 (Douglas, J., concurring).

29. Cooley 1868, p. 392 (quoting Locke). See Mott 1926, pp. 275–76. See also Gillman 1993, pp. 55–59. Other commentators indicated that the due process clause required legislatures to govern by general laws; see Tiedeman 1886, pp. 71–72; E. Freund 1904, p. 633; Mott 1926, pp. 273–74. Many state courts used natural law principles or inferences from the separation of powers to strike down local measures granting special privileges to some persons. See Mott 1926, pp. 259–99; Gillman 1993, pp. 59–60.

30. *Traux v. Corrigan*, 257 U.S. 312, 332 (1921). Early cases did hold that some political and civil rights could be conditioned on property holdings. *Breedlove v. Suttles*, 302 U.S. 277 (1937) (poll tax); *Strauder v. West Virginia*, 100 U.S. 303, 310 (1880) (suggesting that states could limit jury duty to freeholders).

31. *Harper v. Virginia Board of Elections*, 383 U.S. 663, 668 (1966). See *Boddie v. Connecticut*, 401 U.S. 371 (1970) (filing fees in divorce cases unconstitutional); *Griffin v. Illinois*, 351 U.S. 12, 17 (1956) (opinion of Black, J.; "in criminal trials a State can no more discriminate on account of poverty than on account of religion, race, or color"). See also *Edwards*, at 160, 184–85 (Jackson, J., concurring).

The Burger Court did substantially narrow *Boddie* by permitting states to require filing fees in cases concerning bankruptcy and welfare rights. See *United States v. Kras*, 409 U.S. 434 (1973); *Ortwein v. Schwab*, 410 U.S. 656 (1973).

32. *Douglas v. California*, 372 U.S. 353, 361 (1963).

33. 372 U.S. 335, 344 (1963).

34. *Griffin v. Illinois*, at 12, 19 (opinion of Black, J.); *Douglas*, at 355. See *Draper v. Washington*, 372 U.S. 487, 496 (1963); *Lane v. Brown*, 372 U.S. 477, 483–84 (1963); *Smith v. Bennett*, 365 U.S. 708, 710–11 (1960); *Eskridge v. Washington Prison Board*, 357 U.S. 214, 216 (1958); *Williams v. Illinois*, 399 U.S. 235, 241 (1970).

35. *Griffin v. Illinois*, at 12, 19 (opinion of Black, J.). See *Williams v. Illinois*, at 235, 241 ("the basic command that justice be applied equally to all persons").

36. *Douglas*, at 357.

37. *Smith v. Bennett*, at 708, 714.

38. See Bork 1979; Winter 1973; Monaghan 1978.

39. S. Lawrence 1990, p. 48 (quoting Jack Greenberg). See Reich 1964, pp. 785–86; Sparer 1971, pp. 82–91; Sparer 1965, pp. 361–66. See also S. Lawrence 1990, pp. 44, 48–49. For summaries of the difference between older and contemporary notion of constitutional poverty rights, see *Douglas*, at 361–62 (Harlan, J., dissenting); Michelman 1971, p. 43.

40. Michelman 1979, p. 659. See Sparer 1971; Michelman 1969; Michelman 1971, especially pp. 42–43 ("acceptable housing [should] be available irrespective of the market returns commanded by one's endowments of talent, influence, or capital, and irrespective even of voluntary choices in one's remote past which have resulted in present inability to pay the true costs of acceptable housing"); Reich 1964; C. Black 1986.

41. In fact, most poor persons are able to obtain safe abortions in a free market. See chap. II.

42. Noonan 1979, p. 65.

43. Noonan 1979, pp. 64–65; Louisell and Noonan 1970, p. 236. Louisell and Noonan do claim that pro-choice advocates wildly exaggerate the scope of that gray market. See chap. I for a discussion of those claims.

44. Louisell and Noonan 1970, p. 243.

45. Louisell and Noonan 1970, p. 244.

46. See chap. II.

47. See chap. II.

48. See Noonan 1979, p. 65; Louisell and Noonan 1970, p. 236.

49. See *United States v. Cruikshank*, 92 U.S. 542 (1875); *Moose Lodge No. 107 v. Irvis*, 407 U.S. 163 (1972). The language of the Thirteenth Amendment and legal precedents do, however, prohibit both private and public actions that reduce persons to slavery. See *Jones v. Alfred H. Mayer Co.*, 392 U.S. 409 (1968).

50. See Symposium 1993. Indeed, the state action doctrine, particularly as applied by the Rehnquist Court, is not immune to originalist and other attacks; see Kaczorowski 1986.

51. See C. Black 1967, pp. 100–3; Wechsler 1959, p. 34; Karst 1980; chap. I.

52. H.R. Joint Comm. Report No. 30, 39th Cong., 1st Sess., p. xvii (1866). See Hyman and Wiecek 1982, pp. 320, 323–24, 414–15, 423–25; Curtis 1986,

p. 158 (quoting Representative Aaron F. Perry of Ohio); *McCleskey v. Kemp*, 481 U.S. 279, 346–47 (1987) (Blackmun, J., dissenting; citing sources); Kennedy 1988, p. 1423.

53. *Wayte v. United States*, 470 U.S. 598, 608 (1985) (quoting *United States v. Batchelder*, 442 U.S. 114, 125 [1979]). See also *Oyler v. Boles*, 368 U.S. 448, 456 (1962).

54. Pro-life commentators suggest that government officials were not constitutionally responsible for establishing or maintaining an exclusive gray market in safe abortions because state actors delegated to the medical community the responsibility for policing statutory bans on abortion (see Louisell and Noonan 1970, pp. 240–41). Both common sense and legal precedent, however, discredit claims that the Fourteenth Amendment contains a loophole that permits states to preserve discriminatory practices by farming out official functions to private parties. All constitutional limitations on official power would be practically worthless if governmental actors could evade those restrictions merely by inducing "private" associations to do the desired dirty work. Thus, when a Virginia county attempted to circumvent *Brown* by closing its public schools and granting funds to segregated private schools, a unanimous Supreme Court promptly declared the policy unconstitutional; *Griffin v. County School Board of Prince Edward County*, 377 U.S. 218, 233 (1964).

Private agents are particularly obligated to respect constitutional rights when they perform what legal precedents describe as a "traditional state function"; see *Marsh v. Alabama*, 326 U.S. 501 (1946). Efforts to determine the precise contours of "traditional state function" have resulted in numerous disputes, but commentators of all political persuasions agree that law enforcement is the paradigmatic task that states traditionally perform. Any person given official responsibility for administering a law is thus a state actor for Fourteenth Amendment purposes. The doctors at most private hospitals before *Roe* may not have thought of themselves as state actors. Nevertheless, to the extent that the law enforcement community allowed physicians to implement official abortion policies, those doctors had the same constitutional obligation as the patrol officer on the beat not to discriminate against poor persons and persons of color.

55. A. Freeman 1990; C. Lawrence 1987; Flagg 1993; Strauss 1989.

56. *Washington v. Davis*, 426 U.S. 229 (1976). See *Arlington Heights v. Metropolitan Housing Corp.*, 429 U.S. 252 (1977); *Personnel Administrator of Massachusetts v. Feeney*, 442 U.S. 256 (1979).

57. See n. 55, above.

58. *Personnel Administrator of Massachusetts v. Feeney*, at 256, 274 (quoting *Arlington Heights v. Metropolitan Housing Corp.*, at 252, 266); *Washington v. Davis*, at 229, 242. See *Batson v. Kentucky*, 476 U.S. 79, 93–94 (1986).

59. *Personnel Administrator of Massachusetts v. Feeney*, at 275. See *Washington v. Davis*, at 229, 246.

The justices have said very little about how plausible the explanation must be to justify policies that severely burden poor persons and persons of color. A number of cases interpreting the antidiscrimination provisions of Title VII of the Civil Rights Act of 1964 suggest that "a mere insubstantial justification . . . will not suffice." The Rehnquist Court, however, has also declared that the challenged practice need not be "essential" or "indispensable"(*Wards Cove Packing Co. v. Atonio*, 490 U.S. 642, 659 [1989]). Congress recently passed the Civil Rights Act of 1991 in order to make Title VII violations somewhat easier to prove (see 105 *U.S. Statutes at Large* 1074 [1991], discussed at n. 63 and the relevant text), but the Court has yet to determine the precise impact of that measure on federal antidiscrimination law. Moreover, the justices maintain that state practices may satisfy the constitutional standards required by the equal protection clause even when they do not satisfy all of the standards laid down by Congress in the federal code. Compare *Griggs v. Duke Power Co.*, 401 U.S. 424 (1971) (discriminatory intent is not a necessary element in employment discrimination cases arising under the Civil Rights Act of 1964) with *Washington v. Davis*, at 229 (discriminatory intent is a necessary element in employment discrimination cases arising under the equal protection clause).

60. *Batson v. Kentucky*, at 79, 93–94; *Castaneda v. Partida*, 430 U.S. 482 (1977); *Carter v. Jury Commission*, 396 U.S. 320 (1970); *Avery v. Georgia*, 345 U.S. 559 (1953).

61. *Washington v. Davis*, at 229, 253 (Stevens, J., concurring).

62. Kennedy 1988, p. 1405; see also pp. 1402–21.

63. 105 *U.S. Statutes at Large* 1074 (1991). The Civil Rights Act of 1991 recognizes that victims of unlawful discrimination frequently cannot point to the discrete moment when their rights were violated. Congress declared that when "the elements of a respondent's decisionmaking process are not capable of separation for analysis, the decisionmaking process may be analyzed as one employment practice" (105 *U.S. Statutes at Large* 1074 [1991]).

64. *Powers v. Otto*, 499 U.S. 400, 429 (1991). See *Rose v. Mitchell*, 443 U.S. 545, 555 (1979): Kennedy 1988, p. 1409.

65. Though as noted in n. 59, federal statutes may impose stricter antidiscrimination rules than those required by the equal protection clause.

66. *Gomillion v. Lightfoot*, 364 U.S. 339, 340–41 (1960).

67. See chap. II.

68. Noonan 1979, p. 52.

69. Except to the significant extent that the arrest and subsequent procedures in themselves constitute punishment. See Feeley 1992, and chap. II.

70. *McCleskey*, at 279, 287. See also at 355 (Blackmun, J., dissenting; "20 out of every 34 defendants in McCleskey's mid-range category would not have been sentenced to be executed if their victims had been black"); at 321 (Brennan, J., dissenting). For the surveys used in *McCleskey*, see Baldus, Woodworth, and Pulaski 1990.

71. *McCleskey*, at 292.

72. *McCleskey*, at 292.

73. Note 1988, pp. 1621–22. See Kennedy 1988, pp. 1405, 1420–21; Baldus, Woodworth, and Pulaski 1990, p. 370.

74. *Turner v. Murray*, 476 U.S. 28, 35 (1986) (opinion of White, J.). See *Rose v. Mitchell*, at 545, 558–59.

75. Compare *McCleskey*, at 297 ("discretion is essential to the criminal process") with 294 ("the capital sentencing process was different").

76. *McCleskey*, at 313, with n. 36; see also at 315 n. 37.

77. See chap. II.

78. Clearly, the Rehnquist Court is not likely to so interpret *McCleskey*.

79. Hengstler, Moss, and Goldberg 1988, p. 139; Morris 1992, p. 361.

80. See Kennedy 1988, p. 1394 n. 20.

81. Kennedy 1988, p. 1389; Calabresi 1991, p. 117 n. 109; Jeffries 1994, pp. 361–64. Professor Kennedy's attack on *McCleskey* supports equal choice contentions that Americans are more likely to support claims that the law should treat people equally than claims that all persons have a certain right. Significantly, two of the four dissenters in *McCleskey*, Justices Stevens and Blackmun, maintained that fairly administered capital sentencing procedures pass constitutional muster. See *McCleskey*, at 365 (Blackmun, J., dissenting); at 367 (Stevens, J., dissenting).

82. *McCleskey*, at 293.

83. The Burger and Rehnquist Courts usually rejected claims of unconstitutional discrimination, but only on the ground that state procedures served legitimate public purposes. See cases cited in n. 56, above.

84. *McCleskey*, at 346–47 (Blackmun, J., dissenting). See Carter 1991b, p. 4.

85. Nieman 1991, p. 63. See *Caldwell v. Mississippi*, 472 U.S. 320, 343 (1985) (O'Connor, J., concurring); *Gregg v. Georgia*, 428 U.S. 153, 195 n. 46 (1976) (opinion of Stewart, Powell, and Stevens, JJ.); *Godfrey v. Georgia*, 446 U.S. 420, 427 (1980) ("penalty of death may not be imposed under sentencing procedures that create a substantial risk that the punishment will be inflicted in an arbitrary and capricious manner").

86. See Nieman 1991, pp. 66–68. Some law enforcement officials appointed by President Andrew Johnson prosecuted only "blatant discriminatory" practices (Nieman 1991, p. 69). The Johnson administration, however, opposed those measures that were later incorporated into the Fourteenth Amendment.

87. See the discussion in chap. II of the implementation and impact of post-*Casey* regulations.

88. Just as equal choice is agnostic on whether women have a constitutional right to an abortion, so equal choice is agnostic on whether states may pass laws that unduly burden women seeking abortion.

89. Though as noted in chap. II, n. 263, hospitalization requirements might be administered in ways that have very little impact on legal abortion rates.

90. See *Hunter v. Underwood*, 471 U.S. 222 (1985).

91. See, e.g., *City of Akron v. Akron Center for Reproductive Health, Inc.*, 462 U.S. 416, 454–56 (1983) (O'Connor, J., dissenting).

92. The *Washington v. Davis* test is hardly etched in stone. Many commentators criticize both the intentional discrimination requirement and the demanding standards the present Court requires for meeting it (see sources cited in n. 55, above). While I sympathize with some progressive critiques of present Fourteenth Amendment doctrine, using more liberal interpretations of equal protection would defeat the rhetorical value of equal choice. This book purports to offer a better and more persuasive attack on pro-life policies than conventional pro-choice broadsides. That promise cannot be fulfilled by arguments that merely replace controversial theories about the meaning of the due process clause with controversial theories about the meaning of intentional discrimination.

93. American Public Health Association 1980, p. 654. See American College of Obstetricians and Gynecologists 1982, p. 54.

94. See Wilkinson 1989; *Ragsdale v. Turnock*, 941 F.2d 501 (7th Cir. 1991).

95. The canonical works in the democratic process tradition are *United States v. Carolene Products*, 304 U.S. 144, 152–53 n. 4 (1938); Lusky 1942; Lusky 1975; Ely 1980; Calabresi 1991. See also Monaghan 1981; Farber and Frickey 1991, p. 117. The best known of these works, John Hart Ely's *Democracy and Distrust*, unfortunately conflates a democratic process model of judicial review with a theory of constitutional interpretation that insists that the Constitution, for the most part, only protects rights to a certain kind of democratic process (see Ely 1980, pp. 88–101). *Rethinking Abortion* makes no such claim, suggesting only that justices should be particularly responsible for correcting those constitutional violations that result from particular failings of democratic processes. I do not argue that rights to fair political processes are the only or most important rights guaranteed by the constitution.

96. *Ervine's Appeal*, 16 Pa. St. 256, 268 (1851).

97. *Carolene Products*, at 152–53 n. 4; Lusky 1942, p. 21.

98. Calabresi 1991, pp. 91–93. See Ely 1980, pp. 77–87; see also Farber and Frickey 1991, p. 117.

99. Dahl 1989, p. 97. See Mill 1962, p. 58.

100. Hamilton, Madison, and Jay, 1961, p. 80.

101. Ely 1973; Lusky 1975, p. 20. But see Calabresi 1991 (suggesting that pro-life policies do not treat the concerns of women with equal concern and respect).

102. See generally Calabresi 1991, p. 91.

103. Dahl 1989, p. 108. See Calabresi 1991, p. 93. Majorities not hostile to minority interests may nevertheless be indifferent to or ignorant of the disparate social costs of partial laws. "When power resides in an exclusive class," John Stuart Mill observed, "the interest of the excluded is always in danger of being overlooked; and when looked at, is seen with very different eyes from those of the persons whom it directly concerns" (Mill 1962, pp. 59–60).

104. Calabresi 1991, p. 136.

105. Ely 1980, p. 173. See *Railway Express Agency v. New York*, 336 U.S. 106, 112–13 (1949) (Jackson, J., concurring); Farber and Frickey 1991, p. 138.

106. Ely 1980, p. 74.

107. See Ely 1980, pp. 145–72.

108. State failures to fund abortions for indigent women, in contrast, manifest unconstitutional favoritism only when the state at the same time funds abortions for more affluent women.

109. Fewer than half of all voters with family incomes less than $30,000, but nearly two out of every three voters with incomes above $50,000, cast their ballots in 1988 for George Bush (Stanley and Niemi 1992, p. 108). See Abramson, Aldrich, and Rhode 1990, pp. 125–27. For a general breakdown of voting and social class in presidential elections, see Gallup 1988, pp. 4–7.

110. Zimmerman 1977, p. 64. See E. Freeman 1977, p. 505; E. Freeman 1978, p. 152; Lamanna 1980, p. 140. See also Luker 1984b, pp. 174–75.

111. A. Guttmacher 1959, p. 215.

112. See Luker 1984b, pp. 86–88.

113. 492 U.S. 490 (1989).

114. See chap. V.

115. 14 *U.S. Statutes at Large* 27 (1866).

116. See nn. 26–27 and the relevant text.

117. Reconstruction Republicans correctly recognized that (affluent) white citizens would almost always be the beneficiaries of class legislation. Still, the Fourteenth Amendment does not require courts or other constitutional authorities to determine whether "top-down" or "bottom-up" remedial policies are better for the formerly disfavored class. Perhaps pro-life groups are correct when they assert that abortion exploits women, that women are better off when they cannot choose to terminate a pregnancy. Such claims, however, have no bearing on the constitutional remedy for an equal choice violation. If white women are free to choose abortion, then all women must have the same choice, even if all women would be better off having no choice at all.

118. 305 U.S. 337 (1938).

119. 411 U.S. 677 (1973).

120. *Palmer v. Thompson*, 403 U.S. 217 (1971). States that respond to desegregation orders by closing public facilities, however, cannot fund or otherwise support private facilities that discriminate. See *Griffin*, at 218.

121. *Furman v. Georgia*, 408 U.S. 238 (1972).

122. *Gregg*, at 153; *Woodson v. North Carolina*, 428 U.S. 280 (1976); *Lockett v. Ohio*, 438 U.S. 586 (1978).

123. See *Payne v. Tennessee*, 501 U.S. 808 (1991); *McCleskey*, at 279; *Barefoot v. Estelle*, 463 U.S. 880 (1983).

124. The history of equal protection politics and litigation suggests that when elected officials are forced to remedy violations of the equal protection clause, they almost always prefer making the disadvantaged class better off to making the favored class worse off. With few exceptions, southern states responded to attacks on segregation by permitting integrated facilities rather than abandoning public facilities. Many states bankrupted themselves in the years before *Brown* by increasing spending on black schools; no district responded to the imminent destruction of Jim Crow by substantially reducing the quality of education available to white children.

Some segregated communities did stop providing all citizens with some public good or service when affluent white citizens could obtain those benefits in the private sector. When required to desegregate, Jackson, Mississippi, shut down all public pools and Prince Edward County, Virginia, abandoned public schooling. Privatization, however, should not trouble pure equal choice advocates. Equal choice only calls for a free market in abortion services. Not only does that free market satisfy the formal criterion of the equal protection clause, but also, as chapter II makes clear, decriminalization more than any other pro-choice policy results in substantial increases in access to safe abortion services for poor women and women of color.

125. Kant 1965, p. 100.

126. Morris 1992; Note 1988.

127. Louisell and Noonan 1970, pp. 236–37.

128. See *McCleskey*, at 314–15 (federal justices would soon be overwhelmed "with similar claims as to other types of penalties" should the Supreme Court rule that "racial bias had impermissibly tainted the capital sentencing process").

129. See, e.g., *Bakke*; *Korematsu v. United States*, 323 U.S. 214 (1944).

130. See *Turner*, at 28, 36 (opinion of White, J.).

131. *McCleskey* is a constitutional abomination because an important distinction available to the Court was not made. Given the unique severity and finality of the death penalty, the justices should have relied on legal precedents proclaiming that "death is different" (*Gregg*, at 187) to rule that discrimination that had to be accepted in some areas of the law would not be tolerated in the capital sentencing process.

132. See chap. II.

133. Hamilton, Madison, and Jay 1961, pp. 352–53.

134. *Wally's Heir v. Kennedy*, 2 Yeager 554, 555–56 (Tenn. 1831). See Gillman 1993, pp. 53–54 ("the common assumption" among Jacksonian jurists "was that the rights of nonmajorities would be best protected not by having justices divine a set of 'preferred freedoms' . . . but rather by simply insisting that laws be generally applicable").

135. *Railway Express Agency*, at 106, 112–13 (Jackson, J., concurring).

136. Joffe 1991, p. 53. See chap. II.

137. For evidence that pro-life laws would have been repealed had they been enforced, see nn. 111–13 and the relevant text.

138. Kant 1959, p. 39.

Chapter IV
Rule by Law

1. Pro-life advocates cannot parry equal choice attacks by noting that police officers and prosecutors failed to harass many physicians who performed abortions for the general public. Equal protection rights are violated whenever government officials privilege or harm *some* persons because of their race or socioeconomic status: victims of unconstitutional discrimination need not demonstrate that all or even most members of their class or caste have suffered disparate treatment. Warren McCleskey's constitutional rights would have been violated had he been the only victim of race discrimination in the history of Georgia.

2. Sartori 1962, pp. 861–62.

3. See nn. 17–18 and the relevant text.

4. Chivers 1992, p. 480; Jeffries 1985, p. 197. See Amsterdam 1960, p. 108.

5. See D. Bell 1993, p. 18.

6. Legal commentators and practitioners debate the extent to which judges interpreting statutes should be guided by the actual intentions of the enacting legislature, the plain meaning of statutory language, or the conditions that gave rise to the demand for the legislation in question (see Farber and Frickey 1991, pp. 88–115). No accepted method of statutory interpretation, however, supports the ways in which statutory bans on abortion were enforced before *Roe*.

7. Jeffries 1985, p. 226; *Roberts v. United States Jaycees*, 468 U.S. 609, 629 (1984). See *Kolender v. Lawson*, 461 U.S. 352, 357–61 (1983); *Grayned v. City of Rockford*, 408 U.S. 104, 108 (1972); Amsterdam 1960, pp. 80–81, 88–91.

8. Hentoff 1992a, p. 344.

9. Amsterdam 1960, p. 90.

10. *Smith v. Goguen*, 415 U.S. 566, 575 (1974). See generally Ely 1980, pp. 131–34; Calabresi 1991, p. 104.

11. *Roberts v. United States Jaycees*, at 609, 629; *Kolender*, at 358; *Smith v. Goguen*, 415 U.S. 566, 575 (1974). See *Grayned v. City of Rockford*, at 104, 108–9 ("a vague law impermissibly delegates basic policy matters to policemen, judges and juries"). See also Amsterdam 1960, p. 90.

12. *Wayte v. United States*, 470 U.S. 598, 608 (1985). See *Bordenkircher v. Hayes*, 434 U.S. 357, 363 (1978) (quoted in the text); *United States v. Goodwin*, 457 U.S. 368, 372–73 (1982); *Thigpen v. Roberts*, 468 U.S. 27, 31 (1984).

13. See Note 1935, pp. 87–88 nn. 1–2; Buell 1991, p. 1786.

14. For discussions of the influence of nativism on late-nineteenth-century opponents of abortion, see Mohr 1978, pp. 166–67; Siegal 1992, pp. 297–99.

15. Legislative paralysis does, however, provide an additional justification for judicial review of unconstitutional laws. In particular, judicial review does not seem to be countermajoritarian—inconsistent with the preferences of most elected officials—when badly divided legislatures invite courts to resolve policy disputes. See Graber 1993b.

For an interesting argument that courts should have the power to declare unconstitutional obsolete laws that could not be reenacted by present majorities, see Calabresi 1982.

16. Ely 1980, p. 133. See Calabresi 1991, p. 104. See also *Watkins v. United States*, 354 U.S. 178, 203–4 (1957).

17. Bickel 1962, p. 161; Calabresi 1991, p. 120. See Calabresi 1991, pp. 103–8, 119–20, 141–43; Bickel 1962, pp. 156–69; Farber and Frickey 1991, pp. 122, 125.

18. *Greene v. McElroy*, 360 U.S. 474, 507 (1959). See *United States v. Rumely*, 345 U.S. 41, 46 (1953) ("Congress [must] demonstrat[e] its full awareness of what is at stake by unequivocally authorizing an inquiry of dubious limits"); *Peters v. Hobby*, 349 U.S. 331, 347 (1955); *Ex Parte Endo*, 323 U.S. 283, 301–2 (1944); *Watkins v. United States*, at 178, 198, 205; *Kent v. Dulles*, 357 U.S. 116, 129–30 (1958).

19. Packer 1968, pp. 304–5. See Note 1986, p. 648; American Law Institute 1955, p. 278; Frase 1990, p. 568; Note 1991, pp. 1661–62. Connecticut prosecutors enforced statutory bans on birth control only when public clinics offered contraceptive services to poorer persons. Authorities never bothered physicians who provided their private patients with contraceptive information. See Carpenter 1989.

20. For a general discussion of the Mann Act in action, see Beckman 1984.

21. See, e.g., *Terry v. Ohio*, 392 U.S. 1 (1968).

22. Note 1988, p. 1496. See S. Johnson 1983, pp. 225–37; G. H. Williams 1991, p. 583; D. Harris 1994, pp. 660, 677–81. See generally Kerner Commission 1968, pp. 158–60.

23. See, e.g., S. Johnson 1983, pp. 256–57.

24. Indeed, the Georgia law sustained in *Bowers v. Hardwick*, 478 U.S. 186 (1986), forbade both heterosexual and homosexual sodomy.

Chapter V
Realizing Equal Choice

1. *Planned Parenthood v. Casey*, 505 U.S. ___, 120 L. Ed. 2d 674 (1992), inspired a minor renaissance within the professoriat on the joys of an independent judiciary. Ronald Dworkin declared that the ruling "refute[s] the cynics who insist that since Supreme Court appointments are politically motivated the Court is inevitably just another political institution" (1992a, p. 33). See also R. Kahn 1994, pp. 255–60. Nevertheless, even Dworkin's paean to judicial independence (1992a, p. 33) emphasized Justice Blackmun's statement in *Casey* that the future status of *Roe* would depend on who appoints the next justice to the Supreme Court; see *Casey*, at 758 (Blackmun, J., concurring in part and dissenting in part).

2. R. Dworkin 1989b, p. 49.

3. See especially Estrich and Sullivan 1989, p. 123 (the article was written "to convince an audience of one [Justice O'Connor] to stand up to those who are turning their backs on women").

4. For lengthy descriptions of the pro-choice movement's tactics, see Staggenborg 1991; Garrow 1994.

5. Staggenborg 1991, p. 41.

6. Garrow 1994, pp. 350 (quoting Lawrence Lader), 411. See Garrow 1994, pp. 300, 304, 306, 334, 353, 410–11, 415, 420, 423, 432, 482–83, 495, 567; L. Epstein and Kobylka 1992, pp. 154–55.

7. See Staggenborg 1991, pp. 133–36.

8. See Rosenberg 1991, pp. 339–40; Graber 1993b, p. 57.

9. See Staggenborg 1991, pp. 37–40; L. Epstein and Kobylka 1992, pp. 211–12.

10. The law students who initiated *Roe* thought that all they needed for their lawsuit was "about fifteen dollars and an attorney" (Garrow 1994, p. 395).

11. 347 U.S. 483 (1954).

12. *Eisenstadt v. Baird*, 405 U.S. 438, 453 (1972). See *Loving v. Virginia*, 388 U.S. 1 (1967); *Griswold v. Connecticut*, 391 U.S. 145 (1968). See also Garrow 1994, pp. 304, 310, 334, 337, 564–65; Rosenberg 1991, pp. 181–82. These predictions were supported by the numerous state and lower federal court decisions handed down in the late 1960s and early 1970s that struck down local bans on abortion. See chap. II, n. 192.

13. *Thornburgh v. American College of Obstetricians & Gynecologists*, 476 U.S. 747 (1986) (informed consent law declared unconstitutional); *Planned Parenthood of Kansas City v. Ashcroft*, 462 U.S. 476 (1983) (striking down requirement that second trimester abortions be performed in hospitals); *City of Akron v. Akron Center for Reproductive Health, Inc.*, 462 U.S. 416 (1983) (striking down hospi-

talization, consent, notification, and waiting period requirements); *Bellotti v. Baird*, 443 U.S. 622 (1979) (striking down a parental consent statute); *Colautti v. Franklin*, 439 U.S. 379 (1979) (striking down a fetal protection statute); *Bellotti v. Baird*, 428 U.S. 132 (1976) (striking down a parental consent measure); *Planned Parenthood of Central Missouri v. Danforth*, 428 U.S. 552 (1976) (striking down a fetal protection measure).

14. *Board of Education v. Barnette*, 319 U.S. 624, 638 (1943).

15. Bork 1990, p. 264.

16. Tribe 1990a, p. 241; Estrich and Sullivan 1989, pp. 151, 131–32. See Colker 1992, pp. 121 ("we cannot trust legislatures"), 159.

17. Colker 1992, p. 125; Staggenborg 1991, p. 38. See Garrow 1994, p. 701.

18. Estrich and Sullivan 1989, p. 155.

19. R. Dworkin 1985, p. 33.

20. Rhode 1989, pp. 210–11; Olsen 1989, pp. 133–34. See Colker 1992, p. 116 ("because I believe there are some universal ethical principles that shape our notions of justice, I believe that judicial intervention can lead us closer to our aspiration of wisdom").

21. See Rosenberg 1991, pp. 178–80.

22. For a fuller summary of the impact of legalization, see chap. II. Even Professor Gerald Rosenberg, who is correctly skeptical about the ability of courts to produce social change, recognizes that *Roe* had an extraordinary impact on maternal health; see Rosenberg 1991, p. 355.

23. See sources cited in chap. I, n. 28; Garrow 1994, p. 616 (citing sources).

24. Luker 1984b, p. 94. Judicial decisions striking down restrictions on abortion also significantly increased the number of legal abortions performed annually in Wisconsin (200 to 4,661) and in the District of Columbia (4,579 to 18,897; Tyler 1973, p. 29).

25. See Tribe 1990a, pp. 49–50; L. Epstein and Kobylka 1992, p. 151; Garrow 1994, pp. 423, 482–83, 487, 495–96, 506–7, 545–47, 576–77.

26. By keeping abortion legal for twenty years, *Roe* helped create a cultural environment in which terminating a pregnancy was increasingly perceived as a normal act. This perception probably influenced the slow but steady increase in public support for pro-choice policies during the late 1970s and 1980s.

27. *Maher v. Roe*, 432 U.S. 464 (1977); *Harris v. McRae*, 448 U.S. 297 (1980).

28. The problems pro-choice legal advocates face when attempting to secure better access to legal abortion go beyond mere judicial hostility to their constitutional claims. Much evidence suggests that the litigation campaign for abortion rights would not have fully succeeded in actually securing abortion providers for all interested women even had NARAL or Planned Parenthood lawyers been able to persuade the justices to declare that the Constitution protects the right to a guaranteed abortion on demand. Judicial decrees that require hostile elected officials to take unwanted actions are rarely implemented. Most American children were still praying in public schools long after the Supreme Court declared such policies unconstitutional; similarly, ten years after *Brown v. Board of Education*, barely 2 percent of all black children in the South were attending racially mixed schools (see Rosenberg 1991, pp. 42–71, especially p. 50). For other discussions

of judicial failures to secure compliance with important decisions, see Horowitz 1977; C. Johnson and Canon 1984; Dolbeare and Hammond 1971; Becker 1969. *Roe* had a significant effect on abortion practices only because independent entrepreneurs in abortion clinics were willing to provide legal abortion services (see Rosenberg 1991, pp. 195–201). Had the Court ordered state officials to pay for abortions and locate abortion services so that they were accessible to all citizens, history suggests the probable result would have been much foot-dragging, some outright disobedience, and very little implementation.

29. See chap. II, nn. 220, 227–30 and the relevant text.

30. See Staggenborg 1991, pp. 4, 150–53. See also L. Epstein and Kobylka 1992, p. 292.

31. See Sunstein 1991 pp. 206–7; Mansbridge 1986.

32. Staggenborg 1991, p. 152. See Kirp 1992, p. 759 ("it is wishful thinking . . . to imagine that, had they simply stayed out of court, abortion proponents could have slipped the issue by the right-to-life contingent much longer"). Professors Susan Howell and Robert Sims observe that "those most threatened seem more likely to take their abortion attitudes into account in making their vote decision" (Howell and Sims 1993, p. 161).

33. Garrow 1994, pp. 576–77.

34. Garrow 1994, pp. 483–84, 545–47, 561.

35. Kirp 1992, p. 759.

36. See Staggenborg 1991, p. 149; Craig and O'Brien 1993, p. 43; Rosenblatt 1992, pp. 16–17; L. Epstein and Kobylka 1992, pp. 206–7. Similar declines occurred in 1983, after the justices reaffirmed *Roe* (Staggenborg 1991, pp. 126–27).

37. Wolfinger and Rosenstone 1980, pp. 13–36.

38. See Cook, Jelen, and Wilcox 1992, p. 161.

39. See Stanley and Niemi 1992, p. 108; sources cited in chap. III, n. 109.

40. See Murphy 1990; O'Brien 1988; *Bowers v. Hardwick*, 478 U.S. 186 (1986).

41. R. Dworkin 1989b, p. 52.

42. *Webster v. Reproductive Health Services*, 492 U.S. 490, 521 (1989).

43. *Hodgson v. Minnesota*, 497 U.S. 417 (1990); *Ohio v. Akron Center for Reproductive Health*, 497 U.S. 502 (1990); *Planned Parenthood v. Casey*.

44. 500 U.S. 173 (1991).

45. Title X's statutory command that "[n]one of the funds appropriated under this subchapter shall be used in programs where abortion is a method of family planning" (84 *U.S. Statutes at Large* 1506, 1508 [1970]), does not necessarily justify executive orders declaring that persons who receive Title X moneys will not be allowed to "encourage, promote or advocate abortion as a method of family planning" (53 Fed. Reg. 2945 [1988]), even to the extent of referring clients who wish to terminate a pregnancy to a nonfederally funded organization that provides those services. Indeed, one might read Title X as affirmatively requiring federally funded programs to inform clients where they could procure the abortion that their organization could not lawfully provide.

46. Farber 1991, pp. 573–74. See *Rust*, at 204–7 (Blackmun, J., dissenting); *Rust*, at 220–23 (Stevens, J., dissenting); *Rust*, at 223–24 (O'Connor, J., dissenting); Burt 1992, pp. 361–62; Mayo 1992, pp. 310–12. See also McCloskey 1960,

pp. 198–99. Many commentators thought that Bush administration policies violated the free speech rights of family practitioners. The gag rule, after all, prohibited persons who expressed certain opinions about the morality or constitutionality of abortion from receiving government benefits. See *Rust*, at 207–15 (Blackmun, J., dissenting); Sunstein 1992, pp. 297–99; Calabresi 1991, pp. 141–42; Blanchard 1992, p. 469; Mayo 1992, p. 313.

47. Canons 2 and 3 of the Code of Judicial Conduct for United States Judges require judges to perform judicial duties "without bias or prejudice," and "not [to] allow family, social, or other relationships to influence [their] judicial conduct or judgment" (28 USCS §372 [1994]).

48. 28 USCS §372 (1994).

49. 418 U.S. 683 (1974).

50. Abraham 1992, p. 14; see also pp. 298, 301–2, 320–21.

51. See Tribe 1985a, p. 63.

52. On the other hand, by not overruling *Roe* in *Casey*, Justices O'Connor, Kennedy, and Souter may have improved Republican electoral chances by partially defusing the abortion issue (Toner 1992; M. Schwartz and Balz 1992).

53. This list may be too generous. The presidents who appointed Story, McReynolds, Warren, and Brennan were all aware of their appointees' judicial philosophies. See generally Tribe 1985, pp. 60–92.

54. 193 U.S. 197 (1903).

55. Abraham 1992, p. 69.

56. Judge Richard Posner, a Reagan appointee known for his conservative economic views, has written a book supporting the result in *Roe* (Posner 1992).

57. Bork 1990, pp. 115–16, 11.

58. See Staggenborg 1991, pp. 138–46.

59. See Cook, Jelen, and Wilcox 1994; Abramowitz 1995.

60. See Dodson and Burnbauer 1990; Staggenborg 1991, pp. 139–40.

61. Staggenborg 1991, pp. 137–38, 143–46.

62. Staggenborg 1991, pp. 140–41. See Cook, Jelen, and Wilcox 1992, p. 166 (pro-choice conversions of Jesse Jackson and Richard Gephardt); Tatalovich and Schier 1993, pp. 118–19.

63. See Halva-Neubauer 1990; Halva-Neubauer 1991; Rosenblatt 1992, pp. 14–17.

64. Sunstein 1991, pp. 206–7; see also pp. 226–27.

65. Greenhouse 1992, pp. A1, A17. Pro-choice activists insisted that lesser standards of judicial scrutiny would prevent poor women and women of color from obtaining legal abortions (p. A17). As we have seen in chapter II, however, merely keeping abortion legal does more than any other policy to increase the actual ability of poor women and women of color to terminate an unwanted pregnancy. Moreover, if *Roe* were overruled and elected officials given full control of abortion policy, the most favorable abortion policies that the federal government might adopt will still leave as many poor women and women of color unable to terminate an unwanted pregnancy as the present *Casey* standard. As discussed in n. 66, below, the present alternative to a watered-down judicial protection of abortion rights is probably a watered-down legislative protection of abortion rights.

Bold pro-choice declarations that *Roe* is better abandoned than modified are best understood as being directed toward the general public rather than toward the judiciary. The Rehnquist Court rarely seems interested in what left-wing lawyers and law professors have to say. Thus, little reason exists for thinking that the precise pleas made by pro-choice lawyers will determine whether that Court overrules *Roe* or merely chips away at its foundations. Claims that a modified version of *Roe* is unacceptable, however, may arouse pro-choice voters if the general public can be convinced that such modification in practical terms means that judicial solicitude for abortion rights has been abandoned. Citizens who might not join a pro-choice coalition if no more than spousal notification was at stake in the next election might become more involved in the political arena if they believed abortion was about to be recriminalized.

Rhetorical flourishes aside, most pro-choice activists in the spring of 1992 correctly recognized that they were not really choosing between watered-down judicial and watered-down legislative protection of abortion rights. Had President Bush won reelection in 1992, *Roe* would have eventually been overruled and the Freedom of Choice Act would have been vetoed. Hence, no matter what the Court did in the near future, efforts to create a pro-choice legislative majority, however weak that majority might turn out to be, seemed the only way to protect abortion rights. In this political environment, taking the slight risk that *Roe* would be abandoned a year earlier than might have otherwise been the case was clearly a reasonable price to pay for improving the chance of capturing the presidency.

66. Consider the Freedom of Choice Act (FCA). Under the heading "Right to Choose," Section 2 of that bill declares

(a) IN GENERAL.—Except as provided in subsection (b), a State may not restrict the right of a woman to choose to terminate a pregnancy——

(1) before fetal viability; or

(2) at any time, if such termination is necessary to protect the life or health of the woman.

(b) MEDICALLY NECESSARY REQUIREMENTS.—A State may impose requirements medically necessary to protect the life or health of women referred to in subsection (a).

The FCA clearly outlaws state laws that prohibit abortion and prevents states from establishing unreasonable cutoff dates after which no women could abort a pregnancy. Interpreted as only forbidding state bans on abortion, however, the FCA merely codifies existing Rehnquist Court practice as set out in *Casey*.

The Freedom of Choice Act does not clearly prohibit those regulations the Supreme Court currently permits states to enact. The FCA may ban state laws that require parental notification and/or approval prior to a minor's abortions. Some pro-life judges, however, might read "the right of a woman to choose" as consistent with parental notification requirements (and perhaps consent provisions). Whether the Court would interpret the FCA as banning waiting periods, informed consent laws, or special viability tests will depend on whether the justices regard such regulations as efforts to restrict access to abortion or, as *Casey* suggests, good faith attempts to ensure that abortion decisions are intelligently made and

NOTES TO CHAPTER V 203

that no viable fetus is aborted. Moreover, the FCA does not require that states fund abortions or allow organizations that use state funds to provide abortions, although a pro-choice justice might find funding restrictions inconsistent with the statute. Finally, Congress is clearly not commanding any state official to establish the facilities necessary for women to locate an abortionist willing to terminate their pregnancy.

Passage of the Freedom of Choice Act will not decrease access to abortion. Indeed, the measure would prove valuable insurance should the present judicial majority completely abandon *Roe*. However ambiguous the FCA may be on some matters, nothing in that bill can be fairly interpreted as granting federal permission for states to prohibit women from having abortions. Nevertheless, jettisoning *Roe* in return for the increased probability of obtaining legislation resembling the FCA seems a questionable political strategy. Pro-choice advocates should not reject a modified version of *Roe* because present judicial practice does not provide many poor women with the resources necessary to secure access to legal abortion. If the FCA is the best that a contemporary pro-choice majority can produce, then present political practice is as unlikely as present judicial practice to provide poor women with the resources necessary to secure access to legal abortion.

67. Hamilton, Madison, and Jay 1961, p. 465. See Rosenberg 1991.

68. See Dahl 1957; Graber 1993b.

69. Compare *United States v. Darby*, 312 U.S. 100 (1941) and *West Coast Hotel Co. v. Parrish*, 300 U.S. 379 (1937) with *Carter v. Carter Coal Co.*, 298 U.S. 238 (1936) and *Morehead v. New York ex rel. Tipaldo*, 298 U.S. 587 (1936).

70. Or perhaps the coalition might be led by Presidents Bill Clinton, Albert Gore, and Hillary Clinton.

71. 19 Howard 393 (1857).

72. Compare the welfare policies preferred by the Eisenhower and Nixon administrations with those advanced by the Hoover and Reagan administrations.

73. Perot apparently was the major beneficiary of the Bush campaign's pro-life stance; see Abramowitz 1995, p. 180.

74. Toner 1993; Friedman 1992.

75. A survey taken by *Time* found that Clinton voters thought that the environment, health, jobs, and the economy were all more important than abortion (Barrett 1992, p. 48).

76. Sunstein 1991, pp. 206–7. That the movement for abortion rights may weaken other movements for progressive reform is, of course, less troubling to persons who are economically conservative or think that reproductive policies are the most important issue facing the country. Many "New Democrats" would rather support *Roe* than progressive taxation.

77. For women, see chap. I. For persons of color, see Dugger 1991, pp. 570, 583; Abramowitz 1995, pp. 181–82. Early surveys of public opinion found that persons of color tended to be less supportive of abortion than their white counterparts, but more recent research suggests that racial difference in attitudes toward abortion are narrowing to the vanishing point. See Cook, Jelen, and Wilcox, 1992, pp. 46–48; Blake and Del Pinal 1980, p. 34.

78. See generally, Cook, Jelen, and Wilcox 1992, p. 166; Tatalovich and Schier 1993, pp. 119–21. My sense is that the GOP started drifting toward pro-

life positions before the Democrats started drifting toward pro-choice positions, but I have not done the research necessary to support this hunch.

79. Cook, Jelen, and Wilcox 1992, pp. 170–71; Daynes and Tatalovich 1992, pp. 549–55.

80. J. Jackson and Vinovskis 1983, p. 68. See Rossi and Sitaraman 1988, p. 277; Fried 1988, p. 152; Cook, Jelen, and Wilcox 1992, pp. 164–65, 176; Tatalovich and Schier 1993, p. 111.

81. See Abramowitz 1995; Cook, Jelen, and Wilcox 1994.

82. Traugott and Vinovskis 1980, p. 242; J. Jackson and Vinovskis 1983, p. 75. See Daynes and Tatalovich 1992, pp. 555–58; Cook, Jelen, and Wilcox 1992, p. 166 ("abortion attitudes were not significantly associated with vote choice before 1984," but did seem to have some influence in 1984 and 1988), 173 ("congressional elections seldom turn on the abortion issue"); Vinovskis 1980a; Rossi and Sitaraman 1988, p. 277 (elections from 1974 to 1986); Legge 1983, p. 489; Traugott and Vinovskis 1980, p. 245; J. Jackson and Vinovskis 1983; Steiner 1983b, p. 92; Petchesky 1990, p. xi; Jaffe, Lindheim, and Lee 1981, pp. 107–8; Fried 1988, p. 162.

83. Dodson and Burnbauer 1990, pp. 88–91, 154–60. See Richard 1991, pp. 17–18 (similar findings in Ohio); Abramowitz 1995, p. 180 (half the citizenry did not know what the 1992 major party nominees for the presidency thought about abortion).

84. Dodson and Burnbauer 1990, p. 162. But see Cook, Jelen, and Wilcox 1992, p. 177 (suggesting that voters in other states may be more attentive to different candidate positions on abortion).

85. Cook, Jelen, and Wilcox 1992, pp. 164–65.

86. D. Granberg 1987, p. 59. See L. Epstein and Kobylka 1992, p. 232; Vinovskis 1980a, pp. 200–201 (discussing 1976).

87. Cook, Jelen, and Wilcox 1992, p. 162.

88. The two elected officials most supportive of abortion rights in the years before *Roe*, Senator Robert Packwood of Oregon and Governor Nelson Rockefeller of New York, were both Republicans.

89. See Rosenberg 1991, p. 183.

90. See n. 86, above.

91. See Garrow 1994, pp. 471–72.

92. See Barnes 1994; Rich 1994. For a discussion of pro-life legislative goals in the 104th Congress, see A. Rubin 1995.

93. Dodson and Burnbauer 1990, pp. 100, 106–7.

94. Interview with Tim Wright, executive director, New Jersey NARAL, June 8, 1992. The epilogue to the 1989 Virginia gubernatorial election should also trouble pro-choice advocates. Personal squabbling between leading Democrats was partly responsible for Virginians electing in 1993 a very conservative governor with ties to the Christian Coalition.

Of course, the flip side of this coin is also true. Because the two parties are increasingly divided along abortion lines, any recession, foreign policy crisis, or scandal that harms the Republican party is likely to benefit pro-choice policies.

95. The abortion issue clearly favored pro-choice candidates who campaigned in the immediate aftermath of *Webster*; see nn. 59–60, above. Recent election

returns are less conclusive; see Cook, Jelen, and Wilcox 1992, pp. 161–62, 176. Preliminary findings suggest that the abortion issue may have slightly favored President Bush in the 1992 election; see Barrett 1992, p. 48.

96. See McPherson 1988, pp. 301, 349–50, 361, 365, 423–27, 464, 468–70, 539–40, 543–44, 652.

97. McClellen quoted in McPherson 1988, p. 426.

98. Were the English language more accommodating, the strategy advocated in this section would be described as "departisanization" rather than "depoliticization." As I make clear later in this chapter, I do not maintain that abortion rights advocates should stop talking about abortion.

99. Michelman 1988, p. 1537; Fiss 1989, p. 255; *Chambers v. Florida*, 309 U.S. 227, 241 (1940). For a criticism of this view, see nn. 49–57 and the relevant text.

100. See nn. 77, 102–3.

101. Manier 1977, p. 15. See sources cited in n. 103, below.

102. Surveys also show that elites are much more likely than other citizens to hold strong pro-civil liberties and civil rights views; see McClosky and Brill 1983.

103. Skerry 1978, p. 70. See especially Lasch 1991, pp. 491 (abortion "is first and foremost a class issue"), and more generally 488–92; Blake 1971, p. 544; Blake 1973, pp. 452–54; Blake 1977, pp. 67–98, 78; Pomeroy and Landman 1973, pp. 486, 488; Jones and Westoff 1973, p. 473; Tatalovich and Daynes 1981, pp. 6, 38, 84, 117, 124–25; Luker 1984b, pp. 27–28; D. Granberg 1978, pp. 417–18; Skerry 1978, p. 75; Baker, Epstein, and Forth 1981, pp. 94–95; Manier 1977, pp. 15, 24; J. Jackson and Vinovskis 1983, p. 71; Tedrow and Mahoney 1979, pp. 185–86; D. Granberg and B. Granberg 1980, p. 253; Dodson and Burnbauer 1990, p. 23.

104. Lerner, Nagai, and Rothman 1990, pp. 11–12. See McClosky and Brill 1983, pp. 218–19 (noting that community leaders and legal elites are more supportive than the mass public of legal abortion).

105. See Jeffries 1994, p. 317; Woodward and Armstrong 1979, pp. 196, 205, 272; Garrow 1994, pp. 473–74; L. Epstein and Kobylka 1992, p. 190. No member of the *Roe* Court seems to have had any personal association with pro-life advocates.

106. McClosky and Brill 1983, especially pp. 415–38. Indeed, historically, judicial review has always favored elite opinion; see Graber 1993b, pp. 65–66.

107. Garrow 1994, p. 539; L. Epstein and Kobylka 1992, p. 539. See also Garrow 1994, pp. 605–6 (noting that in 1973 leading newspapers overwhelmingly supported the result in *Roe*).

108. Increased turnout in the 1992 election had everything to do with Ross Perot and the recession and nothing to do with abortion policy.

109. See Broder 1993, pp. A6–7.

110. Toner 1990; Stone 1992.

111. See Verba and Nie 1972, pp. 95–101; Wolfinger and Rosenstone 1980, pp. 13–36; Lerner, Nagai, and Rothman 1990, p. 14.

112. See n. 40 and the relevant text.

113. My arguments also attempt to dispirit some pro-life advocates by pointing out that George Bush and like-minded members of his party had and have no

intention of promoting any policy that will actually affect the private family planning practices of country club Republicans.

114. See sources cited in chap. III, n. 110.

115. See Graber 1993b, pp. 53–61; Garrow 1994, pp. 408, 482, 485, 491; Barnes 1993, p. 10; Craig and O'Brien 1993, pp. xv, 109; L. Epstein and Kobylka 1992, p. 264.

116. For a good discussion of how state officials avoided making abortion policies in the wake of *Webster*, see Halva-Neubauer 1991; Halva-Neubauer 1990; Richard 1991, pp. 7–8. A Minnesota state legislator who sought to force a floor vote on abortion was threatened with the loss of benefits to his district by other representatives not eager to take public stands on abortion (Halva-Neubauer 1991, p. 14).

117. Of course, if pro-life forces successfully ban abortion, then the burden of changing the status quo will return to proponents of legal abortion.

118. See n. 104 and the relevant text.

119. Given that most members of the executive and legislative branches of government also enjoy elite status and are thus likely to be tacitly pro-choice, whatever inside information publicly neutral officials possess on candidates for the federal judiciary will probably be used to select a jurist privately known to support legal abortion.

Indeed, pro-life activists who read *Rethinking Abortion* might object to a seemingly neutral judicial nominee on the grounds that any graduate of a prestigious law school probably holds pro-choice views. Without more concrete evidence that the nominee favors *Roe*, however, such claims will not excite the vast majority of citizens who are ambivalent about abortion. As the difference between the Bork and Kennedy hearings demonstrates, only a nominee who clearly expresses opinions on *Roe* is likely to mobilize the opponents necessary for a Senate vote against confirmation.

120. Indeed, in the wake of the 1989 elections, many Republican governors began calling for their party to be more inclusive on abortion issues; see Oreskes 1989.

121. The difference at present between what weak and strong pro-choice candidates are likely to accomplish is not worth considering.

122. See Colker 1992, p. 124.

123. For discussions of the rise and fall of that political order, see Fraser and Gerstle 1989; Burnham 1982; Phillips 1969; T. Edsall 1984; T. Edsall and M. Edsall 1991; Ferguson and Rogers 1986; Phillips 1990.

124. Ely 1973, p. 947; M. Shapiro 1978, pp. 181–82.

Conclusion
The Allure of Pro-Life

1. *Woodson v. North Carolina*, 428 U.S. 280, 305 (1976) (opinion of Stewart, Powell, and Stevens, JJ.).

2. See *Planned Parenthood v. Casey*, 505 U.S. ___, 120 L. Ed. 2d 674, 782 (1992) (Scalia, J., concurring in part and dissenting in part: "the Constitution says absolutely nothing about [abortion] and . . . the longstanding traditions of Amer-

ican society have permitted [abortion] to be legally proscribed"). Pro-choice advocates insist that the common law left persons free to terminate a pregnancy before quickening; see, e.g., Spillenger, Larson, and Law 1989, pp. 170–71. No scholar, however, suggests that antebellum Americans thought this legal permission was grounded in a more basic human or constitutional right. Nineteenth-century courts explicitly affirmed legislative power to alter the common law's permissive attitude toward early abortion. "If the good of society requires that the evil [of abortion] should be suppressed by penal inflictions," one state judiciary maintained, "it is far better that it should be done by legislative enactments than that courts should, by judicial construction, extend the penal code or multiply the objects of criminal punishment"(*Cooper v. State*, 2 Zab. 52, 58 [N.J. 1849]). See Grossberg 1985, p. 163.

3. Noonan 1970.

4. See chap. I, nn. 43–45 and the relevant text.

5. Even painless acts of altruism seem beyond the capacity of most citizens. Everybody who reads about the Kitty Genovese murder knows that they would have called the police had they heard her screams. Yet none of the New Yorkers in her apartment complex did.

Abernathy, James R., Greenberg, Bernard G., and Horvitz, Daniel G., 1970, "Estimates of Induced Abortion in Urban North Carolina," 7 *Demography* 19.

Abortion Political Network, 1994, "Pennsylvania: Clinics Use Phone Tapes; PA Appeals Ruling," American Political Network, Abortion Report (September 23).

Abraham, Henry J., 1992, *Justices and Presidents: A Political History of Appointments to the Supreme Court* (3rd ed.). Oxford University Press: New York.

Abramowitz, Alan I., 1995, "It's Abortion Stupid: Policy Voting in the 1992 Presidential Election," 57 *Journal of Politics* 176.

Abramson, Paul R., Aldrich, John H., and Rohde, David W., 1990, *Change and Continuity in the 1988 Elections.* CQ Press: Washington, D.C.

Adamek, Raymond J., 1980, "Abortion Policy: Time for Reassessment," *Abortion Parley* (edited by James Tunstead Burtchaell). Andrews and McMeel: Kansas City, Mo.

Adelstein, Harvey M., 1960, "The Abortion Law," 12 *Western Reserve Law Review* 74.

"Ads for London Abortions Stir Legal Questions," 1970, *New York Times* 20 (January 26).

Alan Guttmacher Institute, 1979, *Abortions and the Poor: Private Morality, Public Responsibility.* Alan Guttmacher Institute: New York.

———, 1994, *Sex and America's Teenagers.* Alan Guttmacher Institute: New York.

Althaus, Frances A., and Henshaw, Stanley K., 1994, "The Effects of Mandatory Delay Laws on Abortion Patients and Providers," 26 *Family Planning Perspectives* 228.

American Civil Liberties Union, 1976, *1976 Policy Guide of the American Civil Liberties Union.* American Civil Liberties Union: New York.

American College of Obstetricians and Gynecologists, 1982, *Standards for Obstetric-Gynecologic Services* (5th ed.). American College of Obstetricians and Gynecologists: Washington, D.C.

American Law Institute, 1955, *Model Penal Code* (Tentative Draft No. 4). The American Law Institute: Philadelphia.

American Psychiatric Association, 1994, *Diagnostic and Statistical Manual of Mental Disorders* (4th ed.). American Psychiatric Association: Washington D.C.

American Public Health Association, 1980, "APHA Recommended Program Guide for Abortion Services (Revised 1979)," 70 *American Journal of Public Health* 652.

Amsterdam, Anthony G., 1960, "The Void-for-Vagueness Doctrine in the Supreme Court," 109 *University of Pennsylvania Law Review* 67.

Applebome, Peter, 1992, "Mississippi Law Fails to Reduce Abortion Strife," *New York Times* A14 (October 13).

Aristotle, 1980, *The Nicomachean Ethics* (translated by David Ross). Oxford University Press: Oxford.

Arnold, Thurman Wesley, 1962, *The Folklore of Capitalism.* Yale University Press, New Haven.

Baer, Judith A., 1991, *Women in American Law: The Struggle toward Equality from the New Deal to the Present.* Holmes and Meier: New York.

Baker, Ross K., Epstein, Laurily K., and Forth, Rodney, 1981, "Matters of Life and Death: Social, Political, and Religious Correlates of Attitudes on Abortion," 9 *American Politics Quarterly* 89.

Baldus, David C., Woodworth, George, and Pulaski, Charles A., Jr., 1990, *Equal Justice and the Death Penalty: A Legal and Empirical Analysis.* Northeastern University Press: Boston.

Barber, Sotiros A., 1984, *On What the Constitution Means.* Johns Hopkins University Press: Baltimore.

Barnes, Fred, 1992, "No Womb for Debate: Do Pro-Life Democrats Exist?" 207 *New Republic* 36 (July 27).

———, 1993, "Bush II," 209 *New Republic* 10 (October 11).

———, 1994, 'Life of the Party," 211 *New Republic* 10 (December 5).

Barrett, Laurence I., 1992, "A New Coalition for the 1990s," 140 *Time* 47 (November 16).

Bart, Pauline B., 1987, "Seizing the Means of Reproduction: An Illegal Feminist Abortion Collective—How and Why It Worked," 10 *Qualitative Sociology* 339.

Bartlett, Katharine T., 1990, "Feminist Legal Methods," 103 *Harvard Law Review* 829.

Bates, Jerome E., 1957, "The Abortion Mill: An Institutional Study," 45 *Journal of Criminal Law and Criminology* 157.

Bates, Jerome E., and Zawadski, Edward S., 1964, *Criminal Abortion: A Study in Medical Sociology.* Charles C. Thomas: Springfield, Ill.

Becker, Theodore L., ed., 1969, *The Impact of Supreme Court Decisions.* Oxford University Press: New York.

Beckman, Marlene D., 1984, "The White Slave Traffic Act: The Historical Impact of a Criminal Law Policy on Women," 72 *Georgetown Law Journal* 1111.

Beckwith, Francis J., 1992, "Utilitarian Arguments, Abortion Rights, and Justice Blackmun's Dissent in *Webster*: Some Philosophical Observations," 11 *The Simon Greenleaf Review* 5.

Bell, Daniel, 1993, "The Old War: Corruption in Democracies," 209 *New Republic* 18 (August 23).

Bell, Robert R., 1971, *Social Deviance: A Substantive Analysis.* The Dorsey Press: Homewood, Ill.

Benedict, Michael Les, 1985, "Laissez-Faire and Liberty: A Re-Evaluation of the Meaning and Origins of Laissez-Faire Constitutionalism," 3 *Law and History Review* 293.

Bennett, Robert W., 1983, "The Burger Court and the Poor," *The Burger Court: The Counter-Revolution That Wasn't* (edited by Vincent Blasi). Yale University Press: New Haven.

Benshoof, Janet, 1993, "*Planned Parenthood v. Casey:* The Impact of the New

Undue Burden Standard on Reproductive Health Care," 269 *Journal of the American Medical Association* 2249.

Berger, Raoul, 1977, *Government by Judiciary: The Transformation of the Fourteenth Amendent*. Harvard University Press: Cambridge.

Berkman, Michael B., and O'Connor, Robert E., 1993, "Do Women Legislators Matter?: Female Legislators and State Abortion Policy," *Understanding the New Politics of Abortion* (edited by Malcolm L. Goggin). Sage Publications: Newbury Park, Calif.

Bickel, Alexander M., 1955, "The Original Understanding and the Segregation Decisions," 69 *Harvard Law Review* 1.

――――, 1962, *The Least Dangerous Branch: The Supreme Court at the Bar of Politics*. Bobbs-Merrill: Indianapolis.

――――, 1975, *The Morality of Consent*. Yale University Press: New Haven.

Binion, Gayle, 1993, "The Nature of Feminist Jurisprudence," 77 *Judicature* 140.

Binkin, Nancy, Gold, Julian, and Cates, Willard, Jr., 1982, "Illegal-Abortion Deaths in the United States: Why Are They Still Occurring?" 14 *Family Planning Perspectives* 163.

Black, Charles L., Jr., 1967, "Foreword: 'State Action,' Equal Protection and California's Proposition 14," 81 *Harvard Law Review* 69.

――――, 1986, "Further Reflections on the Constitutional Justice of Livelihood," 86 *Columbia Law Review* 1103.

Blake, Judith, 1971, "Abortion and Public Opinion: The 1960-1970 Decade," 171 *Science* 540.

――――, 1973, "Elective Abortion and Our Reluctant Citizenry: Research on Public Opinion in the United States," *The Abortion Experience: Psychological and Medical Impact* (edited by Howard J. Osofsky and Joy D. Osofsky). Harper and Row: Hagerstown, Md.

――――, 1977, "The Supreme Court's Abortion Decisions and Public Opinion in the United States," 3 *Population and Development Review* 46.

Blake, Judith, and Del Pinal, Jorge H., 1980, "Predicting Polar Attitudes toward Abortion in the United States," *Abortion Parley* (edited by James Tunstead Burtchaell). Andrews and McMeel: Kansas City, Mo.

――――, 1981, "Negativism, Equivocation, and Wobbly Assent: Public 'Support' for the Prochoice Platform on Abortion," 18 *Demography* 309.

Blanchard, Margaret A., 1992, *Revolutionary Sparks: Freedom of Expression in Modern America*. Oxford University Press: New York.

Blum, Robert W., Resnick, Michael D., and Stark, Trisha A., 1987, "The Impact of a Parental Notification Law on Adolescent Abortion Decision-Making," 77 *American Journal of Public Health* 619.

――――, 1990, "Factors Associated with the Use of Court Bypass by Minors to Obtain Abortions," 22 *Family Planning Perspectives* 158.

Bobbitt, Philip, 1982, *Constitutional Fate: Theory of the Constitution*. New York: Oxford University Press.

Boling, Patricia, 1991, "Talking about Abortion Rights in a Post-*Roe* World," Paper delivered at the 1991 Annual Meeting of the American Political Science Association, the Washington Hilton, August 29–September 1.

Bonar, Joy Walker, Watson, James Allen, and Koester, Lynne Sanford, 1983, "Abortion Attitudes in Medical Students," 38 *Journal of the American Medical Women's Association* 43.

Boodman, Sandra G., 1993, "The Dearth of Abortion Doctors: Stigma, Low Pay and Lack of Personal Commitment Erodes Ranks," *Washington Post* Z7 (April 20).

Bork, Robert H., 1979, "The Impossibility of Finding Welfare Rights in the Constitution," 1979 *Washington University Law Quarterly* 695.

———, 1990, *The Tempting of America: The Political Seduction of the Law*. Simon and Schuster: New York.

Boston Women's Health Book Collective, 1976, *Our Bodies, Ourselves: A Book by and for Women* (2nd ed.). Simon and Schuster: New York.

"Both Sides See Defeat in Decision," 1992, *St. Louis Post-Dispatch* A1 (June 30).

Bracken, Michael B., Freeman, Daniel M., and Hellenbrand, Karen, 1982, "Hospitalization for Medical-Legal and Other Abortions in the United States 1970–1977," 72 *American Journal of Public Health* 30.

Braucher, Jean, 1991, "Tribal Conflict over Abortion," 25 *Georgia Law Review* 595.

Braudel, Fernand, 1979, *The Structures of Everyday Life: The Limits of the Possible* (translated by Sian Reynolds). Harper and Row: New York.

Brest, Paul, 1980, "The Misconceived Quest for the Original Understanding," 60 *Boston University Law Review* 204.

Broder, David S., 1993, "Lasting Effects of Perot, Religious Right Debated," *Washington Post* A6 (September 6).

Broeman, Peter, and Meier, Jeannette, 1971, "Therapeutic Abortion Practices in Chicago Hospitals—Vagueness, Variation, and Violation of the Law," 4 *Law and Social Order* 757.

Bryson, William C., et al., 1989, "Brief for the United States as *Amicus Curiae* Supporting Appellants," *Webster v. Reproductive Health Services*, 492 U.S. 490.

Buell, Samuel W., 1991, "Criminal Abortion Revisited," 66 *New York University Law Review* 1774.

Burnham, Walter Dean, 1982, *The Current Crisis in American Politics*. Oxford University Press: Oxford.

Burns, Sarah E., et al., 1989, "Brief for the *Amici Curiae* Women Who Have Had Abortions and Friends of *Amici Curiae* in Support of Appellees," *Webster v. Reproductive Health Services*, 492 U.S. 490.

Burt, Robert A., 1992, *The Constitution in Conflict*. Harvard University Press: Cambridge.

Burtchaell, James Tunstead, 1982, *Rachel Weeping: The Case Against Abortion*. Harper and Row: San Francisco.

Calabresi, Guido, 1982, *A Common Law for the Age of Statutes*. Harvard University Press: Cambridge.

———, 1991, "Foreword: Antidiscrimination and Constitutional Accountability (What the Bork-Brennan Debate Ignores)," 105 *Harvard Law Review* 80.

Calabresi, Guido, and Bobbitt, Philip, 1978, *Tragic Choices*. W. W. Norton: New York.

Calderone, Mary Steichen, ed., 1958, *Abortion in the United States: A Conference Sponsored by the Planned Parenthood Federation of America, Inc., at Arden House and the New York Academy of Medicine*. Hoeder-Harper: New York.

Callahan, Daniel, 1984, "The Abortion Debate: Is Progress Possible?" *Abortion: Understanding Differences* (edited by Sidney Callahan and Daniel Callahan). Plenum Press: New York.

———, 1986, "Abortion: Some Ethical Issues," *Abortion, Medicine, and the Law* (3rd ed.) (edited by J. Douglas Butler and David F. Walbert). Facts on File: New York.

Callahan, Sidney, 1984, "Value Choices in Abortion," *Abortion: Understanding Differences* (edited by Sidney Callahan and Daniel Callahan). Plenum Press: New York.

Callahan, Sidney, and Callahan, Daniel, eds., 1984, *Abortion: Understanding Differences*. Plenum Press: New York.

Campbell, Angus, Converse, Philip E., Miller, Warren E., and Stokes, Donald E., 1960, *The American Voter*. University of Chicago Press: Chicago.

Carpenter, Dale A., II, 1989, "Revisiting *Griswold*: An Exploration of Its Political, Social, and Legal Origins," Senior History Essay, Yale University, New Haven.

Carter, Stephen J., 1988, "When Victims Happen to Be Black," 97 *Yale Law Journal* 420.

———, 1991a, "Abortion, Absolutism, and Compromise," 100 *Yale Law Review* 2747 (1991a).

———, 1991b, "Living without the Judge," 101 *Yale Law Journal* 1.

Cartoof, Virginia, and Klerman, Lorraine, 1986, "Parental Consent for Abortion: Impact of the Massachusetts Law," 76 *American Journal of Public Health* 397.

Casey, Robert P., 1992, "What I Would Have Told the Democrats," *Wall Street Journal* A12 (July 31).

Cates, Willard, Jr., 1977, "Legal Abortion: Are American Black Women Healthier Because of It?" 38 *Phylon* 267.

———, 1981, "The Hyde Amendment in Action: How Did the Restriction of Federal Funds for Abortion Affect Low-Income Women?" 246 *Journal of the American Medical Association* 1109.

———, 1982, "Legal Abortion: The Public Health Record," 215 *Science* 1586.

———, 1986, "The First Decade of Legal Abortion in the United States: Effects on Maternal Health," *Abortion, Medicine, and the Law* (3rd ed.) (edited by J. Douglas Butler and David E. Walbert). Facts on File: New York.

Cates, Willard, Jr., and Rochat, Roger W., 1976, "Illegal Abortions in the United States: 1972-1974," 8 *Family Planning Perspectives* 86.

Cates, Willard, Jr., Schulz, Kenneth F., Grimes, David A., and Tyler, Carl W., 1977, "The Effect of Delay and Method Choice on the Risk of Abortion Morbidity," 9 *Family Planning Perspectives* 266.

Charles, Alan, and Alexander, Susan, 1971, "Abortions for Poor and Nonwhite Women: A Denial of Equal Protection?" 23 *Hastings Law Journal* 147.

Chivers, Corey, R., 1992, "Desuetude, Due Process, and the Scarlet Letter Revisited," 1992 *Utah Law Review* 449.

Chopko, Mark E., and Alvare, Helen, 1991, "Legal Issues in a Post-*Webster* World," 34 *Catholic Lawyer* 115.

Cohen, Jane Maslow, 1989, "Comparison-Shopping in the Marketplace of Rights," 98 *Yale Law Journal* 1235.

Colker, Ruth, 1992, *Abortion and Dialogue: Pro-Choice, Pro-Life, and American Law*. Indiana University Press: Bloomington.

Condit, Celeste Michelle, 1990, *Decoding Abortion Rhetoric: Communicating Social Change*. University of Illinois Press: Urbana.

Congressional Record, 95th Cong., 1st sess., 1977. Vol. 123, pt. 10.

Converse, Philip E., 1964, "The Nature of Belief Systems in Mass Publics," *Ideology and Discontent* (edited by David E. Apter). Free Press: New York.

Cook, Elizabeth Adell, Jelen, Ted G., and Wilcox, Clyde, 1992, *Between Two Absolutes: Public Opinion and the Politics of Abortion*. Westview Press: Boulder, Colo.

——, 1994, "Issue Voting in Gubernatorial Elections: Abortion and Post-*Webster* Politics," 56 *Journal of Politics* 187.

Cooley, Thomas M., 1868, *A Treatise on the Constitutional Limitations Which Rest Upon the Legislative Power of the States of the American Union*. Little, Brown: Boston.

Cowles, John E., and Finley, Lucinda M., 1994, "Brief of *Amici Curiae* NOW Legal Defense Fund, et al., in Support of Respondents," *Madsen v. Women's Health Center, Inc.*, 512 U.S. ___, 129 L. Ed. 2d 593 (1994).

Craig, Barbara Hinkson, and O'Brien, David M., 1993, *Abortion and American Politics*. Chatham House: Chatham, N.J.

Culp, Jerome McCristal, Jr., 1994, "Colorbind Remedies and the Intersectionality of Oppression: Policy Arguments Masquerading as Moral Claims," 69 *New York University Law Review* 162.

Curtis, Michael Kent, 1986, *No State Shall Abridge: The Fourteenth Amendment and the Bill of Rights*. Duke University Press: Durham, N.C.

Cushner, Irvin M., Oppel, Wallace C., Unger, Thomas, Athansiou, Robert B., and Yager, Mary J., 1973, "The Johns Hopkins Experience," *The Abortion Experience: Psychological and Medical Impact* (edited by Howard J. Osofsky and Joy D. Osofsky). Harper and Row: Hagerstown, Md.

Dahl, Robert A., 1957, "Decision-Making in a Democracy: The Supreme Court as a National Policy-Maker," 6 *Journal of Public Law* 279.

——, 1989, *Democracy and Its Critics*. Yale University Press: New Haven.

Dalton, Clare, 1985, "An Essay in the Deconstruction of Contract Doctrine," 94 *Yale Law Journal* 997.

David, Henry P., 1980, "The Abortion Decision: National and International Perspectives," *Abortion Parley* (edited by James Tunstead Burtchaell). Andrews and McMeel: Kansas City, Mo.

Davis, Nanette J., 1985, *From Crime to Choice: The Transformation of Abortion in America*. Greenwood Press: Westport, Conn.

Daynes, Byron W., and Tatalovich, Raymond, 1992, "Presidential Politics and Abortion, 1972–1988," 22 *Presidential Studies Quarterly* 545.

Dellinger, Walter, 1992, "Abortion: The Case against Compromise," *Abortion, Medicine, and the Law* (4th ed.) (edited by J. Douglas Butler and David F. Walbert). Facts on File: New York.

Dellinger, Walter, and Sperling, Gene B., 1989, "Abortion and the Supreme Court: The Retreat from *Roe v. Wade*," 138 *University of Pennsylvania Law Review* 83.

D'Emilio, John, and Freedman, Estelle B., 1988, *Intimate Matters: A History of Sexuality in America*. Harper and Row: New York.

Democratic Review, 1954, "An Introductory Statement of the Democratic Principle," *Social Theories of Jacksonian Democracy: Representative Writings of the Period 1825–1850* (edited by Joseph L. Blau). Bobbs-Merrill: Indianapolis.

Diamond, Irene, 1977, *Sex Roles in the State House*. Yale University Press: New Haven.

Dodson, Debra L., and Burnbauer, Lauren D., 1990, *Election 1989: The Abortion Issue in New Jersey and Virginia*. Eagleton Institute of Politics: New Brunswick, N.J.

Donovan, Patricia, 1985, "The Holy War," 17 *Family Planning Perspectives* 5.

Dolbeare, Kenneth M., and Hammond, Philip E., 1971, *The School Prayer Decisions: From Court Policy to Local Practice*. University of Chicago Press: Chicago.

Douglass, Frederick, 1950, *The Life and Writings of Frederick Douglas*, vol. 2, *The Civil War Decade 1850–60* (edited by Philip S. Foner). International Publishers: New York.

Dubin, Leonard, 1961, "The Antiquated Abortion Laws," 34 *Temple Law Quarterly* 146.

Dugger, Karen, 1991, "Race Differences in the Determinants of Support for Legalized Abortion," 72 *Social Science Quarterly* 570.

Dworkin, Andrea, 1983, *Right-wing Women*. Coward-McCann: New York.

Dworkin, Ronald, 1978, *Taking Rights Seriously*. Harvard University Press: Cambridge.

———, 1985, *A Matter of Principle*. Harvard University Press: Cambridge.

———, 1989a, "The Future of Abortion," 36 *New York Review of Books* 47 (September 28).

———, 1989b, "The Great Abortion Case," 36 *New York Review of Books* 49 (June 29).

———, 1992a, "The Center Holds," 39 *New York Review of Books* 29 (August 13).

———, 1992b, "Unenumerated Rights: Whether and How *Roe* Should be Overruled," *The Bill of Rights in the Modern State* (edited by Geoffrey R. Stone, Richard A. Epstein, and Cass R. Sunstein). University of Chicago Press: Chicago.

———, 1993, *Life's Dominion: An Argument about Abortion, Euthanasia, and Individual Freedom*. Alfred A. Knopf: New York.

Edsall, Thomas Byrne, 1984, *The New Politics of Inequality*. W. W. Norton: New York.

Edsall, Thomas Byrne, and Edsall, Mary D., 1991, *Chain Reaction: The Impact of Race, Rights, and Taxes on American Politics*. W. W. Norton: New York.

Eliot, Johan W., Hall, Robert E., Willson, J. Robert, and Houser, Carolyn, 1970, "The Obstetrician's View," *Abortion in a Changing World*, vol. 1 (edited by Robert E. Hall). Columbia University Press: New York.

Ely, John Hart, 1973, "The Wages of Crying Wolf: A Comment on *Roe v. Wade*," 82 *Yale Law Journal* 920.

———, 1980, *Democracy and Distrust: A Theory of Judicial Review*. Harvard University Press: Cambridge.

———, 1991, "Another Such Victory: Constitutional Theory and Practice in a World Where Courts Are No Different from Legislatures," 77 *Virginia Law Review* 833.

Epstein, Lee, and Kobylka, Joseph F., 1992, *The Supreme Court and Legal Change: Abortion and the Death Penalty*. University of North Carolina Press: Chapel Hill.

Epstein, Richard A., 1974, "Substantive Due Process by Any Other Name: The Abortion Cases," 1973 *The Supreme Court Review* 159.

Estrich, Susan, 1987, *Real Rape*. Harvard University Press: Cambridge.

Estrich, Susan R., and Sullivan, Kathleen M., 1989, "Abortion Politics: Writing for an Audience of One," 138 *University of Pennsylvania Law Review* 119.

Farber, Daniel A., 1991, "Free Speech without Romance: Public Choice and the First Amendment," 105 *Harvard Law Review* 554.

Farber, Daniel A., and Frickey, Philip P., 1991, *Law and Public Choice: A Critical Introduction*. University of Chicago Press: Chicago.

Faux, Marian, 1988, *"Roe v. Wade": The Untold Story of the Landmark Supreme Court Decision That Made Abortion Legal*. New York: New American Library.

Feaver, Peter D., Kling, Robert, and Plotchan, Thomas K., Jr., 1992–93, "Sex as Contract: Abortion and Expanded Choice," 4 *Stanford Law and Policy Review* 211.

Feeley, Malcolm M., 1992, *The Process Is the Punishment: Handling Cases in a Lower Criminal Court*. Russell Sage Foundation: New York.

Fein, Bruce A., 1982, "Court Nullification of 'Obsolete' Laws Unnecessary," 5 *Legal Times* 14 (May 10).

Ferguson, Thomas, and Rogers, Joel, 1986, *Right Turn: The Decline of the Democrats and the Future of American Politics*. Hill and Wang: New York.

Finkbine, Sherri, 1967, "The Lesser of Two Evils," *The Case for Legalized Abortion Now* (edited by Alan Guttmacher). Diablo Press: Berkeley, Calif.

Finnis, John M., 1970, "Three Schemes of Regulation," *The Morality of Abortion: Legal and Historical Perspectives* (edited by John T. Noonan Jr.). Harvard University Press: Cambridge.

———, 1994, "'Shameless Acts' in Colorado: Abuse of Scholarship in Constitutional Cases," 7 *Academic Questions* 10 (Fall).

Fiorina, Morris P., 1981, "Short- and Long-Term Effects of Economic Conditions on Individual Voting Decisions," *Contemporary Political Economy* (edited by D. A. Hibbs and H. Fassbender). North Holland: Amsterdam.

Fisher, Russell S., 1951, "Criminal Abortion," 42 *Journal of Criminal Law and Criminology* 242.

———, 1967, "Criminal Abortion," *Abortion in America: Medical, Psychiatric, Legal, Anthropological, and Religious Considerations* (edited by Harold Rosen). Beacon Press: Boston.

Fiss, Owen M., 1982, "Objectivity and Interpretation," 34 *Stanford Law Review* 739.

———, 1989, "The Law Regained," 74 *Cornell Law Review* 245.

Flagg, Barbara, 1993, "'Was Blind, But Now I See': White Race Consciousness and the Requirement of Discriminatory Intent," 91 *Michigan Law Review* 953.

Foner, Eric, 1988, *Reconstruction: American's Unfinished Revolution, 1863–1877.* Harper and Row: New York.

Forrest, Jacqueline Darroch, and Henshaw, Stanley K., 1987, "The Harassment of Abortion Providers," 19 *Family Planning Perspectives* 9.

Forrest, Jacqueline Darroch, Tietze, Christopher, and Sullivan, Ellen, 1978, "Abortion in the United States, 1976–1977," 10 *Family Planning Perspectives* 271.

Francome, Colin, 1986, *Abortion Practice in Britan and United States.* Allen and Unwin: London.

Franklin, Charles H., and Kosaki, Liane C., 1989, "Republican Schoolmaster: The U.S. Supreme Court, Public Opinion, and Abortion," 83 *American Political Science Review* 751.

Frase, Richard S., 1990, "Comparative Criminal Justice as a Guide to American Law Reform: How the French Do It, How We Can Find Out, and Why Should We Care?" 78 *California Law Review* 542.

Fraser, Steve, and Gerstle, Gary, eds., 1989, *The Rise and Fall of the New Deal Order, 1930–1980.* Princeton University Press: Princeton.

Fredrickson, George M., 1971, *The Black Image in the White Mind: The Debate on Afro-American Character and Destiny, 1817–1914.* Harper and Row: New York.

Freeman, Alan, 1990, "Antidiscrimination Law: The View from 1989," *The Politics of Law: A Progressive Critique* (edited by David Kairys). Pantheon Books: New York.

Freeman, Ellen, 1977, "Influence of Personality Attributes on Abortion Experiences," 47 *American Journal of Orthopsychiatry* 503.

———, 1978, "Abortion: Subjective Attitudes and Feelings," 10 *Family Planning Perspectives* 150.

Freund, Ernst, 1904, *The Police Power, Public Policy, and Constitutional Rights.* Callaghan: Chicago, 1904.

Freund, Paul A., 1983, "Storms over the Supreme Court," 69 *American Bar Association Journal* 1474.

Fried, Amy, 1988, "Abortion Politics as Symbolic Politics: An Investigation into Belief Systems," 69 *Social Science Quarterly* 137.

Friedman, Thomas I., 1992, "Aides Say Clinton Will Swiftly Void G.O.P. Initiatives," *New York Times* (national ed.) A1 (November 6).

Fujita, Byron N., and Wagner, Nathaniel N., 1973, "Referendum 20—Abortion Reform in Washington State," *The Abortion Experience: Psychological and Medical Impact* (edited by Howard J. Osofsky and Joy D. Osofsky). Harper and Row: Hagerstown, Md.

Gallup Poll, 1988, "Campaign '88," 278 *The Gallup Report* 2 (November).

Garrow, David J., 1994, *Liberty and Sexuality: The Right to Privacy and the Making of "Roe v. Wade."* MacMillan: New York.

Gebhard, Paul H., Pomeroy, Wardell B., Martin, Clyde E., and Christenson,

Cornelia V., 1958, *Pregnancy, Birth, and Abortion.* Harper and Brothers: New York.

George, B. James, Jr., 1967, "Current Abortion Laws: Proposals and Movements for Reform," *Abortion and the Law* (edited by David T. Smith). Press of Western Reserve University: Cleveland.

Gerhardt, Michael J., 1991, "The Role of Constitutional Decisionmaking and Theory," 60 *George Washington Law Review* 68.

Gilligan, Carol, 1982, *In a Different Voice: Psychological Theory and Women's Development.* Harvard University Press: Cambridge.

Gillman, Howard, 1993, *The Constitution Besieged: The Rise and Demise of Lochner Era Public Powers Jurisprudence.* Duke University Press: Durham, N.C.

Ginsburg, Faye D., 1989, *Contested Lives: The Abortion Debate in an American Community.* University of California Press: Berkeley.

Ginsburg, Ruth Bader, 1985, "Some Thoughts on Autonomy and Equality in Relation to *Roe v. Wade,*" 63 *North Carolina Law Review* 375.

———, 1992, "Speaking in a Judicial Voice," 67 *New York University Law Review* 1185.

Glendon, Mary Ann, 1987, *Abortion and Divorce in Western Law: American Failures, European Challenges.* Harvard University Press: Cambridge.

Gold, Edwin M., Erhardt, Carl L., Jacobziner, Harold, and Nelson, Frieda G., 1965, "Therapeutic Abortions in New York City: A 20-Year Review," 55 *American Journal of Public Health* 964.

Gold, Rachel Benson, 1980, "After the Hyde Amendment: Public Funding for Abortion in FY 1978," 12 *Family Planning Perspectives* 131.

———, 1990, *Abortion and Women's Health: A Turning Point for America?.* Alan Guttmacher Institute: New York.

Gold, Rachel Benson, and Macias, Jennifer, 1986, "Public Funding of Contraceptive, Sterilization, and Abortion Services, 1985," 18 *Family Planning Perspectives* 259.

Goldstein, Joseph, 1960, "Police Discretion Not to Invoke the Criminal Process: Low Visibility Decisions in the Administration of Justice," 69 *Yale Law Journal* 543.

Goldstein, Phillip, and Stewart, Gary, 1972, "Trends in Therapeutic Abortion in San Francisco," 62 *American Journal of Public Health* 695.

Goldstein, Robert D., 1988, *Mother-Love and Abortion: A Legal Interpretation.* University of California Press: Berkeley.

Goodman, Paul, 1975, "The First American Party System," *The American Party Systems: Stages of Political Development* (edited by William Nisbet Chambers and Walter Dean Burnham). Oxford University Press: New York.

Gordon, Linda, 1976, *Woman's Body, Woman's Right: A Social History of Birth Control in America.* Grossman Publishers: New York.

Graber, Mark A., 1993a, "A Constitutional Conspiracy Unmasked: Why 'No State' Does Not Mean 'No State,'" 10 *Constitutional Commentary* 87.

———, 1993b, "The Non-Majoritarian Difficulty: Legislative Deference to the Judiciary," 7 *Studies in American Political Development* 35.

Graglia, Lino A., 1989, "State Action: Constitutional Phoenix," 67 *Washington University Law Quarterly* 777.

Graham, Howard Jay, 1968, *Everyman's Constitution: Historical Essays on the Fourteenth Amendment, the "Conspiracy Theory," and American Constitutionalism.* State Historical Society of Wisconsin: Madison.

Granberg, Donald, 1978, "Pro-Life or Reflection of Conservative Ideology?: An Analysis of Opposition to Legalized Abortion," 62 *Sociology and Social Research* 414.

———, 1981, "The Abortion Activists," 13 *Family Planning Practices* 157.

———, 1987, "The Abortion Issue in the 1984 Election," 19 *Family Planning Perspectives* 59.

Granberg, Donald, and Granberg, Beth Wellman, 1980, "Abortion Attitudes, 1965–1980: Trends and Determinants," 12 *Family Practice Perspectives* 250.

Greenhouse, Linda, 1992, "Abortion Rights Strategy: All or Nothing," *New York Times* A1 (April 24).

———, 1993, "Dr. Milan Vuitch, 78, Fighter for Abortion Rights," *New York Times* 30 (April 11).

Grossberg, Michael, 1985, *Governing the Hearth: Law and the Family in Nineteenth-Century America.* The University of North Carolina Press: Chapel Hill.

Grossvogel, David I., 1987, *Dear Ann Landers: Our Intimate and Changing Dialogue with America's Best Loved Confidante.* Contemporary Books: Chicago.

Guttmacher, Alan F., 1959, *Babies by Choice or by Chance.* Doubleday: Garden City, N.Y.

———, 1960, "The Law That Doctors Often Break," 76 *Readers Digest* 51 (January).

———, 1967a, "Abortion—Yesterday, Today, and Tomorrow," *The Case for Legalized Abortion Now* (edited by Alan Guttmacher). Diablo Press: Berkeley, Calif.

———, 1967b, "The Shrinking Non-Psychiatric Indications for Therapeutic Abortion," *Abortion in America: Medical, Psychiatric, Legal, Anthropological, and Religious Considerations* (edited by Harold Rosen). Beacon Press: Boston.

———, 1973, "Medical Aspects of the Abortion Experience," *The Abortion Experience: Psychological and Medical Impact* (edited by Howard J. Osofsky and Joy D. Osofsky). Harper and Row: Hagerstown, Md.

———, 1986, "The Genesis of Liberalized Abortion in New York: A Personal Insight," *Abortion, Medicine, and the Law* (3rd ed.) (edited by J. Douglas Butler and David E. Walbert). Facts on File: New York.

Guttmacher, M. S., 1967, "The Legal Status of Therapeutic Abortions," *Abortion in America: Medical, Psychiatric, Legal, Anthropological, and Religious Considerations* (edited by Harold Rosen). Beacon Press: Boston.

Hall, Robert E., 1965, "Therapeutic Abortion, Sterilization, and Contraception," 91 *American Journal of Obstetrics and Gynecology* 518.

———, 1967a, "Abortion in American Hospitals," 57 *American Journal of Public Health* 1933.

———, 1967b, "Commentary," *Abortion and the Law* (edited by David T. Smith). Press of Western Reserve University: Cleveland.

Halva-Neubauer, Glen, 1990, "Abortion Policy in the Post-*Webster* Age," 20 *Publius* 27.

Halva-Neubauer, Glen, 1991, "Abortion Policymaking in the Post-*Webster* Age: The Case of Minnesota," Paper delivered at the Midwest Political Science Association Meetings, Palmer House, Chicago, April 18–20.

Hamilton, Alexander, Madison, James, and Jay, John, 1961, *The Federalist Papers.* New American Library: New York.

Hammond, Howard, 1964, "Therapeutic Abortion: Ten Years' Experience with Hospital Committee Control." 89 *American Journal of Obstetrics and Gynecology* 349.

Hansen, Susan B., 1980, "State Implementation of Supreme Court Decisions: Abortion Rates Since *Roe v. Wade*," 42 *Journal of Politics* 372.

———, 1993, "Differences in Public Policies toward Abortion: Electoral and Policy Context," *Understanding the New Politics of Abortion* (edited by Malcolm L. Goggin). Sage Publications: Newbury Park, Calif.

Hardin, Garrett, 1967, "Abortion and Human Dignity," *The Case for Legalized Abortion Now* (edited by Alan Guttmacher). Diablo Press: Berkeley, Calif.

Harper, Fowler V., and Skolnick, Jerome H., 1962, *Problems of the Family* (rev. ed.). Bobbs-Merrill: Indianapolis.

Harris, Angela P., 1990, "Race and Essentialism in Feminist Legal Theory," 42 *Stanford Law Review* 581.

Harris, David A., 1994, "Factors for Reasonable Suspicion: When Black and Poor Means Stopped and Frisked," 69 *Indiana Law Journal* 659.

Hart, Henry M., Jr., 1959, "Foreword: The Time Chart of the Justices," 73 *Harvard Law Review* 84.

Harting, Donald, and Hunter, Helen J., 1971, "Abortion Techniques and Services: A Review and Critique," 61 *American Journal of Public Health* 2085.

Hengstler, Gary A., Moss, Debra Cassens, and Goldberg, Stephanie Benson, 1988, "Racial Bias, Sexism under Fire: House Debates *McCleskey*, Private Clubs, Professionalism," 76 *American Bar Association Journal* 139 (October).

Henriques, Mark Peter, 1990, "Desuetude and Declaratory Judgment: A New Challenge to Obsolete Laws," 76 *Virginia Law Review* 1057.

Henshaw, Stanley K., 1986, "Trends in Abortion, 1982–1984," 18 *Family Planning Perspectives* 34.

———, 1990, "Induced Abortion: A World Review, 1990," 22 *Family Planning Perspectives* 76.

———, 1991, "The Accessibility of Abortion Services in the United States," 23 *Family Planning Perspectives* 246.

———, 1995, "The Impact of Requirements for Parental Consent on Minors' Abortions in Mississippi," 27 *Family Planning Practices* 120.

Henshaw, Stanley K., Forrest, Jacqueline Darroch, and Van Vort, Jennifer, 1987, "Abortion Services in the United States, 1984 and 1985," 19 *Family Planning Perspectives* 63.

Henshaw, Stanley K., and Silverman, Jane, 1988, "The Characteristics and Prior Contraceptive Use of U.S. Abortion Patients," 20 *Family Planning Perspectives* 156.

Henshaw, Stanley K., and Van Vort, Jennifer, 1990, "Abortion Services in the United States, 1987 and 1988," 22 *Family Planning Perspectives* 102.

———, 1994, "Abortion Services in the United States, 1991 and 1992," 26 *Family Planning Practices* 100.

Henshaw, Stanley K., and Wallisch, Lynn S., 1984, "The Medicaid Cutoff and Abortion Services for the Poor," 16 *Family Planning Perspectives* 170.

Hentoff, Nat, 1992a, *Free Speech for Me—But Not for Thee: How the American Left and Right Relentlessly Censor Each Other.* HarperCollins: New York.

———, 1992b, "Pro-Choice Bigots: A View From the Pro-Life Left," 207 *New Republic* 21 (November 20).

Herbert, John G., 1965, "Is Legalized Abortion the Solution to Criminal Abortion?" 37 *University of Colorado Law Review* 283.

Hesburgh, Theodore M., 1980, Foreword to *Abortion Parley* (edited by James Tunstead Burtchaell). Andrews and McMeel: Kansas City, Mo.

Heymann, Philip B., and Barzelay, Douglas E., 1973, "The Forest and the Trees: *Roe v. Wade* and Its Critics," 53 *Boston University Law Review* 765.

Hill, David B., 1981, "Political Culture and Female Political Representation," 43 *Journal of Politics* 159.

Hirschman, Linda R., 1988, "Brontë, Bloom, and Bork: An Essay on the Moral Education of Judges," 137 *University of Pennsylvania Law Review* 177.

Horowitz, Donald L., 1977, *The Courts and Social Policy.* Brookings Institution: Washington, D.C.

Howell, Susan E., and Sims, Robert T., 1993, "Abortion Attitudes and the Lousiana Governor's Election," *Understanding the New Politics of Abortion* (edited by Malcolm L. Goggin). Sage Publications: Newbury Park, Calif.

Hughes, Charles Evans, 1908, *Addresses and Papers of Charles Evans Hughes, Governor of New York, 1906–08.* G. P. Putnam's Sons: New York.

Hyman, Harold M., and Wiecek, William M., 1982, *Equal Justice under Law: Constitutional Development 1835–1875.* Harper and Row: New York.

Imber, Jonathan B., 1986, *Abortion and the Private Practice of Medicine.* Yale University Press: New Haven.

Irwin, Theodore, 1970, "The New Abortion Laws: How Are They Working?" 48 *Today's Health* 21 (March).

Jackson, Andrew, 1963, "Jackson's Veto of the Bank Bill," *Documents of American History*, vol. 1, *To 1898* (7th ed.) (edited by Henry Steele Commager). Appleton-Century-Crofts: New York.

Jackson, John E., and Vinovskis, Maris A., 1983, "Public Opinion, Elections, and the 'Single-Issue' Issue," *The Abortion Dispute and the American System* (edited by Gilbert Steiner). Brookings Institution: Washington, D.C.

Jacobson, Gary C., 1983, *The Politics of Congressional Elections.* Little, Brown: Boston.

Jaffe, Frederick S., Lindheim, Barbara L., and Lee, Philip R., 1981, *Abortion Politics: Private Morality and Public Policy.* McGraw-Hill: New York.

Jeffries, John Calvin, Jr., 1985, "Legality, Vagueness, and the Construction of Penal Statutes," 71 *Virginia Law Review* 189.

———, 1994, *Justice Lewis F. Powell, Jr..* Charles Scribner's Sons: New York.

Jencks, Christopher, et al., 1971, *Inequality: A Reassessment of the Effect of Family and Schooling in America.* Harper and Row: New York.

Joffe, Carole, 1991, "Portraits of Three 'Physicians of Conscience': Abortion before Legalization in the United States," 2 *Journal of the History of Sexuality* 46.

Johnson, Charles A., and Canon, Bradley C., 1984, *Judicial Policies: Implementation and Impact.* CQ Press: Washington, D.C.

Johnson, Sheri Lynn, 1983, "Race and the Decision to Detain a Suspect," 93 *Yale Law Journal* 214.

Jones, Elise F., and Westoff, Charles F., 1973, "Changes in Attitudes toward Abortion: With Emphasis upon the National Fertility Study Data," *The Abortion Experience: Psychological and Medical Impact* (edited by Howard J. Osofsky and Joy D. Osofsky). Harper and Row: Hagerstown, Md.

Jones, Elise F., et al., 1988, "Unintended Pregnancy, Contraceptive Practice, and Family Planning Services in Developed Countries," 20 *Family Planning Perspectives* 53.

Kaczorowski, Robert J., 1986, "Revolutionary Constitutionalism in the Era of the Civil War and Reconstruction," 61 *New York University Law Review* 863.

Kahan, Ronald S., Baker Lawrence D., and Freeman, Malcolm G., 1975, "The Effect of Legalized Abortion on Morbidity Resulting from Criminal Abortion," 121 *American Journal of Obstetrics and Gynecology* 114.

Kahn, James B., Bourne, Judith P., Asher, John D., and Tyler, Carl W., 1971, "Surveillance of Abortions in Hospitals in the United States, 1970," 86 *HSMHA Health Reports* 423.

Kahn, Ronald, 1994, *The Supreme Court and Constitutional Theory, 1953–1993.* University Press of Kansas: Lawrence.

Kant, Immanuel, 1959, *Foundations of the Metaphysics of Morals* (translated by Lewis White Beck). Bobbs-Merrill: Indianapolis.

———, 1965, *The Metaphysical Elements of Justice* (translated by John Ladd). Bobbs-Merrill: Indianapolis.

Karst, Kenneth L., 1977, "Foreword: Equal Citizenship under the Fourteenth Amendment," 91 *Harvard Law Review* 1.

———, 1980, "The Freedom of Intimate Association," 89 *Yale Law Journal* 624.

Kennedy, Randall L., 1988, "*McCleskey v. Kemp*: Race, Capital Punishment, and the Supreme Court," 101 *Harvard Law Review* 1388.

———, 1989, "Racial Critiques of Legal Academia," 102 *Harvard Law Review* 1745.

Kens, Paul, 1990, *Judicial Power and Reform Politics: The Anatomy of "Lochner v. New York."* University Press of Kansas: Lawrence.

Kerner Commission, 1968, *Report of the National Advisory Commission on Civil Disorders.* Bantam Books: New York.

Kifner, John, 1994, "Gunman Kills 2 at Abortion Clinics in Boston Suburb," *New York Times* 1 (December 31).

Kinder, Donald R., and Kiewiet, D. Roderick, 1981, "Sociotropic Politics: The American Case," 11 *British Journal of Political Science* 129.

Kirp, David L., 1992, "How Now, *Brown*," 254 *Nation* 757 (June 1).

Kleegman, Sophia J., 1967, "Planned Parenthood: Its Influence on Public Health and Family Welfare," *Abortion in America: Medical, Psychiatric, Legal, Anthropological, and Religious Considerations* (edited by Harold Rosen). Beacon Press: Boston.

Kopp, Marie E., 1934, *Birth Control in Practice*. Robert M. McBride: New York.

Koppelman, Andrew, 1990, "Forced Labor: A Thirteenth Amendment Defense of Abortion," 84 *Northwestern University Law Review* 480.

Kousser, J. Morgan, 1988, "'The Supremacy of Equal Rights': The Struggle against Racial Discrimination in Antebellum Massachusetts and the Foundations of the Fourteenth Amendment," 82 *Northwestern University Law Review* 941.

Kramer, Gerald H., 1971. "Short-Term Fluctuations in U.S. Voting Behavior," 65 *American Political Science Review* 131.

Krason, Stephen M., 1984, *Abortion: Politics, Morality, and the Constitution: A Critical Study of "Roe v. Wade" and "Doe v. Bolton" and a Basis for Change*. University Press of America: Lanham, Md.

Krason, Stephen M., and Hollberg, William B., 1986, "The Law and History of Abortion: The Supreme Court Refuted," *Abortion, Medicine, and the Law* (3rd ed.) (edited by J. Douglas Butler and David E. Walbert). Facts on File: New York.

Kuhn, Thomas S., 1970, *The Structure of Scientific Revolutions* (2nd ed.). University of Chicago Press: Chicago.

Kummer, Jerome M., 1967, "A Psychiatrist Views Our Abortion Enigma," *The Case for Legalized Abortion Now* (edited by Alan Guttmacher). Diablo Press: Berkeley, Calif.

Kummer, Jerome M., and Leavy, Zad, 1966, "Therapeutic Abortion Law Confusion," 195 *Journal of the American Medical Association* 96.

Lader, Lawrence, 1966, *Abortion*. Bobbs-Merrill: Indianapolis.

————, 1973, *Abortion II: Making the Revolution*. Beacon Press: Boston.

————, 1991, *RU 486: The Pill That Could End the Abortion Wars and Why American Women Don't Have It*. Addison-Wesley: Reading, Mass.

Lamanna, Mary Ann, 1980, "Science and Its Uses: The Abortion Debate and Social Science Research," *Abortion Parley* (edited by James Tunstead Burtchaell). Andrews and McMeel: Kansas City, Mo.

————, 1984, "Social Science and Ethical Issues: The Policy Implication of Poll Data on Abortion," *Abortion: Understanding Differences* (edited by Sidney Callahan and Daniel Callahan). Plenum Press: New York.

Landes, Richard, 1993, "Justice, Work, Study, and Protest: The Biblical Contributions to Modern Democracy," 8 *Tikkun* 67 (July/August).

Landsberg, Brian K., 1982, "Race and the Rehnquist Court," 66 *Tulane Law Review* 1267.

Lapidus, Lenora M., and Albisa, Catherine, 1994, "Brief of the Center for Reproductive Law and Policy, et al., as *Amici Curiae* in Support of Respondents," *Madsen v. Women's Health Center, Inc.*, 512 U.S. ___, 129 L. Ed. 2d 593 (1994).

Lasch, Christopher, 1991, *The True and Only Heaven: Progress and Its Critics*. W. W. Norton: New York.

Law, Sylvia A., 1984, "Rethinking Sex and the Constitution," 132 *University of Pennsylvania Law Review* 955.

Lawrence, Charles R., III, 1987, "The Id, the Ego, and Equal Protection: Reckoning with Unconscious Racism," 39 *Stanford Law Review* 317.

Lawrence, Susan E., 1990, *The Poor in Court: The Legal Services Program and Supreme Court Decision Making*. Princeton University Press: Princeton.

"Lawyer Pleads Not Guilty in Abortion Package Deal," 1970, *New York Times* 40 (February 3).

Leavy, Zad, and Kummer, Jerome M., 1962, "Criminal Abortion: Human Hardship and Unyielding Laws," 35 *Southern California Law Review* 123.

———, 1964, "Criminal Abortion: A Failure of Law," 50 *American Bar Association Journal* 52.

Lee, Luke T., 1973, "International Status of Abortion Legalization," *The Abortion Experience: Psychological and Medical Impact* (edited by Howard J. Osofsky and Joy D. Osofsky). Harper and Row: Hagerstown, Md.

Lee, Nancy Howell, 1969, *The Search for an Abortionist*. University of Chicago Press: Chicago.

Legge, Jerome S., Jr., 1983, "The Determinants of Attitudes toward Abortion in the American Electorate," 36 *Western Political Quarterly* 479.

———, 1985, *Abortion Policy: An Evaluation of the Consequences for Maternal and Infant Health*. State University of New York Press: Albany.

Leggett, William, 1954, "Democratic Editorials," *Social Theories of Jacksonian Democracy: Representative Writings of the Period 1825–1850* (edited by Joseph L. Blau). Bobbs-Merrill: Indianapolis.

Lerner, Robert, Nagai, Althea K., and Rothman, Stanley, 1990, "Abortion and Social Change in America," 37 *Society* 8 (January/February).

Levinson, Sanford, 1988, *Constitutional Faith*. Princeton University Press: Princeton.

Lewin, Tamar, 1992, "Parental Consent to Abortion: How Enforcement Can Vary," *New York Times* A1 (May 28).

Lewis, Anthony, 1964, *Gideon's Trumpet*. Vintage Books: New York.

Lidz, Theodore, 1967, "Reflections of a Psychiatrist," *Abortion in America: Medical, Psychiatric, Legal, Anthropological, and Religious Considerations* (edited by Harold Rosen). Beacon Press: Boston.

Lindheim, Barbara L., and Cotterill, Maureen A., 1978, "Training in Induced Abortion by Obstetrics and Gynecology Residency Programs," 10 *Family Planning Perspectives* 24.

Liu, William T., 1977, "Abortion and the Social System," *Abortion: New Directions for Policy Studies* (edited by Edward Manier, William Liu, and David Solomon). University of Notre Dame Press: Notre Dame.

Llewellyn, K. N., 1960, *The Bramble Bush: On Our Law and Its Study*. Oceana Publications: New York, 1960.

Lofgren, Charles A., 1987, *The Plessy Case: A Legal-Historical Interpretation*. Oxford University Press: New York.

Louisell, David W., and Noonan, John T., Jr., 1970, "Constitutional Balance," *The Morality of Abortion: Legal and Historical Perspectives* (edited by John T. Noonan Jr.). Harvard University Press: Cambridge.

Lucas, Roy, 1968, "Federal Constitutional Limitations on the Enforcement and Administration of State Abortion Statutes," 46 *North Carolina Law Review* 730.

Luker, Kristin, 1975, *Taking Chances: Abortion and the Decision Not to Contracept*. University of California Press: Berkeley.

———, 1984a, "Abortion and the Meaning of Life," *Abortion: Understanding Differences* (edited by Sidney Callahan and Daniel Callahan). Plenum Press: New York.

———, 1984b, *Abortion and the Politics of Motherhood*. University of California Press: Berkeley.

Lupfer, Michael, and Silber, Bohne Goldfarb, 1981, "How Patients View Mandatory Waiting Periods for Abortion," 13 *Family Planning Perspectives* 75.

Lusky, Louis, 1942, "Minority Rights and the Public Interest," 52 *Yale Law Journal* 1.

———, 1975, *By What Right?: A Commentary on the Supreme Court's Power to Revise the Constitution*. Michie Company: Charlottesville, Va.

Macedo, Stephen, 1991, *Liberal Virtues: Citizenship, Virtue, and Community in Liberal Constitutionalism*. Oxford University Press: Oxford.

MacIntyre, Alasdair, 1984, *After Virtue* (2nd ed.). University of Notre Dame Press: Notre Dame.

MacKinnon, Catharine A., 1979, *Sexual Harassment of Working Women: A Case of Sex Discrimination*. Yale University Press: New Haven.

———, 1984, "*Roe v. Wade*: A Study in Male Ideology," *Abortion: Moral and Legal Perspectives* (edited by Jay L. Garfield and Patricia Hennessey). University of Massachusetts Press: Amherst.

———, 1987, *Feminism Unmodified: Discourses on Life and Law*. Harvard University Press: Cambridge.

———, 1989, *Toward a Feminist Theory of the State*. Harvard University Press: Cambridge.

———, 1991, "Reflections on Sex Equality under Law," 100 *Yale Law Journal* 1281.

Maltz, Earl M., 1990a, *Civil Rights, the Constitution, and Congress*. University Press of Kansas: Lawrence.

———, 1990b, "The Constitutional and Nonracial Discrimination: Alienage, Sex, and the Framers' Ideal of Equality," 7 *Constitutional Commentary* 251.

———, 1992, "Abortion, Precedent, and the Constitution: A Comment on *Planned Parenthood of Southeastern Pennsylvania v. Casey*," 68 *Notre Dame Law Review* 11.

Mandy, Arthur J., 1967, "Reflections of a Gynecologist," *Abortion in America: Medical, Psychiatric, Legal, Anthropological, and Religious Considerations* (edited by Harold Rosen). Beacon Press: Boston.

Manier, Edward, 1977, "Abortion and Public Policy in the U.S.: A Dialectical Examination of Expert Opinion," *Abortion: New Directions for Policy Studies* (edited by Edward Manier, William Liu, and David Solomon). University of Notre Dame Press: Notre Dame.

Manier, Edward, Liu, William, and Solomon, David, 1977, "Conclusions," *Abortion: New Directions for Policy Studies* (edited by Edward Manier, William Liu, and David Solomon). University of Notre Dame Press: Notre Dame.

Mannes, Marya, "A Woman Views Abortion," 1967, *The Case for Legalized Abortion Now* (edited by Alan Guttmacher). Diablo Press: Berkeley, Calif.

Mansbridge, Jane J., 1986, *Why We Lost the ERA*. University of Chicago Press: Chicago.

Mayo, Thomas W., 1992, "Abortion and Speech: A Comment," 46 *SMU Law Review* 310.

McClellan, George B., 1989, *The Civil War Papers of George B. McClellan: Selected Correspondence, 1860–1865* (edited by Stephen W. Sears). Ticknor and Fields: New York.

McCloskey, Robert G., 1960, *The American Supreme Court*. University of Chicago Press: Chicago.

McClosky, Herbert, and Brill, Alida, 1983, *Dimensions of Tolerance: What Americans Believe about Civil Liberties*. Russell Sage Foundation: New York.

McConnell, Michael W., 1991a, "How Not to Promote Serious Deliberation about Abortion," 58 *University of Chicago Law Review* 1181.

———, 1991b, "The Selective Funding Problem: Abortion and Religious Schools," 104 *Harvard Law Review* 989.

McCurdy, Charles W., 1984, "The Roots of 'Liberty of Contract' Reconsidered: Major Premises in the Law of Employment, 1867–1937," *Yearbook 1984: The Supreme Court Historical Society*. Supreme Court Historical Society: Washington, D.C.

McPherson, James M., 1988, *Battle Cry of Freedom: The Civil War Era*. Oxford University Press: New York.

McWilliams, Rita, 1991, "Why Aren't Pro-lifers and Pro-choicers Pro-contraception?" 23 *Washington Monthly* 10 (July/August).

Means, Cyril C., 1968, "The Law of New York Concerning Abortion and the Status of the Foetus, 1664–1968," 14 *New York Law Forum* 411.

Meehan, Mary, 1984, "More Trouble Than They're Worth? Children and Abortion," *Abortion: Understanding Differences* (edited by Sidney Callahan and Daniel Callahan). Plenum Press: New York.

Mendelson, Wallace, 1985, *Supreme Court Statecraft: The Rule of Law and Men*. Iowa State University Press: Ames.

Mensch, Elizabeth, and Freeman, Alan, 1991, "The Politics of Virtue: Animals, Theology, and Abortion," 25 *Georgia Law Review* 923.

Messer, Ellen, and May, Kathryn E., 1988, *Back Rooms: Voices from the Illegal Abortion Era*. St. Martin's Press: New York.

Michelman, Frank I., 1969, "Foreword: On Protecting the Poor through the Fourteenth Amendment," 83 *Harvard Law Review* 7.

———, 1971, "The Right to Housing," *The Rights of Americans: What They Are—What They Should Be* (edited by Norman Dorsen). Vintage Books: New York.

———, 1979, "Welfare Rights in a Constitutional Democracy," 1979 *Washington University Law Quarterly* 659.

———, 1988, "Law's Republic," 97 *Yale Law Journal* 1493.

Milbauer, Barbara (in collaboration with Bert H. Obrentz), 1983, *The Law Giveth: Legal Aspects of the Abortion Controversy*. McGraw-Hill: New York.

Mill, John Stuart, 1962, *Considerations on Representative Government*. Gateway Editions: South Bend, Ind.

Miller, Patricia G., 1993, *The Worst of Times*. HarperCollins: New York.

Mills, Don Harper, 1958, "A Medicolegal Analysis of Abortion Statutes," 31 *Southern California Law Review* 181.

Mohr, James C., 1978, *Abortion in America: The Origins and Evolution of National Policy, 1800–1900*. Oxford University Press: New York.

———, 1984, "Patterns of Abortion and the Response of American Physicians, 1790–1930," *Women and Health in America: Historical Readings* (edited by Judith Walzer Leavitt). University of Wisconsin Press: Madison.

Monaghan, Henry Paul, 1978, "Commentary: The Constitution Goes to Harvard," 13 *Harvard Civil Rights–Civil Liberties Law Review* 117.

———, 1981, "Our Perfect Constitution," 56 *New York University Law Review* 353.

Moore, Marvin M., 1963, "Antiquated Abortion Laws," 20 *Washington and Lee Law Review* 250.

Morris, Norval, 1992, "Race and Crime: What Evidence Is There That Race Influences Results in the Criminal Justice System," *Judicial Politics: Readings from "Judicature."* American Judicature Society: Chicago.

Mott, Rodney L., 1926, *Due Process of Law*. Bobbs-Merrill: Indianapolis.

Murphy, Walter F., 1990, "Reagan's Judicial Strategy," *Looking Back on the Reagan Presidency* (edited by Larry Berman). Johns Hopkins University Press: Baltimore.

Myers, Henry J., 1967, "The Problem of Sterilization: Sociologic, Eugenic, and Individual Considerations," *Abortion in America: Medical, Psychiatric, Legal, Anthropological, and Religious Considerations* (edited by Harold Rosen). Beacon Press: Boston.

Nathanson, Bernard N. (with Richard N. Ostling), 1979, *Aborting America*. Doubleday: Garden City, N.Y.

Nathanson, Constance A., and Becker, Marshall H., 1977, "The Influence of Physicians' Attitudes on Abortion Performance, Patient Management, and Professional Fees," 9 *Family Planning Perspectives* 158.

———, 1981, "Professional Norms, Personal Attitudes, and Medical Practice: The Case of Abortion," 22 *Journal of Health and Social Behavior* 198.

National Abortion Federation, 1993, *Summary of Extreme Violence against Abortion Providers as of November 12, 1993*. National Abortion Federation: Washington, D.C.

———, 1994, *Summary of Extreme Violence against Abortion Providers as of November 21, 1994*. National Abortion Federation: Washington, D.C.

Nelson, William E., 1988, *The Fourteenth Amendment: From Political Principle to Judicial Doctrine*. Harvard University Press: Cambridge.

Neubardt, Selig, and Schulman, Harold, 1977, *Techniques of Abortion* (2nd ed.). Little, Brown: Boston.

Newman, Lucile, 1967, "Between the Ideal and Reality: Values in American Society," *The Case for Legalized Abortion Now* (edited by Alan Guttmacher). Diablo Press: Berkeley, Calif.

Nieman, Donald C., 1991, *Promises to Keep: African-Americans and the Constitutional Order, 1776 to the Present.* Oxford University Press: New York.

Niswander, Kenneth R., 1967, "Medical Abortion Practices in the United States," *Abortion and the Law* (edited by David T. Smith). Press of Western Reserve University: Cleveland.

Niswander, Kenneth R., Klein, Morton, and Randall, Clyde L., 1966, "Changing Attitudes toward Therapeutic Abortion," 196 *Journal of the American Medical Association* 1140.

Niswander, Kenneth R, and Porto, Manuel, 1986, "Abortion Practices in the United States: A Medical Viewpoint," *Abortion, Medicine, and the Law* (3rd ed.) (edited by J. Douglas Butler and David E. Walbert). Facts on File: New York.

Noonan, John T., Jr., 1970, "An Almost Absolute Value in History," *The Morality of Abortion: Legal and Historical Perspectives* (edited by John T. Noonan Jr.). Harvard University Press: Cambridge.

———, 1979, *A Private Choice: Abortion in America in the Seventies.* Free Press: New York.

Note, 1935, "A Functional Study of Existing Abortion Laws," 35 *Columbia Law Review* 87.

———, 1957, "The Law of Criminal Abortion: An Analysis of Proposed Reforms," 32 *Indiana Law Journal* 193.

———, 1986, "Survey on the Constitutional Right to Privacy in the Context of Homosexual Activity," 40 *University of Miami Law Review* 521.

———, 1988, "Developments in the Law—Race and the Criminal Process," 101 *Harvard Law Review* 1473.

———, 1991, "Constitutional Barriers to Civil and Criminal Restrictions on Pre- and Extramarital Sex," 104 *Harvard Law Review* 1660.

O'Brien, David M., 1988, "The Reagan Judges: His Most Enduring Legacy?" *The Reagan Legacy: Promise and Performance* (edited by Charles O. Jones). Chatham House: Chatham, N.J.

Olsen, Frances, 1989, "Comment: Unraveling Compromise," 103 *Harvard Law Review* 105.

———, 1993, "Constitutional Law: Feminist Critiques of the Public/Private Distinction," 10 *Constitutional Commentary* 319.

Oppel, Wallace, and Wolf, Sanford, 1973, "Liberalized Abortion and Birth Rate Changes in Baltimore," 63 *American Journal of Public Health* 405.

Oreskes, Michael, 1989, "For G.O.P. Governors, New Look at Abortion," *New York Times* B12 (November 14).

Orr, Margaret Terry, and Forrest, Jacqueline Darroch, 1985, "The Availability of Reproductive Health Services from U.S. Private Physicians," 17 *Family Planning Perspectives* 63.

Packer, Herbert L., 1968, *The Limits of the Criminal Sanction.* Stanford University Press: Stanford.

Packer, Herbert L., and Gampell, Ralph J., 1959, "Therapeutic Abortion: A Problem in Law and Medicine," 11 *Stanford Law Review* 417.

Page, Benjamin I., and Shapiro, Robert Y., 1992, *The Rational Public: Fifty Years of Trends in Americans' Policy Preferences.* University of Chicago Press: Chicago.

Pakter, Jean, O'Hare, Donna, Nelson, Frieda, and Svigir, Martin, 1973, "Two Years Experience in New York City with the Liberalized Abortion Law—Progress and Problems," 63 *American Journal of Public Health* 524.

Pear, Robert, 1995, "Debate in House on Welfare Bill Splits G.O.P. Bloc," *New York Times* A1 (March 23).

"Pennsylvania Abortion Foes Say Law Is Being Undermined," 1994, *New York Times* A14 (September 26).

Perry, Michael J., 1988, *Morality, Politics, and Law*. Oxford University Press: New York.

Petchesky, Rosalind Pollack, 1990, *Abortion and Woman's Choice: The State, Sexuality, and Reproductive Freedom* (rev. ed.). Northeastern University Press: Boston.

Phillips, Kevin P., 1969, *The Emerging Republican Majority*. Arlington House: New Rochelle, N.Y.

———, 1990, *The Politics of Rich and Poor: Wealth and the American Electorate in the Reagan Aftermath*. HarperCollins: New York.

Piercy, Marge, 1988, Foreword to *Back Rooms: Voices from the Illegal Abortion Era* (by Ellen Messer and Kathryn E. May). St. Martin's Press: New York.

Pilpel, Harriet F., 1967, "The Abortion Crisis," *The Case for Legalized Abortion Now* (edited by Alan Guttmacher). Diablo Press: Berkeley, Calif.

Pole, J. R., 1978, *The Pursuit of Equality in American History*. University of California Press: Berkeley.

Pollak, Otto, 1950, *The Criminality of Women*. University of Pennsylvania Press: Philadelphia.

Pomeroy, Richard, and Landman, Lynn C., 1973, "American Public Opinion and Abortion in the Early Seventies," *The Abortion Experience: Psychological and Medical Impact* (edited by Howard J. Osofsky and Joy D. Osofsky). Harper and Row: Hagerstown, Md.

Popkin, Samuel L., 1991, *The Reasoning Voter: Communication and Persuasion in Presidential Campaigns*. University of Chicago Press: Chicago.

Posner, Richard A., 1977, *Economic Analysis of Law* (2nd ed.). Little, Brown: Boston.

———, 1992, *Sex and Reason*. Harvard University Press: Cambridge.

Pound, Roscoe, 1910, "Law in Books and Law in Action," 44 *American Law Review* 12.

Powe, L. A., Jr., 1994, "Does Footnote Four Describe," 11 *Constitutional Commentary* 197.

Powell, Thomas Reed, 1918, "The Logic and Rhetoric of Constitutional Law," 15 *The Journal of Philosophy, Psychology, and Scientific Methods* 645.

Quay, Eugene, 1960–61, "Justifiable Abortion—Medical and Legal Foundations," 49 *Georgetown Law Journal* 173, 395.

Quick, Jonathan B., 1978, "Liberalized Abortion in Oregon: Effects on Fertility, Prematurity, Fetal Death, and Infant Death," 68 *American Journal of Public Health* 1003.

Rae, Douglas, 1981, *Equalities*. Harvard University Press: Cambridge.

Rawls, John, 1971, *A Theory of Justice*. Harvard University Press: Cambridge.

Reagan, Leslie J., 1991a, "'About to Meet Her Maker': Women, Doctors, Dying

Declarations, and the State's Investigation of Abortion, Chicago, 1867–1940," 77 *Journal of American History* 1240.

———, 1991b, "When Abortion Was a Crime: The Legal and Medical Regulation of Abortion, Chicago, 1880–1973," Ph.D. diss., University of Wisconsin.

Reardon, David C., 1987, *Abortion Women: Silent No More*. Crossway Books: Westchester, Ill.

Regan, Donald H., 1979, "Rewriting *Roe v. Wade*," 77 *Michigan Law Review* 1569.

Reich, Charles A., 1964, "The New Property," 73 *Yale Law Journal* 733.

Reiss, Albert J., 1971, *The Public and the Police*. Yale University Press: New Haven.

Rembar, Charles, 1980, *The Law of the Land: The Evolution of Our Legal System*. Simon and Schuster: New York.

Reske, Henry J., 1993, "Developments behind the Scenes," 79 *American Bar Association Journal* 28 (August).

Rhode, Deborah L., 1989, *Justice and Gender: Sex Discrimination and the Law*. Harvard University Press: Cambridge.

———, 1990, "Feminist Critical Theories," 42 *Stanford Law Review* 617.

Rich, Spencer, 1994, "Congress's Antiabortion Blocs Gain," *Washington Post* A1 (December 5).

Richard, Patricia Bayer, 1991, "They'd Rather It Would Go Away: Ohio Legislators and Abortion Policy," Paper delivered at the Annual Meeting of the Midwest Political Science Association, Chicago, April 18–20.

Ridgeway, James, 1963, "One Million Abortions: It's Your Problem, Sweetheart," 148 *New Republic* 14 (February 2).

Rimer, Sara, 1993, "Abortion Clinics Seek Doctors but Find Few," *New York Times* A14 (March 31).

Roberts, Dorothy E., 1992, "The Future of Reproductive Choice for Poor Women and Women of Color," 14 *Women's Rights Law Reporter* 305.

Robertson, John A., 1994, *Children of Choice: Freedom and the New Reproductive Technologies*. Princeton University Press: Princeton.

Rochat, Roger W., Tyler, Carl W., and Schoenbucher, Albert K., 1971, "An Epidemiological Analysis of Abortion in Georgia," 61 *American Journal of Public Health* 543.

Rodman, Hyman, Sarvis, Betty, and Bonar, Joy Walker, 1987, *The Abortion Question*. Columbia University Press: New York.

Roemer, Ruth, 1973, "Legalization of Abortion in the United States," *The Abortion Experience: Psychological and Medical Impact* (edited by Howard J. Osofsky and Joy D. Osofsky). Harper and Row: Hagerstown, Md.

Rosen, Harold, 1967a, "The Emotionally Sick Pregnant Patient: Psychiatric Indications and Contraindications to the Interruption of Pregnancy," *Abortion in America: Medical, Psychiatric, Legal, Anthropological, and Religious Considerations* (edited by Harold Rosen). Beacon Press: Boston.

———, 1967b, "The Hysterectomized Patient and the Abortion Problem," *Abortion in America: Medical, Psychiatric, Legal, Anthropological, and Religious Considerations* (edited by Harold Rosen). Beacon Press: Boston.

———, 1967c, "Psychiatric Implications of Abortion: A Case Study in Social Hypocrisy," *Abortion and the Law* (edited by David T. Smith). Press of Western Reserve University: Cleveland.

Rosen, Jeffrey, 1993a, "Poetic Justice," 208 *New Republic* 25 (March 8).

———, 1993b, "A Womb with a View," 208 *New Republic* 35 (June 14).

Rosenbaum, David E., 1993, "Defying President, Senate Votes to Keep Medicaid Abortion Limit," *New York Times* A19 (September 29).

Rosenberg, Gerald N., 1991, *The Hollow Hope: Can Courts Bring About Social Change?* University of Chicago Press: Chicago.

Rosenblatt, Roger, 1992, *Life Itself: Abortion in the American Mind.* Random House: New York.

Rosenthal, Elisabeth, 1995, "Finances and Fear Spurring Hospitals to Drop Abortions," *New York Times* A1 (February 20).

Rosin, Hanna, 1995, "Invasion of the Church Ladies: The GOP Bid to Close the Gender Gap," 212 *New Republic* 20 (April 24).

Rosoff, Jeannie I., 1988, "The Politics of Birth Control," 20 *Family Planning Perspectives* 312.

Rossi, Alice, 1967, "Public Views on Abortion," *The Case for Legalized Abortion Now* (edited by Alan Guttmacher). Diablo Press: Berkeley, Calif.

Rossi, Alice S., and Sitaraman, Bhavani, 1988, "Abortion in Context: Historical Trends and Future Changes," 20 *Family Planning Perspectives* 273.

Rovinsky, Joseph J., 1971, "Abortion in New York City: Preliminary Experience with a Permissive Abortion Statute," 38 *Obstetrics and Gynecology* 333.

Rubenfeld, Jed, 1989, "The Right of Privacy," 102 *Harvard Law Review* 737.

Rubin, Alissa J., 1992, "Throwing Babies," 207 *New Republic* 19 (October 26).

———, 1995, "As Congress Takes Up Social Issues, Whose Values Will Prevail," *Washington Post* C3 (May 7).

Rubin, Eva R., 1987, *Abortion, Politics, and the Courts: "Roe v. Wade" and Its Aftermath* (rev. ed.). Greenwood Press: New York.

Russell, Keith, 1953, "Changing Indications for Therapeutic Abortion: Twenty Years' Experience at Los Angeles County Hospital," 151 *Journal of the American Medical Association* 108.

Russell, Keith P., and Jackson, Edwin W., 1969, "Therapeutic Abortions in California: First Year's Experience under New Legislation," 105 *American Journal of Obstretrics and Gynecology* 757.

Sands, Michael S., 1966, "The Therapeutic Abortion Act: An Answer to the Opposition," 13 *UCLA Law Review* 285.

Sartori, Giovanni, 1962, "Constitutionalism: A Preliminary Discussion," 56 *American Political Science Review* 853.

Sarvis, Betty, and Rodman, Hyman, 1973, *The Abortion Controversy.* Columbia University Press: New York.

Schattscheider, E. E., 1975, *The Semisovereign People: A Realist's View of Democracy in America.* Dryden Press: Hinsdale, Ill.

Schur, Edwin M., 1965, *Crimes without Victims; Deviant Behavior and Public Policy: Abortion, Homosexuality, Drug Addiction.* Prentice-Hall: Englewood Cliffs, N.J.

Schwartz, Maralee, and Balz, Dan, 1992, "Issue Passes to Politicians; Decision Is Grist for Election-Year Mill," *Washington Post* A1 (June 30).

Schwartz, Richard A., 1986, "Abortion on Request: The Psychiatric Implications," *Abortion, Medicine, and the Law* (3rd ed.) (edited by J. Douglas Butler and David E. Walbert). Facts on File: New York.

Sealey, Raphael, 1987, *The Athenian Republic: Democracy or the Rule of Law*. Pennsylvania State University Press: State College.

Seims, Sara, 1980, "Abortion Availability in the United States," 12 *Family Planning Perspectives* 88.

Sewart, Paul N., Ballard, Charles A., and Ulene, Arthur L., 1973, "The Effect of Legal Abortion at a Large County Hospital," 115 *American Journal of Obstretics and Gynecology* 335.

Shapiro, Ian, 1989, "Gross Concepts in Political Argument," 17 *Political Theory* 51.

Shapiro, Martin, 1978, "The Supreme Court: From Warren to Burger," *The New American Political System* (edited by Anthony King). American Enterprise Institute: Washington, D.C.

Sheeran, Patrick J., 1987, *Women, Society, the State, and Abortion*. Praeger: New York.

Shelton, James D., Brann, Edward A., and Schulz, Kenneth F., 1976, "Abortion Utilization: Does Travel Distance Matter?" 8 *Family Planning Perspectives* 260.

Shestack, Jerome J., 1971, "The Right to Legal Services," *The Rights of Americans: What They Are—What They Should Be* (edited by Norman Dorsen). Vintage Books: New York.

Siegal, Reva, 1992, "Reasoning from the Body: A Historical Perspective on Abortion Regulation and Questions of Equal Protection," 44 *Stanford Law Review* 261.

Simon, Nathan M., Senturia, Audrey G., and Rothman, David, 1967, "Psychiatric Illness Following Therapeutic Abortion," 124 *American Journal of Psychiatry* 59.

Skerry, Peter, 1978, "The Class Conflict over Abortion," 52 *The Public Interest* 69.

Sparer, Edward V., 1965, "The Role of the Welfare Client's Lawyer," 12 *UCLA Law Review* 361.

——, 1971, "The Right to Welfare," *The Rights of Americans: What They Are—What They Should Be* (edited by Norman Dorsen). Vintage Books: New York.

Spillenger, Clyde, Larson, Jane E., and Law, Sylvia A., 1989, "Brief of 281 American Historians as *Amici Curiae* Supporting Appellees," *Webster v. Reproductive Health Services*, 492 U.S. 490.

Staggenborg, Suzanne, 1991, *The Pro-Choice Movement: Organization and Activism in the Abortion Conflict*. Oxford University Press: New York.

Stanley, Harold W., and Niemi, Richard G., 1992, *Vital Statistics on American Politics* (3rd ed.). CQ Press: Washington, D.C..

Starr, Jack, 1965, "1,000,000 a Year: The Growing Tragedy of Illegal Abortion," 29 *Look* 149 (October 19).

Steiner, Gilbert Y., 1983a, "Introduction: Abortion Policy and the Potential for Mischief," *The Abortion Dispute and the American System* (edited by Gilbert Y. Steiner). Brookings Institution: Washington, D.C.

Steiner, Gilbert Y., 1983b, "Reactions of the Symposium," *The Abortion Dispute and the American System* (edited by Gilbert Y. Steiner). Brookings Institution: Washington, D.C.

Steinhoff, Patricia G, 1973, "Background Characteristics of Abortion Patients," *The Abortion Experience: Psychological and Medical Impact* (edited by Howard J. Osofsky and Joy D. Osofsky). Harper and Row: Hagerstown, Md.

Steinhoff, Patricia G., and Diamond, Milton, 1977, *Abortion Politics: The Hawaii Experience*. University Press of Hawaii: Honolulu.

Stephens, Philip, 1983, "Dateline: Brussels, June 30," Reuters North European Service (June 30).

Stewart, Gary K., and Goldstein, Phillip J., 1971, "Therapeutic Abortion in California: Effects on Septic Abortion and Maternal Mortality," 37 *Obstetrics and Gynecology* 510.

Stone, Ann E. W., 1992, "A Way Out for Republicans on Abortion," *New York Times* (national ed.) A19 (April 23).

Strauss, David A., 1989, "Discriminatory Intent and the Taming of *Brown*," 56 *University of Chicago Law Review* 935.

Sunstein, Cass R., 1991, "What Judge Bork Should Have Said," 23 *Connecticut Law Review* 205.

———, 1992, "Neutrality in Constitutional Law (with Special Reference to Pornography, Abortion, and Surrogacy)," 92 *Columbia Law Review* 1.

Swartz, Donald P., 1973, "The Harlem Hospital Center Experience," *The Abortion Experience: Psychological and Medical Impact* (edited by Howard J. Osofsky and Joy D. Osofsky). Harper and Row: Hagerstown, Md.

Sweet, Gail Grenier, ed., 1985, *Pro-Life Feminism: Different Voices*. Life Cycle Books: Toronto, Ont.

Symposium, 1993, "Symposium on the State Action Doctrine," 10 *Constitutional Commentary* 309.

Syska, Barbara J., Hilgers, Thomas W., and O'Hare, Dennis, 1981, "An Objective Model for Estimating Criminal Abortions and Its Implications for Public Policy," *New Perspectives on Human Abortion* (edited by Thomas W. Hilgers, Dennis J. Horan, and David Mall). University Publications of America: Frederick, Md.

Tatalovich, Raymond, and Daynes, Byron W., 1981, *The Politics of Abortion: A Study of Community Conflict in Public Policy Making*. Praeger: New York.

Tatalovich, Raymond, and Schier, David, 1993, "The Persistence of Ideological Cleavage in Voting on Abortion Legislation in the House of Representatives, 1973–1988," *Understanding the New Politics of Abortion* (edited by Malcolm L. Goggin). Sage Publications: Newbury Park, Calif.

Taub, Nadine, and Schneider, Elizabeth M., 1990, "Women's Subordination and the Role of Law," *The Politics of Law: A Progressive Critique* (rev. ed.) (edited by David Kairys). Pantheon Books: New York, 1990.

Taussig, Frederick, 1936, *Abortion: Spontaneous and Induced*. C. V. Mosby: St. Louis.

Taylor, Howard Canning, 1944, *The Abortion Problem*. Williams and Wilkins: Baltimore.

Tedrow, Lucky M., and Mahoney, E. R., 1979, "Trends in Attitudes toward Abortion: 1972–1976," 43 *Public Opinion Quarterly* 181.

TenBroek, Jacobus, 1951, *The Antislavery Origins of the Fourteenth Amendment.* University of California Press: Berkeley.

Thayer, James B., 1893, "The Origin and Scope of the American Doctrine of Constitutional Law," 7 *Harvard Law Review* 129.

Thomas, Sue, 1991, "The Impact of Women on State Legislative Policies," 53 *Journal of Politics* 958.

Thomas, Sue, and Welch, Susan, 1991, "The Impact of Gender on Activities and Priorities of State Legislators," 44 *Western Political Quarterly* 445.

Thomson, Judith Jarvis, 1971, "A Defense of Abortion," 1 *Philosophy and Public Affairs* 47.

Thucydides, 1954, *The Peloponnesian War* (translated by Rex Warner). Penguin Books: Harmondsworth, Middlesex.

Tiedeman, Christopher G., 1886, *Limitations of Police Power.* F. H. Thomas: St. Louis.

Tietze, Christopher, 1968, "Therapeutic Abortions in the United States," 101 *American Journal of Obstetrics and Gynecology* 784.

———, 1973, "Two Years' Experience with a Liberal Abortion Law: Its Impact on Fertility Trends in New York City," 5 *Family Planning Perspectives* 36.

———, 1981, *Induced Abortion: A World Review, 1981* (4th ed.). Population Council: New York.

———, 1984, "The Public Health Effects of Legal Abortion in the United States," 16 *Family Planning Perspectives* 26.

———, 1986, "Demographic and Public Health Experience with Legal Abortion: 1973–80," *Abortion, Medicine, and the Law* (3rd ed.) (edited by J. Douglas Butler and David E. Walbert). Facts on File: New York.

Tietze, Christopher, and Bongaarts, John, 1976, "The Demographic Effect of Induced Abortion," 31 *Obstetrical and Gynecological Survey* 699.

Tietze, Christopher, and Martin, Clyde E., 1957, "Fetal Deaths, Spontaneous and Induced, in the Urban White Population of the United States," 11 *Population Studies* 170.

Tinnelly, Joseph T., 1959, "Abortion and Penal Law," 5 *Catholic Lawyer* 187.

Toner, Robin, 1990, "G.O.P. Group Formed to Change Party's Stance against Abortion," *New York Times* (national ed.) A10 (April 24).

———, 1992, "The Supreme Court: Ruling Eases a Worry for Bush, But Just Wait, His Critics Warn," *New York Times* A1 (June 30).

———, 1993, "Settling In: Easing Abortion Policy," *New York Times* A1 (January 23).

Torres, Aida, and Forrest, Jacqueline Darroch, 1988, "Why Do Woman Have Abortions?" 20 *Family Planning Perspectives* 169.

Traugott, Michael W., and Vinovskis, Maris A., 1980, "Abortion and the 1978 Congressional Elections," 12 *Family Planning Perspectives* 238.

Tribe, Laurence H., 1985a, *Constitutional Choices.* Harvard University Press: Cambridge.

———, 1985b, *God Save This Honorable Court: How the Choice of Supreme Court Justices Shapes Our History.* New American Library: New York.

————, 1990a, *Abortion: The Clash of Absolutes*. W. W. Norton: New York.

————, 1990b, 'A Nation Held Hostage," *New York Times* A13 (July 2).

Trout, Monroe, 1964, "Therapeutic Abortion Laws Need Therapy," 37 *Temple Law Quarterly* 172.

Trussell, James, Menken, Jane, Lindheim, Barbara L, and Vaughan, Barbara, 1980, "The Impact of Restricting Medicaid Financing for Abortion," 12 *Family Planning Perspectives* 120.

Tufte, Edward R., 1975, "Determinants of the Outcomes of Midterm Congressional Elections," 69 *American Political Science Review* 812.

Tyler, Carl W., 1973, "Abortion Services and Abortion-Seeking Behavior in the United States," *The Abortion Experience: Psychological and Medical Impact* (edited by Howard J. Osofsky and Joy D. Osofsky). Harper and Row: Hagerstown, Md.

Uslaner, Eric M., and Ronald E. Weber, 1980, "Public Support for Pro-Choice Abortion Policies in the Nation and States: Changes and Stability after the *Roe* and *Doe* Decisions," *The Law and Politics of Abortion* (edited by Carl E. Schneider and Maris A. Vinovskis). Lexington Books: Lexington, Mass.

Verba, Sidney, and Nie, Norman H., 1972, *Participation in America: Political Democracy and Social Equality*. Harper and Row: New York.

Vinovskis, Maris A., 1980a, "Abortion and the Presidential Election of 1976: A Multivariate Analysis of Voting Behavior," *The Law and Politics of Abortion* (edited by Carl E. Schneider and Maris A. Vinovskis). Lexington Books: Lexington, Mass.

————, 1980b, "The Politics of Abortion in the House of Representatives in 1976," *The Law and Politics of Abortion* (edited by Carl E. Schneider and Maris A. Vinovskis). Lexington Books: Lexington, Mass.

Voyles, James, 1967, "Changing Abortion Laws in the United States," 7 *Journal of Family Law* 496.

Vrazo, Fawn, 1995, "Financial Pressure Changing Abortion Clinic Business," *Times-Picayune* B4 (February 12).

Wechsler, Herbert, 1959, "Toward Neutral Principles of Constitutional Law," 73 *Harvard Law Review* 1.

Weigel, George, and Kristol, William, 1994, "Prudence, Principle, and Abortion," *Washington Post* A21 (August 30).

Weisman, Carol S., Nathanson, Constance A., Teitelbaum, Martha Ann, Chase, Gary A., and King, Theodore M., 1986, "Abortion Attitudes and Performance among Male and Female Obstetricians-Gynecologists," 18 *Family Planning Perspectives* 67.

Welch, Susan, 1985, "Are Women More Liberal Than Men in the U.S. Congress?" 10 *Legislative Studies Quarterly* 125.

West, Robin, 1988, "Jurisprudence and Gender," 55 *University of Chicago Law Review* 1.

————, 1990, "Foreword: Taking Freedom Seriously," 104 *Harvard Law Review* 43.

White House Conference on Child Health and Protection, 1933, *Fetal, Newborn, and Maternal Morbidity and Mortality*. D. Appleton-Century: New York.

Wickenden, Dorothy, 1990, "Drug of Choice," 203 *New Republic* 24 (November 26).

Wilkinson, Isabel, 1989, "Illinois Case on Abortion Settled Prior to Supreme Court Hearing," *New York Times* A1 (November 23).

Williams, Glanville, 1957, *The Sanctity of Life and the Criminal Law*. Alfred A. Knopf: New York.

———, 1966, "Euthanasia and Abortion," 38 *University of Colorado Law Review* 178.

Williams, Gregory Howard, 1991, "The Supreme Court and Broken Promises: The Gradual But Continual Erosion of *Terry v. Ohio*," 34 *Howard Law Journal* 567.

Wilson, David C., 1967, "The Abortion Problem in the General Hospital," *Abortion in America: Medical, Psychiatric, Legal, Anthropological, and Religious Considerations* (edited by Harold Rosen). Beacon Press: Boston.

Wilson, Theodore Brantner, 1965, *The Black Codes of the South*. University of Alabama Press: Tuscaloosa.

Winter, Ralph K., Jr., 1973, "Poverty, Economic Rights, and the Equal Protection Clause," *1972: The Supreme Court Review* (edited by Philip Kurland). University of Chicago Press: Chicago.

Wolfinger, Raymond E., and Rosenstone, Steven J., 1980, *Who Votes?* Yale University Press: New Haven.

Wolpert, Robin, and Rosenberg, Gerald N., 1990, "The Least Dangerous Branch: Market Forces and the Implementation of *Roe*," Paper presented at the 1990 Annual Meeting of the American Political Science Association, San Francisco, August 28–31.

Wood, Gordon S., 1992, *The Radicalism of the American Revolution*. Alfred A. Knopf: New York.

Woodward, Bob, and Armstrong, Scott, 1979, *The Brethren: Inside the Supreme Court*. Avon: New York.

Yates, Susanne, and Pliner, Anita J., 1988, "Judging Maturity in the Courts: The Massachusetts Consent Statute," 78 *American Journal of Public Health* 646.

Ziff, Harvey L., 1969, "Recent Abortion Law Reforms (or Much Ado about Nothing)," 60 *Journal of Criminal Law, Criminology and Police Science* 3.

Zimmerman, Mary K., 1977, *Passage through Abortion: The Personal and Social Reality of Women's Experiences*. Praeger: New York.

General Index

About the Author

MARK A. GRABER, who holds a J.D. degree from Columbia Law School, is Associate Professor of Political Science at the University of Maryland. He is the author of *Transforming Free Speech: The Ambiguous Legacy of Civil Libertarianism.*